depositions

catherine
seavitt nordenson

depositions

roberto burle marx and public landscapes under dictatorship

university of texas press austin

Support for this book was provided by the Graham Foundation for Advanced Studies in the Fine Arts, the Foundation for Landscape Studies, and joint funding from the Professional Staff Congress and the City University of New York.

Printed in the United States of America
First edition, 2018

Requests for permission to reproduce material from this work should be sent to:
Permissions
University of Texas Press
P.O. Box 7819
Austin, TX 78713-7819
utpress.utexas.edu/rp-form

♾ The paper used in this book meets the minimum requirements of ANSI/NISO Z39.48-1992 (R1997) (Permanence of Paper).

LIBRARY OF CONGRESS CATALOGING-IN-PUBLICATION DATA

Names: Seavitt Nordenson, Catherine, author.
Title: Depositions : Roberto Burle Marx and public landscapes under dictatorship / Catherine Seavitt Nordenson.
Description: First edition. | Austin : University of Texas Press, 2018. | Includes bibliographical references and index.
Identifiers: LCCN 2017036834
ISBN 978-1-4773-1573-6 (cloth : alk. paper)
Subjects: LCSH: Burle Marx, Roberto, 1909–1994. | Landscape architects—Brazil—Biography. | Landscape architecture—Conservation and restoration—Brazil. | Architecture, Modern—Social aspects—20th century. | Landscape protection—Government policy—Brazil. | Dictatorship—Social aspects—Brazil—History. | Political culture—Brazil.
Classification: LCC SB470.B87 S43 2018 | DDC 712.092—dc23
LC record available at https://lccn.loc.gov/2017036834

doi:10.7560/315736

for guy, sébastien, and pierre

The landscape gardener . . . Well, you might have heard of him—he's lectured at Harvard—and is called the modern Le Nôtre, and *I* think he is one of the real Brazilian geniuses—Roberto Burle Marx. He gave a big party out at his *fazenda* (his nursery, really—acres and acres of marvelous and somehow sad, flamboyant, and threatening subtropical trees and plants) for our pal the governor and everyone to do with the "fill."

– Elizabeth Bishop, letter to Robert Lowell,
Rio de Janeiro, June 15, 1961

Contents

Introduction

Roberto Burle Marx and the Ecological Modern

FIGURE 0.1.
Roberto Burle Marx at the Sítio Santo Antônio da Bica, Barra de Guaratiba, ca. 1961

Photo by Marcel Gautherot/ Instituto Moreira Salles Collection

The landscape architect Roberto Burle Marx (1909–1994) designed an astonishing wealth of significant public landscapes during the modernist period in Brazil, beginning with a series of municipal plazas in Recife in the 1930s and peaking with the design of large public parks for several Brazilian cities during the early 1960s. He collaborated with an impressive roster of modern architects and was commissioned by powerful members of the Brazilian political elite.[1] With the right-wing military coup of 1964 and his subsequent appointment to a federal advisory council, Burle Marx's decades of experience as a landscape architect would be complemented by his newly voiced activist position of environmental advocacy. Throughout his professional career, Burle Marx developed and maintained close ties with those in power, proving himself to be adept at leveraging those connections in order to play a significant role in the greater project of the cultural construction of a rapidly modernizing country. He consistently positioned the Brazilian landscape as a significant element of Brazil's cultural heritage, arguing vehemently for its protection.

Burle Marx's environmental advocacy was effectively realized in two realms: physical design and political positioning. The latter was most pronounced during Brazil's twenty-one years of authoritarian military dictatorship, initiated by the coup of March 31, 1964. Three years later, in 1967, the first president of the dictatorship, Humberto de Alencar Castelo Branco, appointed Burle Marx to serve as a member of the Conselho Federal de Cultura (CFC, Federal Council of Culture), which operated as an advisory board under the authority of the Ministério da Educação e Cultura (Ministry of Education and Culture). This book examines Burle Marx's eighteen environmental depositions, a series of position pieces written and delivered to this plenary council during the seven years of his tenure from 1967 through 1974—a period that included the regime's most oppressive years. These depositions, addressing such issues as deforestation, national parks and land conservation, urban disfiguration, botanical gardens, ecological devastation, and the unique qualities of the Brazilian landscape, articulate an opposition to the regime's strategy of national economic development.

This book presents the collected depositions, translated into English from the Portuguese and republished here for the first time since they appeared as proceedings in three journals of the Brazilian Ministério da Educação e Cultura: *Cultura*, *Boletim*, and *Revista Brasileira de Cultura*. A close reading of these texts provides new insight into a selection of Burle Marx's earlier public design works, set forth here as visual evidence. The words of the Conselho Federal de Cultura depositions elucidate a little-known but important moment in the trajectory of Burle Marx's oeuvre, from prolific designer to prescient counselor. Yet the complexity of the historical and political context cannot be overlooked—Burle Marx was a voluntary cultural advisor to a regime that would execute a series of brutal human rights violations as well as devastating environmental abuses in the interest of national economic development.

Burle Marx's tenure as cultural counselor from 1967 through 1974 overlapped with a particularly repressive period of Brazil's military dictatorship known as the *anos de chumbo* (years of lead) but also aligned with the years of economic recovery and wealth known as the *milagre econômico brasileiro*—the Brazilian Miracle. It must be acknowledged that the military regime in Brazil successfully seized power with the support of the covert interventionist policies of the United States during the cold war, driven by a fear of the spread of communism in the Western Hemisphere. The military also took advantage of an economic crisis, and the duration of the regime was dependent on its developmentalist agenda and subsequent economic recovery of the so-called Brazilian Miracle. In addition, the authoritarianism of the Brazilian military regime was amply supported by the middle and upper classes during its whole existence, certainly by those who were profiting economically. Redemocratization was not initiated, and was arguably not a viable alternative, until the deterioration of the Brazilian economy in the late 1970s due to massive debt produced by international borrowing.[2]

To maintain its authority, the military regime violently suppressed freedom of speech, freedom of the press, and any political opposition, which included both extreme-left and extreme-right groups. Many significant cultural and political figures were harassed, exiled, tortured, or otherwise driven from Brazil during this period, including Gilberto Gil, Caetano Veloso, Chico Buarque, and Oscar Niemeyer.[3] Yet

FIGURE 0.2.
Military tanks in front of the Ministério da Guerra and Estação Central do Brasil, Rio de Janeiro, April 2, 1964
Photo by Neuza França/Arquivo Nacional do Brasil

M. E.C.

ANO - I

1

JULHO
1967

CULTURA

CONSELHO FEDERAL DE CULTURA

FIGURE 0.3.
Cover of *Cultura* 1, no. 1 (July 1967)
Acervo da Fundação Biblioteca Nacional do Brasil

FIGURE 0.4.
Passeata dos Cem Mil (March of 100,000), Cinelândia, Rio de Janeiro, June 1968
Centro de Pesquisa e Documentação do Jornal do Brasil

FIGURE 0.5.
Roberto Burle Marx (*left*) at a plenary session of the Conselho Federal de Cultura, with fellow counselors Gilberto Freyre, João Guimarães Rosa, and Rachel de Queiroz, ca. 1967
Photographer unknown

many massive civilian protests were organized. The most significant demonstration against the military dictatorship since its onset in 1964 was the Passeata dos Cem Mil (March of 100,000) held on June 22, 1968, in Rio de Janeiro. The regime responded fiercely with the implementation of Ato Institucional Número Cinco (AI-5, Institutional Act No. 5), enacted by the second president of the dictatorship, Artur da Costa e Silva, on December 13, 1968. Among other prohibitions, AI-5 suspended citizens' political rights and any constitutional guarantee of habeas corpus for those accused of politically motivated crimes. It eventually resulted in the institutionalization of the use of torture as a tool of the state. AI-5 marked the beginning of the *anos de chumbo* and the most repressive period of the dictatorship, continuing through the end of Emílio Garrastazu Médici's rule in 1974.

As a cultural counselor, Roberto Burle Marx remained close to the regime, perhaps a conservative stance. He arguably held a powerful platform from which to advise and influence the policies of the regime, yet he was obliged to perform in a situation in which critical speech acts were highly restricted. His appointment to the Conselho Federal de Cultura presented a unique position, ethically compromised though it may have been, from which to develop and assert his ideas of the modern Brazilian landscape, its protection, and its relationship to the public realm, while reflecting a distinctly modernist approach to aesthetics, ecology, and conservation. This book translates, categorizes, and contextualizes Burle Marx's eighteen consular statements through an analysis of their historical and political context. The depositions are framed and introduced by a critical presentation of both pertinent examples of Burle Marx's earlier public landscape projects (organized by decade) and their political milieu.

Chapter 1, "Constructing Culture in Brazil: Politics and the Public Landscape," is an examination of the extended history of the construction and support of landscape as culture through the policies of the Brazilian state, from the 1808 arrival of the Portuguese court in Rio de Janeiro through the establishment of the Conselho Federal de Cultura by the military regime in 1967. Burle Marx's eighteen depositions are subsequently presented in the next five chapters in five thematic groupings, each paired with his key public projects organized both typologically and chronologically by decade. His public parks are thus presented in parallel with the key political and cultural policies that influenced the environmentalist positioning expressed in the selected depositions.

Chapter 2, "Forest Narratives," examines the ecological tableaux developed in Burle Marx's early public plazas in Recife and Rio de Janeiro in parallel with the important Forestry Code of 1934, the Código Florestal Brasileiro, and its subsequent iterations by the military regime.

Chapter 3, "Landscapes of the Baroque Interior," considers the role of the landscape in Brazil's heritage protection laws, established in 1937 by the Serviço do Patrimônio Histórico e Artístico Nacional (Department of National Historic and

Artistic Heritage), known by its acronym SPHAN. With a focus on the state's valorization of the colonial baroque, this chapter examines Burle Marx's early park projects in the interior state of Minas Gerais.

Chapter 4, "Large Parks, Statues, and Disfigurement," analyzes Burle Marx's large metropolitan parks, initiated as commemorative centennial projects, and his ongoing concerns with the disfigurement of urban public spaces.

Chapter 5, "The Scientific Park," examines the typology of the botanical garden, presenting Burle Marx's designs for botanical and zoological gardens as well as his own private experimental nursery and garden at Barra de Guaratiba, Rio de Janeiro. The chapter focuses on his advocacy as counselor for Rio de Janeiro's historic Jardim Botânico as well as other botanical gardens throughout the country.

Chapter 6, "Military Gardens," discusses Burle Marx's gardens for three of Brasília's ministries (International Relations, Justice, and the Army), all commissioned after 1964 by the military regime itself, and concludes with a presentation of his essay "Garden and Ecology," written for the Conselho Federal de Cultura's journal *Revista Brasileira de Cultura*—an excellent summation of his positioning of nature, environmental conservation, and ecology as part of the cultural expression of a modern Brazil.

The epilogue, entitled "The Counselor," analyzes the ethical questions and political motivations of Burle Marx's role as advisor to the military regime.

Burle Marx was a messenger, an early advocate for the environment, and his role as counselor was one of his greatest and most powerful acts as a landscape architect. Through his carefully crafted depositions, he argued for the designation of more national parks and natural reserves, the conservation of cultural landscapes in the historic colonial towns of the interior, the protection of the Jardim Botânico of Rio de Janeiro and its adjacent forest nursery, and a more robust enforcement of the Brazilian Forestry Code in order to protect the country's forests from exploitative deforestation. He spoke from experience, often referring to himself as a witness—indeed, Burle Marx had traveled throughout the country on expeditions he would call *viagens de coleta*, plant collection trips modeled on the earlier missions of naturalists and scientists in the nineteenth and early twentieth centuries throughout various geographic regions of Brazil. At his home and experimental plant nursery at a former plantation site in Barra de Guaratiba, he propagated over 3,500 species of live Brazilian plants, several of which were discovered during his extensive travels and now bear his Latinized name, *burle marxii*.

Burle Marx's prescient depositions raise the specters of both species extinction and climate change. He noted the disappearance of hardwood tree species; the increase of torrential rains, erosion, and mudslides; and the observable changes in the climate. He insisted that the definition of national culture include the Brazilian forest and its diversity of flora as a part of the Brazilian national heritage, which therefore deserved protective legislation. Perhaps at some personal risk, considering several

FIGURE 0.6.
Sítio Santo Antônio da Bica, Burle Marx's home and experimental nursery garden, Barra de Guaratiba, ca. 1970
Photo by Alair Gomes/Acervo da Fundação Biblioteca Nacional do Brasil

implicit critiques of the regime's values and policies present in these texts, Burle Marx leveraged his position as counselor to argue for environmental protection from a government consumed with the modernist drive toward economic development (*desenvolvimento*), occurring at the high cost of environmental destruction.

Burle Marx, the counselor, sought to reconcile the world of the environment with that of the encroaching realities of a new and rapidly urbanizing Brazil, including a massive housing crisis and extreme income inequality. These realities were often at odds with his advocacy of conservation. Burle Marx intended his gardens to provide didactic environments for the public, to expose them to the wealth and beauty of the flora and ecological tableaux of Brazil, the country with the greatest amount of biodiversity on the planet even today. Though he moved within the small circles of the powerful Brazilian elite, Burle Marx remained aware of the fringes and worked to understand complex questions of access, marginality, and the crisis of identity. Yet he tended to support the greater state project of the culture of the environment over individual human rights. Burle Marx's decision to work with the military regime in Brazil was ethically fraught indeed; but this conflux of culture and politics is common, often appearing in the realm of design. Likewise, the intertwining of art and politics during the military dictatorship in Brazil is certainly inextricable from the international collusion of countries like the United States with that regime.

As an American scholar and landscape architect who has had the privilege of living and researching in Brazil for several years, I have had the opportunity of engaging not only with a rich body of work usually inaccessible to English speakers but also with the very cultural institutions that this book examines—the Jardim Botânico, Biblioteca Nacional, Escola Nacional de Belas Artes (ENBA: National School of Fine Arts), and of course Ministério da Educação e Cultura. As a translator and an outsider reckoning with the legacy of the military dictatorship in Brazil whose fascination with Roberto Burle Marx's work and writing has spanned two decades, it is an honor to give voice to his eighteen speeches. Fifty years have passed since his first address to the full plenary session of the Conselho Federal de Cultura at the Palácio da Cultura in Rio de Janeiro. Burle Marx spoke five languages in addition to his native Portuguese but wrote predominantly in Portuguese, and very few translations of his primary texts have been made available in English. These eighteen spoken depositions, delivered over a period of seven years, constitute a unique assemblage. The statements, transcribed by a stenographer before being published in the ministry's meticulous journals, have undergone several layers of translation prior to landing in this book. The deposition, as a particular speech act, includes both locutionary and illocutionary components—a challenge for any translator. How does one translate words that are withheld?

The translation task here has thus been manifold. It is probable that much of the content of Burle Marx's depositions was not formally written as a complete text before oral delivery to the full council. I suspect (though I do not have archival evidence) that he probably worked from an outline or notes, adding emphatic rhetorical emphasis where needed. Even when the depositions appear to be more formally structured, he connects with his listeners: the audience is present and palpable in our own reading of these speeches. Indeed, the depositions are best interpreted as speech acts when read aloud. I have thus attempted to capture the cadence and power of Burle Marx's dramatic voice in these English translations.

On several occasions, Burle Marx develops a position piece around something that he has just read in the newspaper or expands his thoughts in reference to commentary delivered by another counselor at a previous meeting. He reflects upon a recent Ministério da Agricultura (Ministry of Agriculture) conference held in Brasília and shares his comparative impressions of Brazil with other countries upon his return from a trip abroad. Burle Marx's depositions are meant to convince: his speeches, while circuitous, often conclude with a direct proposition to change or implement specific policy. These are entertaining oral presentations. Like any good storyteller, Burle Marx implements the meander as a way of pouncing upon a conclusion that is sharp, acerbic, and direct.

Though meandering, the depositions are specific enough that they consistently require contextualization. This has led me to cast a wider net around the speeches, situating them within the key policies that Burle Marx evokes: the Forestry Code and SPHAN legislation both provide useful lenses through which the depositions are best interpreted. The contents of the speeches also require a curated visual context. I am grateful to the numerous archives and individuals in Brazil who so willingly shared their rich collections. These visual exhibits, including my new scaled drawings of Burle Marx's public parks, situate the depositions and illuminate the counselor's speech. Indeed, they often reveal what is not said, providing evidence for a cross-examination. As focused and activist opinion pieces very much of their time, the depositions are inextricably anchored to an incredibly rich history of Brazilian culture, covering the period from the arrival of the Portuguese royal family on Brazilian soil to the present day—yet they speak evocatively to our time as well. The deposition is a particular speech act with a promise to uphold the truth, and this collation offers the reader an opportunity to take Burle Marx at his word.

FIGURE 1.0.

Portrait of Dom Pedro II, emperor of Brazil, seated at the Paço de São Cristóvão, Quinta da Boa Vista, Rio de Janeiro, ca. 1885

Photo by Marc Ferrez/Gilberto Ferrez Collection/Instituto Moreira Salles

CHAPTER 1

Constructing Culture in Brazil

Politics and the Public Landscape

Roberto Burle Marx came of age in the 1930s, a decade of significant political and cultural transformation in Brazil, during which a distinctly modern Brazilian cultural identity was increasingly promoted for a rapidly industrializing nation. Throughout his professional career, Burle Marx emphasized the importance of conserving and valorizing the biodiversity of the environment, developing an ecologically positioned defense of the Brazilian public landscape as an integral component of cultural heritage. Yet Brazil's identity has been intertwined with the representation and imagination of its landscape since the colonial period, particularly its rich tropical flora. The Brazilian state has long been the leading force in culture and education—the patron of modern buildings, plazas, and parks as well as a sponsor of the conservation of natural and architectural patrimony. This cultural patrimony was an essential component of Brazilian state policy from the arrival of Prince Regent João VI of Portugal to Rio de Janeiro in 1808 through the coup that established the military dictatorship under Humberto de Alencar Castelo Branco in 1964. As a member of the Conselho Federal de Cultura and advisor to the military regime from 1967 through 1974, Burle Marx tapped directly into this history in order to influence the direction of the regime's policies toward the environment. Although his tenure as counselor coincided with the most repressive years of the dictatorship, his ecological defense of the public landscape ran boldly counter to the economic development policies of the regime. Burle Marx transformed a conservationist spirit into a prescient environmentalist position that constructed Brazilian modernity as inseparable from an ecological positioning of nature.

The Arrival of the Royal Court, 1808–1821

The construction of culture and education by a government apparatus, with an undercurrent that embraces nature as a critical aspect of that culture, has an extended history in Brazil, which was colonized by the kingdom of Portugal beginning with the arrival of Pedro Álvares Cabral on April 22, 1500. The very name "Brazil" is drawn from the colony's first major export, the hardwood tree species pau-brasil or brazilwood (*Caesalpinia echinata*), prized for its red dye. Massive colonial extraction of pau-brasil from Brazil's coastal forests nearly led to its extinction—the early Portuguese colonization was funded through this exploitative deforestation. Yet with the arrival of the Portuguese royal family and court three hundred years later, seeking refuge from Napoleon Bonaparte's invasion of Portugal during the Peninsular War, a state-sponsored program of both education and culture was initiated in Brazil. The enhancement and support of the natural environment, now seen as a valuable asset of the new tropical kingdom, was considered an imperative.

In 1808 Queen Maria I of Portugal, her son Prince Regent João, and the entire Portuguese court of approximately 20,000 people arrived in Rio de Janeiro in a massive flotilla, escorted by the British navy. The royal family established itself on a large property north of the city center, the Quinta da Boa Vista, and expanded the site's sumptuous manor house that would become known as the Paço de São Cristóvão. The same year, João established the Jardim Botânico of Rio de Janeiro as the Horto Real, an acclimatization garden for the propagation of tropical plants, spices, and tea from the Portuguese colonies of the East Indies, China, and Africa.[1] Seeds of the majestic royal palm (*Roystonea oleracea*) were given to João by Luís de Abreu Vieira e Silva in 1809, who obtained them clandestinely from the acclimatization gardens of the French colony of Mauritius. Planted at the Jardim Botânico and named the *palma mater*, the palm grew to a height of almost forty meters and eventually flowered in 1829. Its seeds were used to establish the Jardim Botânico's stunning 750-meter long allée of 134 royal palms. The original *palma mater* was destroyed by lighting in 1972 after surviving 163 years, but its descendants thrive in parks and gardens throughout Brazil. Another prized species was *Victoria amazonica*, the giant water lily, discovered in 1837 along the Amazon River in British Guiana. The specimens at the Jardim Botânico were cultivated from seeds brought to the garden from the state of Mato Grosso by the botanist Frederico Carlos Hoehne in 1901. The lilies, often reaching over two meters in diameter, are grown in an artificial pond at the garden, created in 1825, now known as the Lago Frei Leandro in honor of the

FIGURE 1.1.
Nicolas-Antoine Taunay, *Passage of the Royal Cortege over the Maracanã Bridge*, ca. 1817–1820
Museu Nacional/Universidade Federal do Rio de Janeiro

garden's first director. These two species, the royal palm and the giant water lily, would continue to evoke a vision of a particularly regal Brazilian landscape through the modern period.

In 1815 João elevated the colony of Brazil to become part of the new transatlantic United Kingdom of Portugal, Brazil, and the Algarves. Upon the death of Maria I in 1816, the prince regent became king: Dom João VI would rule the kingdom from a throne in Brazil for the next five years. In addition to the establishment of the Jardim Botânico, Dom João VI created many new cultural institutions to enhance the economic and cultural standing of the former colony (including a publishing house, museum, library, educational institutions, and scientific academies), thus laying the groundwork for what would become the modern Brazilian state. Perhaps the king's most profound and lasting cultural initiative was his engagement of a number of French artists within his court beginning in 1816, a group known as the

FIGURE 1.2.
Paço de São Cristóvão, Quinta da Boa Vista, Rio de Janeiro, ca. 1862
Photo by Augusto Stahl/Instituto Moreira Salles Collection

Missão Artística Francesa (French Artistic Mission). These artists would together establish the Escola Real de Ciências, Artes e Ofícios (Royal School of Sciences, Arts, and Crafts) and an official system of state-supported artistic education.[2] This royal patronage of a group of French painters, sculptors, engineers, and the architect Auguste-Henri-Victor Grandjean de Montigny (1776–1850) grew out of Dom João VI's genuine concern for cultural development in the former colony, which had so rapidly been transformed into the capital of the Portuguese kingdom. All members of the Missão had studied at the École des Beaux-Arts in Paris and had been forced into

FIGURE 1.3.
Palma mater at the Jardim Botânico, Rio de Janeiro, 1875
Photo by Alberto Henschel/Acervo da Fundação Biblioteca Nacional do Brasil

FIGURE 1.4.
Allée of royal palms at the Jardim Botânico, Rio de Janeiro, 1885
Photo by Marc Ferrez/Gilberto Ferrez Collection/Instituto Moreira Salles Collection

FIGURE 1.5.
Victoria amazonica at the Jardim Botânico, Rio de Janeiro, ca. 1914
Photo by Antônio Ribeiro/Acervo da Fundação Biblioteca Nacional do Brasil

exile after the fall of Napoleon. The artists brought with them a particularly academic European neoclassical style, but this approach was paired with a contemporaneous European interest in the English picturesque garden in the case of the architect Grandjean de Montigny. His compositional deployment of the picturesque garden as a dynamic counterpoint to the formal neoclassical palace can be seen in his 1808 sketch of the palace and gardens for Jérôme Bonaparte, king of the short-lived Napoleonic realm of Westphalia in northwestern Germany. This interest prefigures the picturesque transformation of several of Rio de Janeiro's public gardens by another Frenchman fascinated by the *jardin à l'anglaise* (English garden), Auguste François Marie Glaziou, by over fifty years.

Dom João VI sponsored not only a culture of artistic education but also a culture of scientific exploration, reflecting his interest in learning more about and protecting the vast territory of Brazil. Exploration into the interior had occurred in the seventeenth century during the era of Portuguese *bandeirantes*, adventurers who effectively expanded the colony's borders in the central and southern hinterlands. In 1783 Queen Maria I sponsored an exploratory scientific, economic, and territorial expedition to the

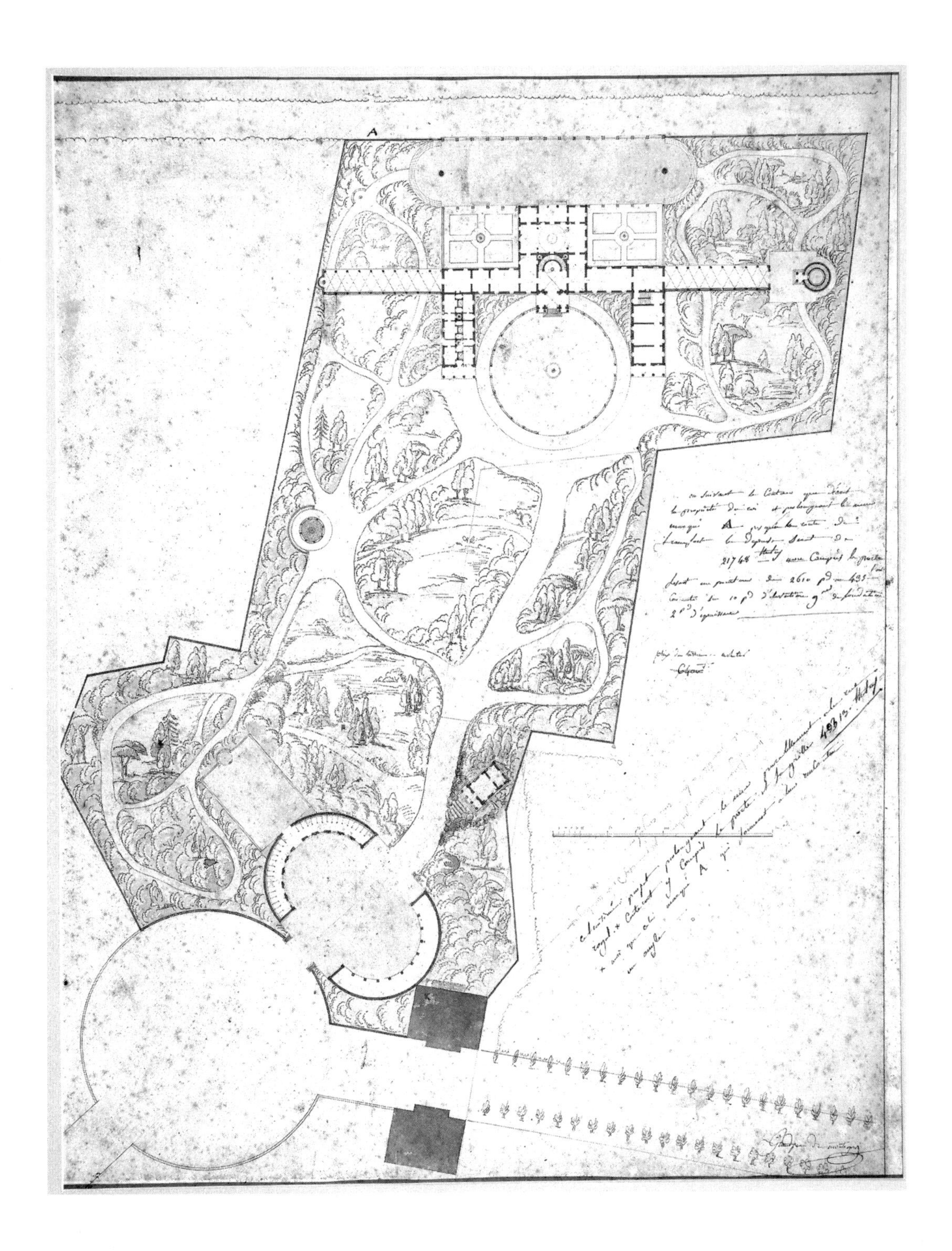

FIGURE 1.6.
Auguste-Henri-Victor Grandjean de Montigny, sketch of the palace and gardens for Jérôme Bonaparte in Westphalia, Prussia, ca. 1808–1813
Coleção Museu Nacional de Belas Artes/Instituto Brasileiro de Museus/Ministério da Cultura

Amazon and Mato Grosso river basins by the Bahian native Alexandre Rodrigues Ferreira (1756–1815), who had traveled to Portugal to study at the University of Coimbra. The maps, artifacts, and documents of Ferreira's subsequent nine-year expedition, the Viagem Filosófica (Philosophical Journey), were remitted to Portugal.[3] But the territory's floral wealth was not rigorously collected, documented, and classified until the beginning of the nineteenth century, when Dom João VI opened Brazil to European scientific expeditions in 1816.[4] He welcomed the Missão Científica Austríaca (Austrian Scientific Mission) to Brazil in 1817, which joined Archduchess Maria Leopoldina of Austria, the daughter of the first emperor of Austria, as promised bride to Dom João's son Pedro in a strategic union of new and old worlds. Botanist Carl Friedrich Phillip von Martius (1794–1868) and zoologist Johann Baptist von Spix (1781–1826), the mission's leaders, commenced a three-year scientific expedition from Rio de Janeiro in 1817, traveling first overland northward through the eastern inland provinces and then westward along the Amazon River to Tabatinga and finally departing for Europe from Belém in 1820. Brazil's exotic tropical wealth of flora and fauna was collected, classified, and remitted to Europe. *Flora brasiliensis*, initiated in 1840 by Martius but only completed postmortem in 1902 by his colleagues, was the expedition's monumental publication, documenting over 8,000 species of native flora with thousands of lithographic prints.[5] The work included Martius's map that classified the country into five ecological or phytogeographic regions as well as over fifty plates illustrating typical landscapes throughout the country. Martius's private collection of flora specimens, the Herbarium Martii, contained 300,000 specimens at the time of his death, including over 12,000 collected during his scientific mission to Brazil.[6]

The Rise of the Empire, 1822–1889

Dom João VI returned to Portugal in 1821 after thirteen years in Brazil, at the demand of liberal revolutionaries in Portugal. He left his son and heir-apparent, Pedro, in Rio de Janeiro to serve as regent of the Kingdom of Brazil. On September 7, 1822, Pedro claimed Brazilian independence from Portugal, declaring himself Emperor Pedro I of Brazil and instituting a constitutional monarchy two years later. Pedro I transformed the Escola Real de Ciências, Artes e Ofícios into the Academia Imperial de Belas Artes (Imperial Academy of Fine Arts) in 1827, appointing Grandjean de Montigny as both the architect of its new building in Rio de Janeiro and the first director of its School of Architecture.[7] Grandjean de Montigny's influence as the only professor to teach architecture at the Academia Imperial, where he served until his death in 1850, is significant. In a climate of rising tensions in Brazil and unrest in Portugal, however, Dom Pedro I abdicated in 1831 and returned to Europe, leaving his five-year-old son, Dom Pedro II, as the emperor of Brazil, under a rule of regents between 1831 and 1840. Pedro II was declared of age in 1841 and ruled as emperor in a political model approaching a parliamentary democracy until 1889, when he was

FIGURE 1.7.
Auguste-Henri-Victor Grandjean de Montigny, Escola Nacional de Belas Artes (formerly Academia Imperial de Belas Artes), Rio de Janeiro, ca. 1891
Photo by Marc Ferrez/Gilberto Ferrez Collection/Instituto Moreira Salles

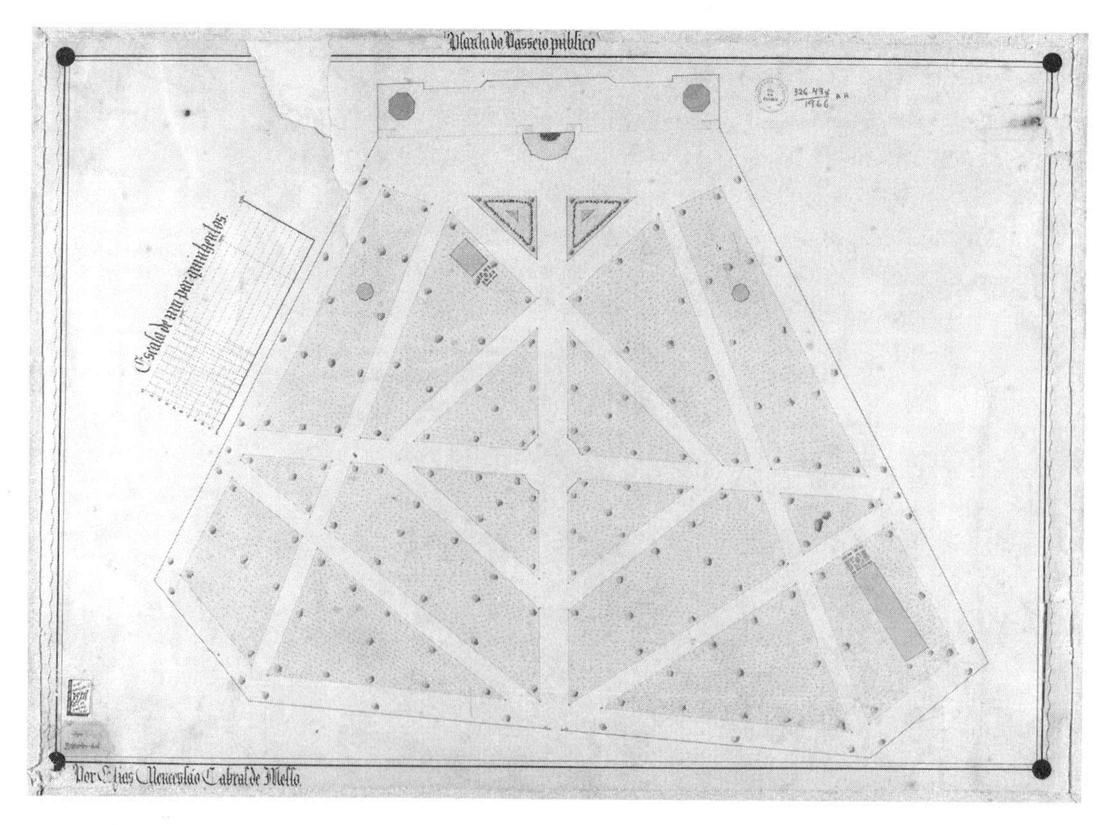

FIGURE 1.8.
Plan of Mestre Valentim's Passeio Público, Rio de Janeiro, drawn by Elias Wenceslão Cabral de Mello, ca. 1850
Acervo da Fundação Biblioteca Nacional do Brasil

FIGURE 1.9.
Waterfront belvedere of the Passeio Público, Rio de Janeiro, ca. 1910
Photo by Augusto Malta/Gilberto Ferrez Collection/Instituto Moreira Salles

ousted by a bloodless coup that led to the República Velha (Old Republic, also called the First Republic) of Brazil, which would last until 1930.

Like those of his father and grandfather before him, Pedro II's contributions to cultural development in parallel with a deep interest in defining and valorizing the natural world in Brazil were profound. During his reign as emperor, he transformed the Museu Real (Royal Museum) into an internationally regarded scientific research museum, reforested an entire watershed serving Rio de Janeiro's supply of drinking water, and transformed the urban parks and plazas of Rio through the establishment of the Diretoria de Parques e Jardins da Casa Imperial (Imperial Directorate of Parks and Gardens). For almost fifty years, Pedro II devoted himself to the support of culture, education, and science, building the values of a nation-state that he hoped would ensure its future progress and prosperity.[8]

Pedro II's invitation to the French hydraulic engineer and botanist Auguste François Marie Glaziou (1828–1906) to Rio de Janeiro to direct the new agency of the Parques e Jardins da Casa Imperial was an extension of Dom João VI's interest in French-influenced culture through the patronage of the Missão Artística Francesa. But beyond painting, sculpture, and architecture, Pedro II supported the design of urban public parks at the infrastructural scale of the city. Glaziou arrived in Brazil in 1858 after having worked in Paris with Adolphe Alphand, the designer of the Parc des Buttes-Chaumont and Parc Monceau. In 1860 Glaziou was tasked by Pedro II with the renovation of the Passeio Público, a formal public garden in the historic center of Rio de Janeiro opening up to the waterfront of the Baía de Guanabara. An irregular hexagonal site bounded by the hills of São Bento to the north, the hill of Santo Antônio to the south, and Rua da Vala to the west, the park was commissioned in 1779 by the Portuguese viceroy of colonial Brazil, Luís de Vasconcelos e Sousa, and built in 1783 by the sculptor and architect Valentim da Fonseca e Silva (ca. 1745–1814), known as Mestre Valentim.[9] He designed the Passeio Público in the formal French garden style, with an elaborate entrance gate and two octagonal pavilions along the waterfront belvedere, a wide terraced promenade extending the length of the park's eastern frontage along the Baía de Guanabara. The entrance gate led to orthogonal diagonal allées intersecting within the irregular hexagon-shaped park. The flora within the park was selected for its ability to provide broad expanses of shade from hot tropical sun, with trees including tropical natives such as mango, tamarind, and palms as well as cedars and pines.[10] The enclosed park also featured a pond with islands, ornamental sculptural elements, and a fountain adorned with bronze caimans and egrets.

Glaziou's 1860 renovation transformed Valentim's axial design with the romantic sensibility of an English garden, inserting sinuous planting beds and curving paths. Commentary in the *Almanak Laemmert* at the time expressed fascination with the park's novelty: "This plan represents a garden known as 'English' or 'landscape,' of the style adopted by the most forward-looking civilizations, for its natural and gracious singularity . . . enlarging the horizon to its very limits."[11]

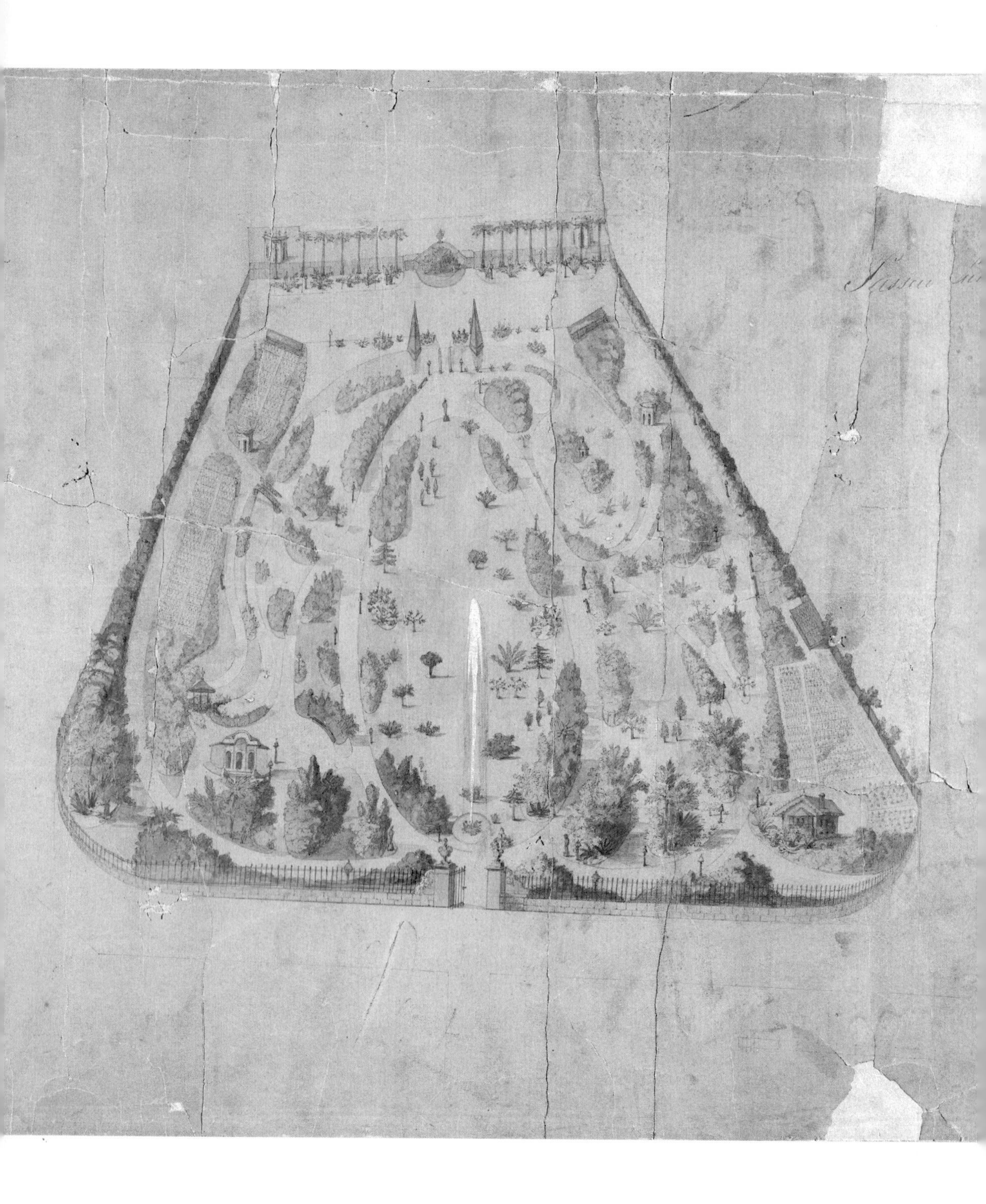

FIGURE 1.10.
Auguste François Marie Glaziou, landscape plan for the renovation of the Passeio Público, Rio de Janeiro, ca. 1862

Acervo da Fundação Biblioteca Nacional do Brasil

FIGURE 1.11.
Entrance to the Passeio Público, Rio de Janeiro, ca. 1862
Photo by Augusto Stahl/Instituto Moreira Salles Collection

In 1869 Glaziou began a renovation of the gardens of the Paço de São Cristóvão at the Quinta da Boa Vista—previously the palace of Dom João VI and Emperor Dom Pedro I and now the imperial residence of his patron, Emperor Dom Pedro II. Glaziou sculpted a picturesque landscape around the palace anchored by a formal central allée of sapucaias (*Lecythis pisonis*), native Brazilian trees with a spectacular spring display of pink leaves and purple flowers. The allée bisected the grounds into two curvilinear gardens with interconnected lakes and rustic grottos. In 1874 Glaziou initiated a transformation of the Campo de Santana, a former marshland near the historic center of Rio de Janeiro, creating a public park renamed the Campo da Aclamação (Field of Acclamation, now known as the Praça da República) to commemorate its significance as the site of Dom Pedro I's 1822 proclamation of Brazilian independence.[12] Modeled on the great picturesque parks of Paris—Parc Monceau, Parc des Buttes-Chaumont, and the Bois de Boulogne—the park was completed in 1880 and inaugurated by Dom Pedro II himself. Sinuous lines guided the design, and picturesque features were constructed within the park, including large rocks, tunnels, grottos, lakes, and waterfalls.[13]

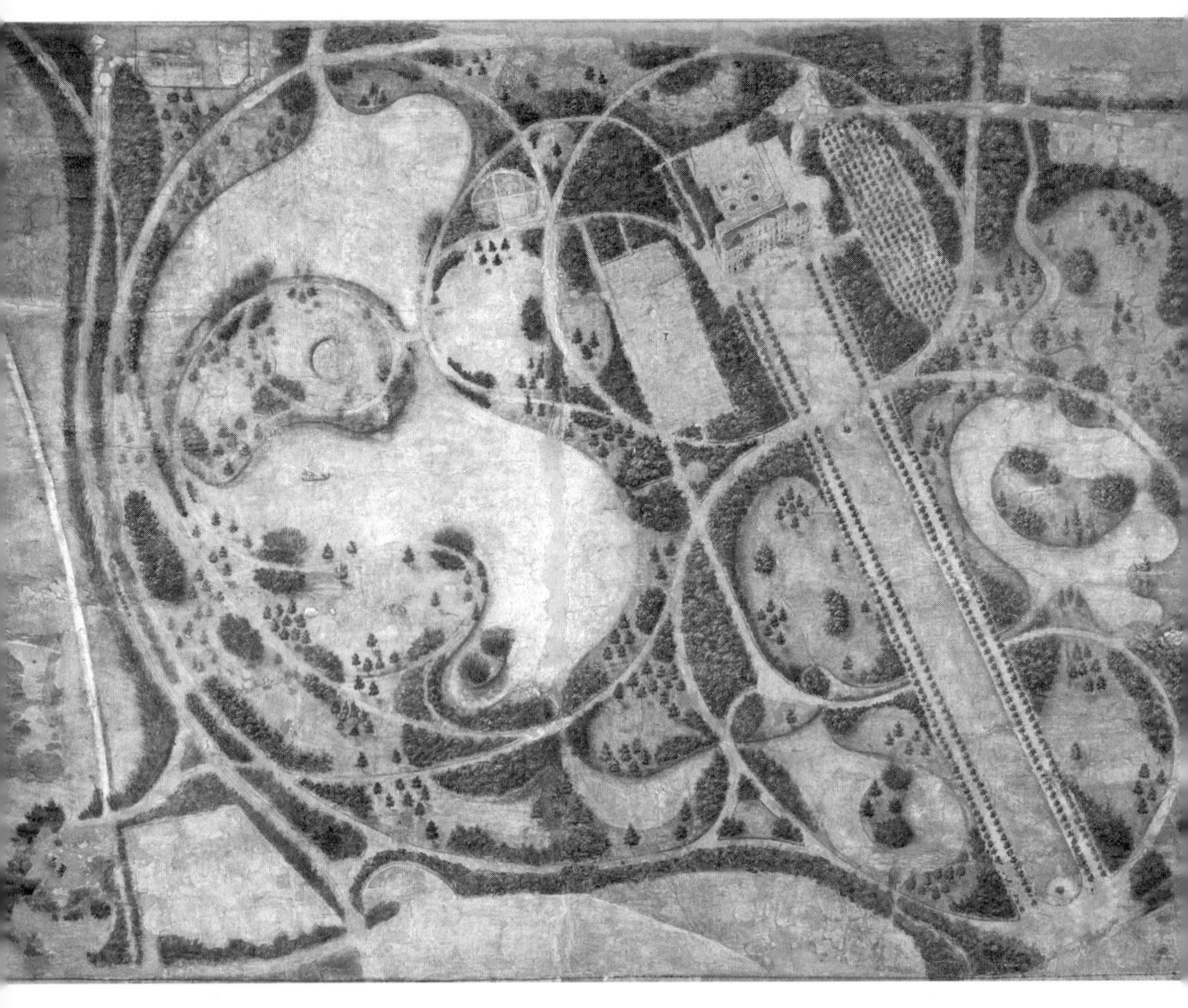

FIGURE 1.12.
Auguste François Marie Glaziou, landscape plan of the Quinta da Boa Vista, Rio de Janeiro, 1866
Photo by Caique Bellato/Governo do Estado do Rio de Janeiro/Secretaria de Estado de Cultura/Fundação Anita Mantuano de Artes do Estado do Rio de Janeiro/Casa da Marquesa de Santos–Museu da Moda Brasileira

In addition to the construction of these large imperial parks, Glaziou completed the designs of several urban plazas and streetscapes. His beautification program for the Avenida do Mangue and the Largo do Machado from 1869 through 1875 included the planting of native fig and palm species.[14] Glaziou often used local tropical flora in his planting schemes, specimens that he had collected himself on numerous botanical expeditions. He maintained a collection of live plants at the imperial summer palace in Petrópolis, a village north of Rio de Janeiro. As the first director of Parques e Jardins, he influenced an impressive line of successors, including Paul Villon, Luiz

FIGURE 1.13.
Lake with Ilha dos Amores and the ruins of a temple by Auguste François Marie Glaziou, Quinta da Boa Vista, Rio de Janeiro, ca. 1920
Acervo Arquivo Geral da Cidade do Rio de Janeiro

FIGURE 1.14.
Auguste François Marie Glaziou, Campo da Aclamação with the neoclassical Museu Imperial (*left*), Rio de Janeiro, 1880
Photo by Marc Ferrez/Acervo da Fundação Biblioteca Nacional do Brasil

Emygdio de Mello Filho, and Fernando Magalhães Chacel. In 1872 Glaziou accompanied Princesa Isabel, the eldest daughter of Dom Pedro II, on a plant-collecting expedition to the massif of Itatiaia, a mountainous region between the cities of Rio de Janeiro and São Paulo.[15] After gathering plant specimens (including several rare species of ferns), Glaziou later prepared a commemorative book of the plants collected during their expedition, entitled *Plantes cueillies sur l'Itatiaia au mois de juillet 1872* and presented it to the princess. Glaziou returned to France in 1897; after his death in 1906, his personal herbarium consisting of over 24,000 Brazilian species was given to the Muséum National d'Histoire Naturelle in Paris, France, where Princesa Isabel's book also resides.

Dom Pedro II extended his support of the natural world beyond the urban to the regional scale. He was responsible for the first successful tropical forest restoration at the Floresta da Tijuca in the highlands of the city of Rio de Janeiro from 1860 to 1887. The Floresta da Tijuca, covering over thirty-three square kilometers and ranging in elevation between eighty and one thousand meters above sea level, is today the

FIGURE 1.15.
Auguste François Marie Glaziou, Largo do Machado with the Igreja Nossa Senhora da Glória, Rio de Janeiro, 1906
Photo by Augusto Malta/Instituto Moreira Salles Collection

largest urban forest in the world, a fragment of the remaining *mata atlântica* (Atlantic rainforest) biome that extends along the entire Atlantic coast of Brazil.[16] Much of the forest had been cut down during the colonial period to establish the extensive coffee and sugar plantations that produced the colony's major exports along the Tijuca Massif, the ridge highlands that surrounded the city. By the 1820s, with the rapid urban growth that followed the arrival of the Portuguese royal family and court, the region was experiencing serious watershed damage, compounded by droughts that affected Rio de Janeiro's water supply. Despite the literal translation of its name, "River of January," no major river serves the city. It was the small streams and waterfalls descending from the Tijuca highlands, principally the Carioca, Comprido, and Maracanã, that first provided the city's drinking water. The main supply of water was delivered through a large aqueduct, completed in 1732, that carried the waters of a diverted Rio Carioca to a series of public fountains at the center of Rio de Janeiro.

Following a particularly severe drought in 1844, a number of tree planting and forest protection measures were begun through the imperial government's purchase of private lands within the Floresta da Tijuca watershed, but it was not until Dom Pedro II's issue of an imperial order in 1860 that a massive government replanting effort was begun in the Tijuca and Paineiras forests. A new agency, Secretaria de Estado dos Negócios da Agricultura, Comércio e Obras Públicas (State Department of Agriculture, Commerce, and Public Works) was established in 1860. Almost 100,000 native tree seedlings were planted between 1862 and 1887 by approximately twelve slaves working for the department under the directorship of Manuel Gomes Archer. Archer's systematic planting scheme included combinations of seedlings of many native tree species, often drawn from the nursery plants of the Jardim Botânico.[17] In 1874 Archer reported that over 60,000 trees had been successfully planted and stated that more laborers were needed.[18] In 1877 his successor, Gastão de Escragnolle, planted over 20,000 more seedlings and engaged Auguste Glaziou to begin the work of transforming the Floresta da Tijuca into a large public park, building access roads, plazas, belvederes, fountains, trails, and bridges. In 1879 Dom Pedro II contracted the engineers Francisco de Paula Bicalho and subsequently Paulo de Frontin and Raimundo Teixeira Belfort Roxo to tap the watershed of the Serra do Tinguá and the Rio São Pedro, reducing the importance of the streams of the Floresta da Tijuca for Rio de Janeiro's water supply. However, the forest restoration was substantially complete by the time these other sources of drinking water were established, for no significant tree planting was done after 1887.

Dom Pedro II reigned as emperor of Brazil for half a century, supporting science, culture, and the exploration of the extents of Brazil. He significantly expanded the collections of the Museu Imperial, first established in 1818 by his grandfather Dom João VI as the Museu Real at the Campo de Santana in Rio de Janeiro. Martius, Spix, Auguste de Saint-Hilaire, Prince Alexander Philipp Maximilian of Wied-Neuwied, and other European explorers invited by Dom João VI and Pedro I had contributed

FIGURE 1.16.
Waterfall at the Floresta da Tijuca, Rio de Janeiro, ca. 1885
Photo by Marc Ferrez/Gilberto Ferrez Collection/Instituto Moreira Salles

significantly to the museum's collections. Pedro II enhanced it with anthropological, archaeological, and paleontological findings from his own trips both in Brazil and abroad, including a voyage to Egypt in 1871. He also invited scientists from abroad to work at the museum, establishing a veritable international scientific study center. Pedro II shifted the naturalists' interest in the tropical novelty of Brazil's flora and fauna toward a scientific interest in a rich environment and complex ecology that was yet to be fully understood but was appreciated as uniquely and inextricably Brazilian.

The Entrance of the Republic, 1889–1930

On November 15, 1889, General Manuel Deodoro da Fonseca initiated a military coup at the Campo da Aclamação, the Proclamação da República (Proclamation of the Republic), exiling Dom Pedro II and the imperial family to France and initiating the period known as the República Velha, from 1889 through 1930.[19] The Républica Velha would continue until another military coup, the Revolução de 1930 (Revolution of 1930), which installed Getúlio Vargas as Brazil's president.

The new Brazilian Constitution of 1891 renamed the country the República dos Estados Unidos do Brasil (Republic of the United States of Brazil), establishing a somewhat centralized form of federalism that transformed the former provinces into states led by elected governors.[20] The transition from empire to Republic led to many radical changes in the leadership of cultural institutions as well as a rising interest in scientific positivism through an educated military elite that encouraged significant new exploration of the country's vast interior. Nationalism, industrialization, urbanization, immigration, and a developmental vision of expansion and settlement throughout the Brazilian territory—all with significant impact on natural resources—increased rapidly during the period of the República Velha.

One of the most significant elements of the Constitution of 1891 was its third article, which suggested that the capital of Brazil be moved from Rio de Janeiro to a more central location on the country's interior plateau—predating the construction of Brasília by more than sixty years. But this vision of an interior capital was not new. In 1883 the mystical Italian priest Giovanni Melchiorre Bosco, popularly known as Dom Bosco, had recorded his dream of an inconceivably rich land in central Brazil, between the fifteenth and twentieth latitudes, noting that "there will appear in this place the Promised Land, flowing with milk and honey."[21] Even earlier, José Bonifácio, advisor to the emperor Pedro I, had suggested in 1827 that a new city named Brasília be established to the west of the densely settled Atlantic coast. Responding to the 1891 Constitution's directive to demarcate the territory of this future federal capital, two state-supported expeditions to the central highlands of Brazil were established by Congress, first the 1892 Comissão Exploradora do Planalto Central do Brasil (Commission to Explore the Central Plateau of Brazil) then the 1894 Comissão de Estudos da Nova Capital da União (Commission to Study the New Capital of the

Union). The goal of the two missions, led by the Belgian-born astronomer Luíz Cruls (1848–1908), the director of the National Observatory, was to plat a 160-kilometer by 90-kilometer rectangle on the high central plateau of Brazil, capturing the sources of the three major Brazilian river basins: the Amazon, the São Francisco, and the Paraná. Within this "Quadrilátero Cruls," subsequently included on every national map until 1956, would rise the future capital city of Brasília at the Distrito Federal.[22]

FIGURE 1.17.

Map of Brazil indicating the location of the "Quadrilátero Cruls" at the Planalto Central, 1893 Luíz Cruls, *Relatorio parcial apresentado ao ministro da indústria, viação e obras públicas* (Rio de Janeiro: H. Lombaerts, 1893)

FIGURE 1.18.
Members of the Missão Cruls, Goiás, 1892
Photo by Henrique Morize/Arquivo Público do Distrito Federal

Auguste François Marie Glaziou, the former imperial director of parks and gardens, joined the expedition team of the Missão Cruls as its field botanist. In his 1894 report to Cruls, Glaziou wrote admiringly of the rich diversity of the *cerrado* (tropical savanna) species endemic to this ecoregion of the central plateau. In addition he suggested the creation of an artificial lake to ease the elevated central plateau's dryness, which was realized years later during the implementation of Brasília with the construction of a dam across the Rio Paranoá and the subsequent formation of Lago Paranoá.[23]

The República Velha continued to embrace education, science, and culture as state concerns, though they were now imbued with an especially nationalist spirit. In 1890 Grandjean de Montigny's Academia Imperial de Belas Artes was renamed the Escola Nacional de Belas Artes (ENBA: National School of Fine Arts). Though the school remained aesthetically eclectic, nationalist proponents of a particularly Brazilian neocolonial style of architecture had emerged by the early twentieth century, presented as an appropriate alternative to the dominant European neoclassical style. The leading advocate of the neocolonial in Rio de Janeiro was José Marianno Filho (1881–1946), a wealthy aristocrat and architectural critic trained as a physician. Though he never taught courses at the ENBA, Marianno Filho was its director from

1926 to 1927. Several years earlier, he had promoted two architectural competitions for students, Casa Brasileira (Brazilian House) in 1921 and Solar Brasileira (Brazilian Manor) in 1924. The young Lúcio Costa, graduating from ENBA in 1924, was awarded a prize in the second competition. This began his mentorship by Marianno Filho, who would sponsor his first visit to the colonial mining towns in the state of Minas Gerais. Costa would immerse himself in neocolonial theory, though he would soon rupture this affiliation and his relationship with Marianno Filho, emerging as one of the proponents of the new vanguard of Brazilian modernism in the 1930s, along with other ENBA students such as Cândido Portinari, Oscar Niemeyer, and Roberto Burle Marx.[24]

In the realm of science, the República Velha renamed Pedro II's beloved Museu Imperial as the Museu Nacional. Its holdings were transferred from their original building at the Campo de Santana to the vacated imperial palace at the Quinta da Boa Vista, now named the Palácio de São Cristóvão. Science had replaced the emperor. Ladislau de Souza Mello e Netto, the museum's director since 1874, retained his position during this transition of power, but many of the foreign scientists once welcomed at the museum were dismissed in a mood of nationalist retrenchment. Leadership at the Jardim Botânico was also reconfigured with the 1890 appointment of João Barbosa Rodrigues as director. The Jardim Botânico was transformed into an important scientific research institution during his directorship between 1890 and 1892 and again from 1903 until 1909. Barbosa Rodrigues augmented the garden's collection of live plants and addressed the necessity of conservation, particularly for native Brazilian species. A specialist in Brazilian palms, he founded a herbarium, museum, and library at the garden and published an influential reference work on the palm species of Brazil, entitled *Sertum palmarum brasiliensium*. The Jardim Botânico served as host to a number of traveling expeditions, many led by European scientists, dispatched to expand the garden's collection of Brazilian plants.

Despite their frequent involvement of European scientists, the Jardim Botânico's exploratory expeditions were becoming a particularly Brazilian endeavor, in which the state sought to integrate the vast hinterlands of the new Republic. In parallel with a massive wave of immigration, rapid urbanization, and increased industrialization, especially in the southern regions of Brazil, the country's natural wealth was positioned as part of its new modern identity. No longer merely the object of a curious emperor's scientific interests, these resources defined Brazil's identity.

In 1906 the Ministério da Agricultura, Indústria e Comércio (Ministry of Agriculture, Industry, and Commerce) was established, and the scientific institutions of the Museu Nacional and the Jardim Botânico were placed under its purview. In 1907 this new ministry joined forces with the positivist Ministério da Guerra (Ministry of War) for an exploratory joint venture, the Comissão de Linhas Telegráficas Estratégicas de Mato Grosso ao Amazonas (CLTEMTA: Commission for a Strategic Telegraph Line from Mato Grosso to Amazonas). It was placed under the leadership of 1st Lt.

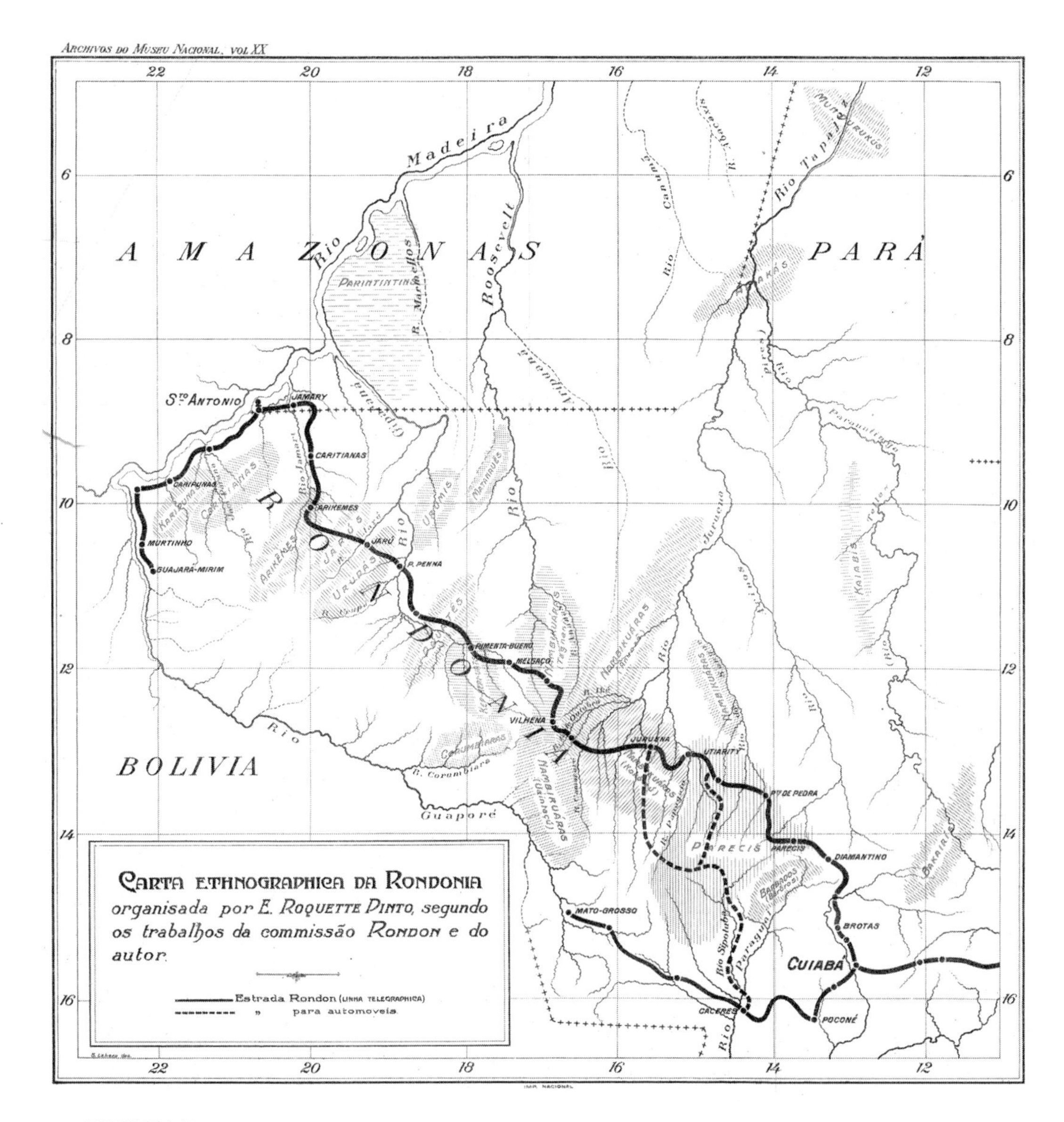

FIGURE 1.19.

Carta ethnographica da Rondônia, showing the path of the telegraph line connecting Cuiabá to Santo Antônio, 1917

Edgar Roquette-Pinto, *Rondônia: Anthropologia—Ethnographia*, Archivos do Museu Nacional do Rio de Janeiro, vol. 20 (Rio de Janeiro: Imprensa Nacional, 1917)

Cândido Mariano da Silva Rondon (1865–1958) of the Corpo de Engenheiros Militares, appointed by President Afonso Pena. The nine-year project, extending from 1907 to 1916, became known as the Comissão Rondon. The purpose of the commission was to construct a telegraph line between the cities of Cuiabá in the state of Mato Grosso and Santo Antônio do Rio Madeiro (now Porto Velho) in the state of Amazonas. It was envisioned that the peoples and territories of the faraway hinterlands of Brazil (the *sertão*) would thus be incorporated into the Republic, transforming what had developed as a coastal nation governed by urban Rio de Janeiro. However, the expedition was not planned merely to lay a telegraph line between the states of Mato Grosso and Amazonas. It was also a scientific expedition, this time conducted by Brazilians for the purposes of understanding and unifying their vast country, particularly the westernmost reaches of the Amazon basin and the northern *sertão*.

The botanist Frederico Carlos Hoehne (1882–1959), then the head gardener at the Museu Nacional, joined the Comissão Rondon from 1908 through 1909, identifying and collecting fifty-eight new plant species.[25] His role as the expedition's botanist was very similar to Auguste Glaziou's during the Missão Cruls expeditions of 1892 and 1894. The Comissão Rondon also studied areas of the *sertão* that might be suitable

FIGURE 1.20.
The Comissão Rondon, clearing a path for roads and telegraph line connections, Mato Grosso, ca. 1910
Photo by Argentina Reis/Acervo do Museu do Índio/Fundação Nacional do Índio, Brasil

for colonization, agriculture, and grazing. As part of his team's scientific activity, Rondon collected rich visual data, particularly on the indigenous peoples of Mato Grosso, through its innovative Cinematography and Photography Section, led by Maj. Thomaz Reis.[26]

This spirit of scientific inquiry evident in the intellectual atmosphere generated by the military-led Comissão Rondon reflected the growing influence of positivism throughout military academies during the República Velha.[27] Positivism, developed by the French philosopher Auguste Comte in the 1820s, was widely adopted in Latin America and particularly popular in Brazil. By the early 1880s, when the Igreja Positivista do Brasil (Positivist Church of Brazil) was founded, Comte's ideas were seen as particularly attractive within Brazil's technical schools and military academies, where many of the rising middle class were being educated. The emphasis on the idea of progress and development through a measured, rational methodology of economic development appealed to this new elite as the means through which Brazil might end colonial domination and achieve economic independence.[28] Positivism embraced strategies of technical progress and modernization, particularly the construction of railroads and industrialization. Appropriately, the motto on the new flag raised by the República Velha was "Ordem e Progresso" (Order and Progress)—the positivist creed of Comte—which embraced this vision of advancement through the rational work of science.[29]

The positivists also embraced nature as part of this scientific and rational world view. Alberto Torres (1865–1917), an intellectual and politician whose advocacy for a strong interventionist state would be influential in destabilizing the elites toward the end of the República Velha, was one of the first Brazilians to address the topic of the conservation of nature.[30] In his 1915 book *As fontes da vida no Brasil*, he states: "Civilization has a duty to conserve the unexploited resources of the earth, reserves destined for future generations, and to defend those which are in production against improvident exploitation, just as it has a duty to protect all races and nationalities against forms of competition that might threaten their vital interests, as well as the security, property, and prosperity of their posterity."[31] His political ideas were adopted by Getúlio Vargas and other leaders of the Revolução de 1930, who emphasized the importance of a strong state to achieve national unity.

Given the context of rapid industrialization and immigration, the task of defining a shared conception of modern national identity during the República Velha was a vexing one for the Brazilian elite. More than 2.6 million immigrants who arrived in Brazil between 1890 and 1919 (a rural labor force that immigrated after the 1888 abolition of slavery) set to work with the *fazendeiros*, the large estate owners growing coffee, sugar, and cotton for export. An ideology of *branqueamento*, the so-called whitening of the nation, was supported through a national policy that supported and subsidized European immigration.[32] But subsequent economic growth also led to rapid urban development and industrialization. Native-born Brazilians of Portuguese

FIGURE 1.21.
Emiliano di Cavalcanti, cover of the exhibition catalog of the *Semana de Arte Moderna* (São Paulo: Theatro Municipal de São Paulo, 1922)

© Estate of Emiliano di Cavalcanti/ International Center for the Arts of the Americas, Museum of Fine Arts, Houston

FIGURE 1.22.
Mina Klabin, native plant and cactus gardens for the house by Gregori Warchavchik for Luiz da Silva Prado, Rua Bahia, São Paulo, 1927–1928

Acervo Gregori Warchavchik/ Biblioteca da Faculdade de Arquitetura e Urbanismo, Universidade de São Paulo descent now mingled with upwardly mobile Italian, Spanish, German, Chinese, Japanese, Syrian, and Lebanese immigrants, a challenge for both the established middle class and the ruling elite. The oligarchs of the agricultural estates of São Paulo and Minas Gerais and the regime of "café com leite" (coffee with milk) gradually lost power to an industrializing São Paulo.[33] With this urban industrialization and a rising immigrant working class, Brazil saw the emergence of trade unions, strikes, discontent with the oligarchy, and the establishment of the Communist Party in 1922.

Thus the concept of *brasilidade* (Brazilianness) emerged as part of these modernizing processes. A concern of both the upper classes of ruling elites and cultural intellectuals, it is both discriminatory and inclusive in regard to the growing immigrant population. As a positioning of identity, *brasilidade* oscillated between poles of a fixed essence and an ongoing, transformable construct.[34] Critical posturing of *brasilidade* grew from a festival of avant-garde art and literature held at the Theatro Municipal in São Paulo in 1922, the Semana de Arte Moderna (Modern Art Week), featuring the artists and poets Emiliano di Cavalcanti, Anita Malfatti, Mário de Andrade, and Oswald de Andrade. The collective was later joined by the painter Tarsila do Amaral. This vanguard proved influential on the São Paulo architect Gregori Warchavchik as well as his wife Mina Klabin, whose designs for cactus gardens provided the appropriate foil of color and texture to the abstract cubic volumes of Warchavchik's modern villas.[35]

The hero of this self-conscious search for a modern Brazilian cultural identity, which looked as much to the folklore and flora of the Brazilian countryside as to the urban elite, was a compelling character named Macunaíma, the shape-shifting hero of the 1928 novel of the same name by Mário de Andrade.[36] *Macunaíma* represented a blended possibility for the construction of *brasilidade*—a semiwild jungle boy embodying the three Brazilian peoples (African, Indian, and Iberian)—several years before Gilberto Freyre's 1933 publication of *Casa-grande e senzala*, celebrating the racial and cultural miscegenation practiced by the Portuguese in Brazil, who had their own mixed heritage of North African Arabs and Sephardic Jews.[37]

Another key text of the São Paulo modernists was Oswald de Andrade's 1928 *Manifesto antropófago*, an argument for a metaphorical cultural cannibalism: anthropophagy. Drawing from the 1554 incident in which the first bishop of Brazil, Pedro Fernandes Sardinha, was eaten by the Tupi Caeté tribe, the modernists interpreted the consumption of the priest not as a slaughter but as the tribe's assimilation of the virtues of the "other." Likewise, the modernists argued for a metaphorical cannibalism and assimilation of both inherited Western culture and New World knowledge.[38] *Brasilidade* was also driven by the cultural observations and critiques of Europeans, including the poet Blaise Cendrars, the architect Le Corbusier, and the anthropologist Claude Lévi-Strauss.[39] The manifesto's witty phrase "Only Cannibalism unites us . . . Tupi, or not Tupi, that is the question" became the mantra of a generation of vanguard artists and writers. This cultural argument influenced the development of a particularly Brazilian modernist identity in the work of many architects as well, including Gregori Warchavchik, Lúcio Costa, Oscar Niemeyer, and Affonso Eduardo Reidy, and would emerge in the rich oeuvre of the landscape architect Roberto Burle Marx as well.[40]

The Vargas Era, 1930–1945

The rise of Getúlio Vargas (1882–1954), a former governor of the southern state of Rio Grande do Sul who would become Brazil's longest serving president, led the successful Revolução de 1930 that brought an end to the República Velha. The revolution, a military coup deposing President Washington Luís, was supported by discontented sectors of the military and civilian Brazilian population during the Republic's waning years. The growing urban bourgeoisie, dissatisfied with the political power of the elite landowners from the states of São Paulo and Minas Gerais, was calling for democratic changes and was supported by oppositional military movements that rose from within the officers' corps of the army and navy.[41]

Vargas led the military junta that took control in 1930 and remained in power through 1945. He sought to continue the economic, industrial, and agricultural growth of the country through a strong centralized state, with a renewed interest in the development of the vast interior. His leadership consisted of three successive phases. From 1930 to 1934 Vargas governed by decree as the head of the Provisional Government, pending the adoption of a new Constitution. During the second period of the Constitution of 1934, from 1934 to 1937, Vargas governed as president, sharing power with a democratically elected legislature. The third phase, the Estado Novo (New State) period from 1937 to 1945, was initiated by a coup, after which Vargas imposed a new authoritarian Constitution and shut down Congress, assuming dictatorial powers. His deposition from power in 1945 and the subsequent redemocratization of Brazil with yet another Constitution in 1946 marked the end of the Vargas era and the beginning of a democratic period that would last until the military coup of 1964.

During the first years after the 1930 revolution, Vargas sought to merge the urbanized coastal regions with the vast hinterland *sertão*, bringing modernizing projects and social services to the country's farthest reaches. But this unifying ambition, particularly in Brazil's tropical forest region, was greatly hindered by disease, particularly mosquito-borne malaria. Interior expansion and colonization were thus dependent on the reduction of disease. This led to Vargas's establishment of a new ministry on November 14, 1930: the Ministério da Educação e Saúde Pública (Ministry of Education and Public Health), joining the existing Ministério da Guerra and Ministério da Agricultura, Indústria e Comércio—the two agencies responsible for the Comissão Rondon during the República Velha.[42] Echoing the Comissão Rondon telegraph project, Vargas unified and centralized the post office and telegraph sectors

FIGURE 1.23.
Ministério da Educação e Saúde building under construction, Rio de Janeiro, ca. 1938

Arquivo Gustavo Capanema/ Fundação Getúlio Vargas, Centro de Pesquisa e Documentação/ Fundação Oscar Niemeyer © 2017 Artists Rights Society (ARS), New York/AUTVIS, São Paulo

FIGURE 1.24.
Gustavo Capanema (*third from left*) and Getúlio Vargas (*fourth from left*) at the minister's private roof garden with Celso Antônio's sculpture *Moça reclinada* during the opening celebrations of the Ministério de Educação e Saúde, Rio de Janeiro, 1944

Arquivo Gustavo Capanema/ Fundação Getúlio Vargas, Centro de Pesquisa e Documentação/ Fundação Oscar Niemeyer © 2017 Artists Rights Society (ARS), New York/AUTVIS, São Paulo

in 1931, establishing the Departamento de Correios e Telégrafos (Department of Post and Telegraphs). In 1934 Vargas appointed the charismatic and progressive intellectual Gustavo Capanema (1900–1985) as his second minister of education and public health, who would serve until the end of the Vargas era in 1945. Capanema's vanguard leadership at the ministry established complex links among science, nature, education, health, and culture.[43]

Vargas's state support of the pedagogical mission of the Ministério da Educação e Saúde Pública (MES) was reflected in his acceptance of Capanema's visionary commissioning of modern architects for significant public buildings, projecting a progressive image of Brazilian modernity and culture onto an international stage.[44] The architectural projects sponsored by the MES—the ministry's own new headquarters building in Rio de Janeiro, the project for a new University of Brazil, and the Brazilian Pavilion of the 1939 New York World's Fair, among others—embraced the notion that architecture and indeed nature could be mobilized both operationally and expressively to support a cultural construct. They drew from the unifying principles of the International Style while transforming it through a particularly Brazilian concern for formal diversity.[45]

In parallel with Capanema's ambitious modern building program, Vargas executed two extremely important pieces of conservationist and preservationist legislation that would prove critical to future environmental movements in Brazil: the Código Florestal Brasileiro (Brazilian Forestry Code) in 1934 and the Serviço do Patrimônio Histórico e Artístico Nacional (SPHAN: Department of National Historic and Artistic Heritage) in 1937.[46] These two legislative acts continued to evolve from their initiation during the Vargas era through the military dictatorship that began in 1964 and would become the legal anchors for Burle Marx's later arguments for environmental and cultural conservation and protection. Vargas's outreach to the hinterlands did not only concern economic development, access to resources, and strategic border protection. His government supported the conservation of natural areas as part of a greater modernizing project, with the Código Florestal Brasileiro as a catalyst that led to the designation of the country's first national park in 1937.

Lúcio Costa (1902–1998), the architect, urban planner, and mentor to a young Roberto Burle Marx, was a significant figure in the modernization program implemented by Vargas. In December 1930 the first minister of the Ministério da Educação e Saúde Pública, Francisco Campos, appointed the 29-year-old Costa, a 1924 graduate of the Escola Nacional de Belas Artes, as the new director of the school. From this pedagogical platform Costa confirmed his radical break with the neocolonial style supported by José Marianno Filho, abandoning eclecticism in favor of the new European "International Style" modernism.[47] He also proposed that courses in urbanism and landscape be taught at the school; throughout his career, Costa was a staunch defender of the integration of architecture and the landscape. He also argued for the establishment of a distinct school of architecture, separate from the ENBA.

FIGURE 1.25.
Roberto Burle Marx, roof garden of the Alfredo Schwartz residence by architects Lúcio Costa and Gregori Warchavchik, Rio de Janeiro, 1932
Acervo Lúcio Costa and Acervo Gregori Warchavchik/Biblioteca da Faculdade de Arquitetura e Urbanismo, Universidade de São Paulo

He invited the São Paulo architect Gregori Warchavchik to teach the architecture course at the school. The two men formed an architectural practice in Rio de Janeiro for three years, employing the young Oscar Niemeyer and commissioning Burle Marx's first garden, the roof terrace of their Casa Schwartz in Copacabana in 1932, with its echoes of Mina Klabin's cactus gardens. However, Costa's tenure at the ENBA lasted less than one year before he was forced out in September 1931 by the conservative faculty, who deplored the radical new modernist curricular approach that he sought for the staid institution. The students—including Roberto Burle Marx and the architects Oscar Niemeyer, Affonso Eduardo Reidy, Carlos Leão, and Jorge Moreira—went on strike in support of Costa, but he would never return to ENBA to teach.

In 1936 Costa was commissioned by Capanema to work on two significant projects for Rio de Janeiro: the new headquarters building for the Ministério da Educaçao e Saúde Pública and a new campus for the Universidade do Brasil, a proposed transformation of the existing Universidade do Rio de Janeiro that would unify its many separate schools and faculties. The proposed site for the new university campus was the former imperial palace grounds at the Quinta da Boa Vista.[48] At Costa's suggestion, Capanema invited the internationally known Swiss modernist architect Charles-Édouard Jeanneret (known as Le Corbusier), who had lectured at ENBA in 1929, to come to Brazil from Paris in 1936 to consult with the local Brazilian architectural teams for both projects. Though the project for the University of Brazil at the Quinta da Boa Vista was abandoned, the ministry headquarters in the Castelo district of downtown Rio de Janeiro would become one of the most important modern buildings in Latin America, celebrated internationally as the featured building of the 1943 "Brazil Builds" exhibition at the Museum of Modern Art, New York.

The Serviço do Patrimônio Histórico e Artístico Nacional (SPHAN) was established in 1937 by Vargas's Decreto-Lei No. 25 under the jurisdiction of the Ministério da Educação e Saúde Pública, an agency that would provide a legal mechanism for classifying and protecting the country's cultural heritage.[49] In 1937 Capanema appointed Rodrigo Mello Franco de Andrade (1898–1969) as the first director of SPHAN. Costa would participate in SPHAN as well: in addition to his ongoing architectural work commissioned by Capanema, Mello Franco de Andrade appointed Costa as a specialized regional research technician for SPHAN in 1939. In 1946 Costa was designated the national director of the Divisão de Estudos e Tombamento (Division of Research and Registration)—a position that he would maintain until 1972. Costa brought a deep knowledge and appreciation of colonial architecture along with an impassioned support of Brazilian modernism. Together, Mello Franco de Andrade and Costa shaped a consistent vision of Brazilian cultural heritage for decades.

Decreto-Lei No. 25 broadly defined Brazil's historic and artistic patrimony as "those assets, moveable or immovable . . . whose conservation is of public interest due to their exceptional value."[50] It instituted four registration books (*livros do tombo*) to list these assets by category. Significantly, in its description of the national patrimony, Decreto-Lei No. 25 explicitly cites natural monuments and remarkable landscapes—immovable assets—as worthy of conservation and protection. This law is particularly noteworthy because it acknowledged the importance of the environment within the frame of cultural patrimony—a notion that Burle Marx would build upon years later as a cultural counselor.

Good Neighbors: The Brazilian Pavilion

In 1938, during the ongoing development of the new headquarters building of the Ministério da Educação e Saúde Pública and the campus of the University of Brazil, a new competition was launched by the Ministério do Trabalho, Indústria e Comércio (Ministry of Labor, Industry, and Commerce).[51] For Vargas, the Pavilhão Brasileiro (Brazilian Pavilion) for the 1939 New York World's Fair had the potential to propagate an aura of Brazilian cultural and economic wealth to an interested North American audience.[52] With the Axis powers on the rise in Germany and Italy, Franklin D. Roosevelt was courting Vargas with the United States' "Good Neighbor" policy in South America. In Vargas's political revolution of 1937 he evoked fear of a Communist threat, dissolved the legislative Congress, and imposed a new authoritarian Constitution, shifting his presidency to a veritable dictatorial regime: the Estado Novo. Despite Roosevelt's recognition of Vargas's authoritarianism, Brazil's allegiance to the Allies was critical for the development of a Pan-American political bloc.

Though Vargas's architectural taste was eclectic, the jury for the pavilion competition—composed of members of the Ministério do Trabalho and the Instituto de Arquitetos do Brasil (Institute of Architects of Brazil)—embraced modernist architecture over the neocolonial style for this World's Fair, with its theme of "The World of Tomorrow." The selection criterion was described as "an architectural form capable of translating an expression of the Brazilian environment."[53] Lúcio Costa, who received the first prize for his pavilion's "espírito de brasilidade" (Brazilian spirit),

FIGURE 1.26.
Lúcio Costa, perspective sketch of the courtyard and lily pond from his competition entry for the Pavilhão Brasileiro, New York World's Fair Exhibition, 1938
Acervo Lúcio Costa

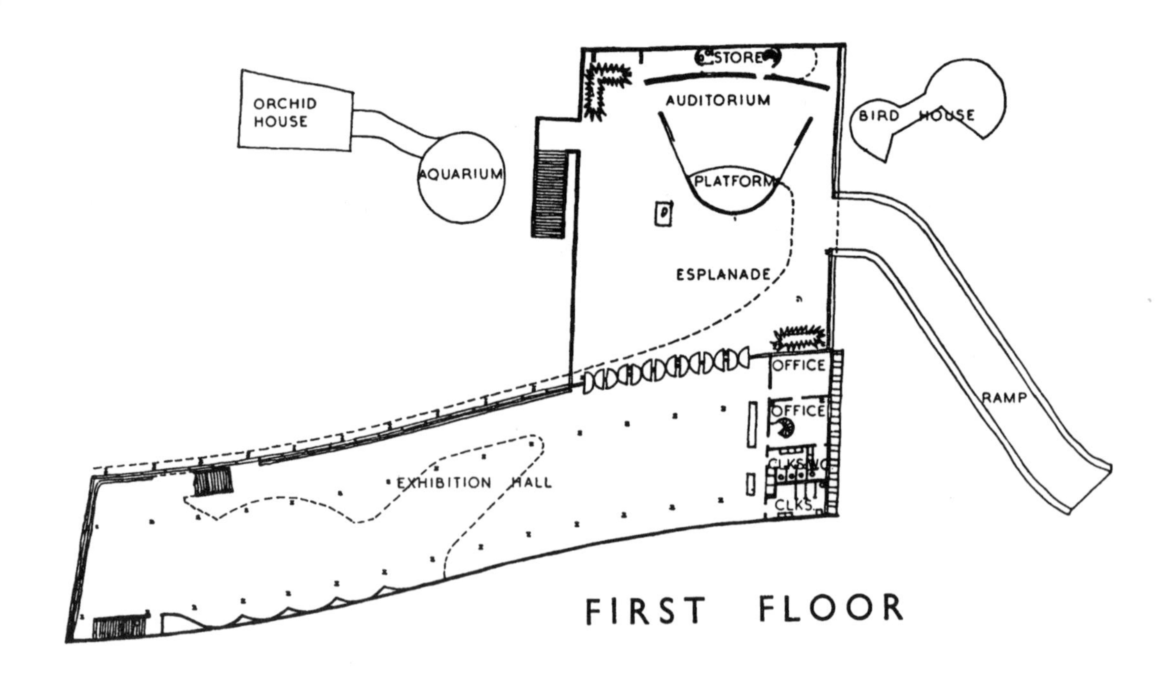

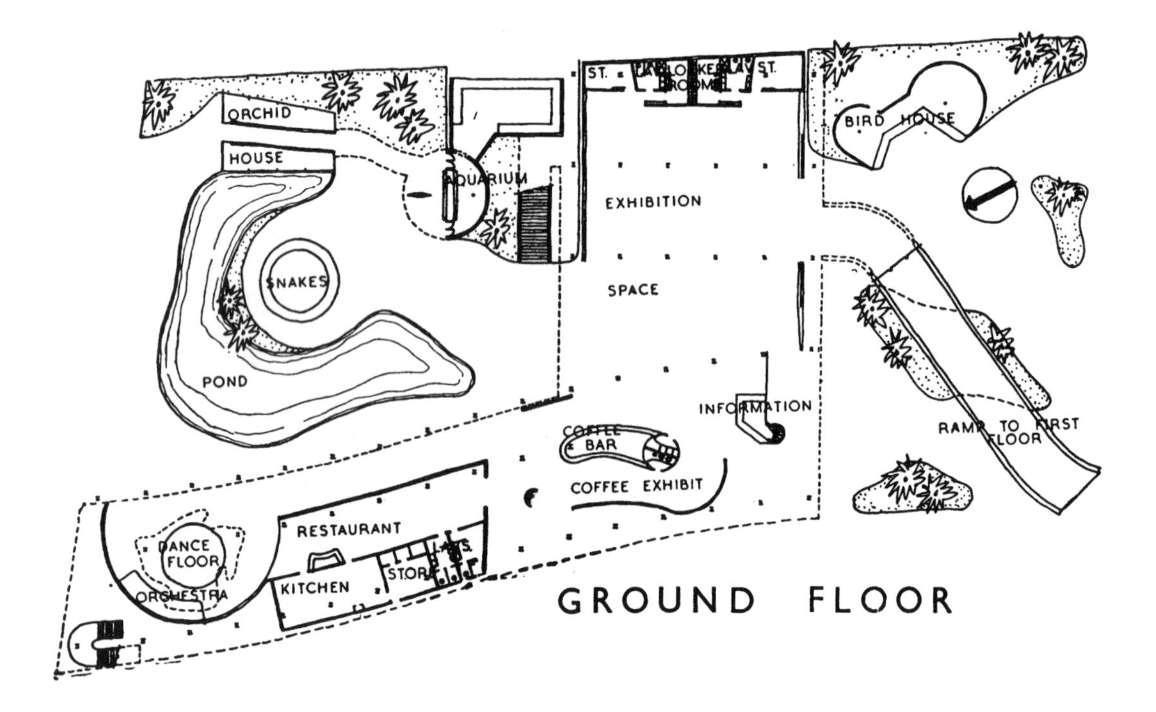

FIGURE 1.27.

Lúcio Costa and Oscar Niemeyer, plans of their collaborative project for the Pavilhão Brasileiro, New York World's Fair Exhibition, 1939

Acervo Lúcio Costa and Fundação Oscar Niemeyer/Digital Image © The Museum of Modern Art/ Licensed by SCALA/Art Resource, New York and © 2017 Artists Rights Society (ARS), New York/ AUTVIS, São Paulo elected to collaborate with Oscar Niemeyer (1907–2012), the second-place winner. Located on a curved rectangular site in Flushing Meadows, a former wetland and ash dump in Queens, New York, their pavilion consisted of a gently curved L-shaped two-story structure with a sweeping ramp leading to the second level of the building's exhibition hall. The pavilion was later described by Philip Goodwin in the Museum of Modern Art's 1943 *Brazil Builds* exhibition catalogue as "light-heartedly elegant," with "fluid space treatment and fresh detail."[54] Yet what Costa evoked most skillfully in his own competition entry and with Niemeyer in the final pavilion was an integration of the landscape and tropical climate into this iteration of a distinctly Brazilian and state-supported vision of modernist architecture.

The pavilion's architecture aimed to express a particularly Brazilian modernism with its gentle curves, the use of operable *quebra-sol* (sun shade) panels along the south façade, evocative of the intense tropical sun, and its floor-to-ceiling glazing of the double-height interior exhibition hall facing the courtyard, creating a transparent connection between indoor and outdoor space. Perhaps most significantly, the courtyard evoked a tropical paradise, echoing the long Brazilian history of the neoclassical palace set within a dynamic picturesque garden. The garden, even in Costa's first competition entry, was anchored by a free-form amoeboid pond with aquatic plants, including the famed *Victoria amazonica* giant water lilies, along with an orchid house, an aviary with tropical birds, an aquarium with tropical fish, and a dramatic snake pit.[55] The snake pit and orchid house were not built, but the astonishing presence of the giant water lilies in this former marshland in Queens evoked the majesty of the Amazon region and native Brazilian vegetation.

Burle Marx did not participate in the design of the gardens of the Pavilhão Brasileiro, though by 1938 he was beginning work in Rio de Janeiro with Costa on the roof and plaza gardens of the Ministério da Educação e Saúde Pública. Nevertheless, he would certainly have been aware of the New York project, not only because of his close association with Costa but also because of his brother Walter Burle Marx's participation as the director of the pavilion's musical programming. The pavilion's gardens were drawn by the American landscape architect Thomas Drees Price (1901–1989). Price was born in Brazil to missionary parents and later emigrated to the United States, where he studied landscape architecture. In 1932 he was recruited to work at the New York City Department of Parks and Recreation, where he was subsequently appointed a staff member for the 1939 World's Fair Commission. As Price was considered a Brazilian landscape architect at the Parks Department, he was selected to work with the Brazilian architects on the development of plans for the gardens of the Pavilhão Brasileiro.

The exhibition content of the Pavilhão Brasileiro emphasized the Estado Novo's nationalist modernizing project of integrating the extents of Brazil's territory and consolidating the wealth of its natural resources. The country's commodity production was showcased, with elements of the mining industry—large samples of nickel, chrome, and iron ore—placed at the base of a large bust of Vargas. The pavilion also included exhibits about Brazil's vast forests, particularly the stands of native Brazilian pine, *Araucaria angustifolia*, reputed for its excellent timber and paper pulp production. The "luxury woods" of Brazil were also described, including Brazilian walnut (*Ocotea porosa*), Brazilian rosewood (*Dalbergia nigra*), and ipê-peroba (*Paratecoma peroba*), noting that these hardwood forest commodities would be valuable exports to the United States and other foreign partners. Mineral, timber, and rubber exports were particularly desirable for the Allies' ongoing war effort.[56] Yet more and more Brazilians were concerned with the consequences of this rapid modernization, extractive mining, and forest exploitation: a nascent conservationist movement was growing. Meanwhile, Roosevelt's efforts to gain Brazil's support of the Allies in World War II through the Good Neighbor policy would prove successful—Vargas reversed his neutral stance in 1941, agreeing to align with any continental American nation in the event of attack.

FIGURE 1.28.
Lúcio Costa and Oscar Niemeyer, lily pond of the Pavilhão Brasileiro, New York World's Fair Exhibition, 1939
Photo by Fay S. Lincoln/Eberly Family Special Collections Library, Pennsylvania State University Libraries/Fundação Oscar Niemeyer © 2017 Artists Rights Society (ARS), New York/AUTVIS, São Paulo

FIGURE 1.29.
Promotional literature on Brazil's export commodities distributed at the Pavilhão Brasileiro, New York World's Fair Exhibition, 1939
Donald G. Larson Collection on International Expositions and Fairs, Special Collections Research Center, Henry Madden Library, California State University, Fresno

Experiments in Democracy, 1945–1964

The United States entered World War II on December 7, 1941, after the Japanese bombing of the American fleet in Pearl Harbor, Hawaii. In August 1942 Vargas joined the Allies in declaring war on the Axis powers after the sinking of Brazilian merchant ships by German submarines. However, Brazil's participation in the war strengthened popular pressure against the Estado Novo regime in favor of redemocratization and free elections. Vargas was not able to retain sufficient support for the continuation of his authoritarian presidency and was deposed by his own military in a surprise coup on October 29, 1945.

After Vargas's regime was overthrown, Brazil entered into a democratic period that would last until 1964. In 1946 Gen. Eurico Gaspar Dutra was elected president for a five-year term and the country's fifth Constitution was adopted, marking the return to democracy. Vargas would return a second time to the presidency in 1951 through a democratic election, and he embraced a new program of economic developmentalism based on the establishment of state-owned industrial monopolies. Due to increasing popular dissatisfaction with his presidency, he ended his political career with a bullet to the heart in 1954, leaving a dramatic suicide note and an indelible legacy.

Brazil experienced a period of rapid economic growth during Juscelino Kubitschek's five-year presidency, beginning in 1956 and culminating with the inauguration of the new central capital of Brasília, inscribed into the landscape of Brazil's central plateau, in 1960. With the transfer of the federal capital to Brasília, Rio de Janeiro lost some of its political and cultural clout, while São Paulo continued to rise as a cultural capital, a trajectory that had begun in the 1950s with the state and municipal support of museums, parks, and the new biennial art and architecture exhibitions at Parque do Ibirapuera. Meanwhile, Rio restructured itself as the Estado da Guanabara (State of Guanabara), the designation of the city from 1960 to 1975. Again the state and municipal government initiated the large landfill project of the Parque do Flamengo, with Burle Marx's public gardens transforming the waterfront of the Baía de Guanabara. But, following Kubitschek, the institutional crises prompted by the rapid presidential succession of Jânio Quadros, Ranieri Mazzilli, and João Goulart were coupled with high inflation and popular discontent. These factors, along with the support of the United States government and its embassy in Brazil, led to the successful Brazilian military coup of March 31, 1964.

FIGURE 1.30.
Aerial view of the Esplanada dos Ministérios, Brasília, ca. 1958
Photo by Mario Fontenelle/Arquivo Público do Distrito Federal/Fundação Oscar Niemeyer © 2017 Artists Rights Society (ARS), New York/AUTVIS, São Paulo

FIGURE 1.31.
Landfill construction at Parque do Flamengo, Rio de Janeiro, ca. 1961
Photo by Marcel Gautherot/Instituto Moreira Salles Collection

The Military Regime, 1964–1985

Marshal Humberto de Alencar Castelo Branco was selected by the Congress to serve as the first president of the military regime after the 1964 coup and would serve through March 1967. During the first years of the dictatorship that would last until 1985, intense economic growth was spurred by the regime. But this so-called *milagre econômico brasileiro* (Brazilian Miracle) was enabled not only by the government's heavy investment in infrastructure and energy production but also by a new Constitution that stifled freedom of speech and political opposition. The military's hard-line stance on popular dissent resulted in the censorship, torture, imprisonment, and deportation of thousands of Brazilian citizens. Nonetheless, during this time, the regime continued the pattern of state-supported nationalist culture, with the establishment of a new Conselho Federal de Cultura (Federal Council of Culture) as an elite civilian advisory counsel to the recently renamed Ministério da Educação e Cultura (Ministry of Education and Culture).

The Council

Though a first Conselho Nacional de Cultura (National Council of Culture) had been established in 1938 under Vargas, it had been largely dormant since 1945. It was revived on February 23, 1961, during the brief presidency of Jânio Quadros with Decreto-Lei No. 50.293, consisting of a council of twenty-nine members, but was suspended for political reasons in 1964 by the military regime.[57] Under Castelo Branco's presidency, the council was reconfigured as the Conselho Federal de Cultura (Federal Council of Culture) on November 21, 1966, with Decreto-Lei No. 74 and would henceforth consist of twenty-four counselors appointed by the president of the Republic to one of four separate councils, each representing a specialty subject area—arts, letters, social sciences, and national historic and artistic patrimony.[58] The counselors, given the task to "formulate a national culture policy," were to be "eminent personalities of Brazilian culture and of well-known repute."[59] Like Vargas's original Conselho Nacional de Cultura, this Conselho Federal de Cultura was organized by the Ministério da Educação e Cultura and served a greater intellectual project of formulating a unified state-sponsored national culture. During the military dictatorship that began in the 1960s, however, the traditional conception of culture was overlaid with a new nationalism designed to suppress the radical artistic production critical of the regime.

In February 1967 the Conselho Federal de Cultura was inaugurated by President Humberto de Alencar Castelo Branco.[60] Appointed as a member of the Câmara de Artes (Arts Council), Roberto Burle Marx served actively on the council from 1967 through 1974 alongside other well-known members of the Brazilian cultural elite, including sociologist Gilberto Freyre, novelists Rachel de Queiroz and João

Guimarães Rosa, and the art historian Rodrigo Mello Franco de Andrade, the former director of SPHAN, the public agency responsible for the protection of Brazil's historic and artistic heritage.[61] By then the concept of "culture" had been embedded into the very structures and personages of the government. The Palácio da Cultura (Palace of Culture) was the new name given to Lúcio Costa's landmark building of the Ministério da Educaçao e Saúde Pública upon the transfer of this ministry to the new federal capital of Brasília in 1960. The name of the ministry itself was changed in 1967 to the Ministério da Educaçao e Cultura after the health division had been extracted into its own agency. The minister himself was accordingly renamed the minister of education and culture.

During frequent meetings at the Palácio da Cultura in Rio de Janeiro, the Conselho Federal de Cultura acted in an advisory and consultative role to the minister of education and culture, supporting cultural programming and awarding funding and grants to both public and private cultural institutions. The twenty-four counselors had dissimilar allegiances and motivations for accepting their appointments, but each had a certain authority within a particular field—in the case of Roberto Burle Marx, this was in the realm of the natural and constructed Brazilian landscape. In this respect, he was a unique figure on the council, which focused on traditional artistic realms of cultural production. Burle Marx's advocacy as counselor shifted well beyond cultural support to embrace the realm of environmental protection and even activism—positions clearly indicated in the council's published record of his depositions.

The counselors were a highly productive group and met often. As part of its mandate in Decreto-Lei No. 74, the Ministério da Educação e Cultura published a journal of the council's meeting minutes: *Cultura* was launched in July 1967 as a monthly periodical and was renamed *Boletim do Conselho Federal de Cultura* in 1971 and published quarterly. Both publications provide an invaluable record of the work of the council. Each of the issues included the full bureaucratic proceedings of the meetings, including the official opinions ("Pareceres"), minutes of the legislative and funding votes of the full plenary sessions ("Atas"), and reprints of reports of the council's work appearing in the Brazilian media ("Noticiário"). The richest part of these journals, however, was the section entitled "Estudos e proposições," a record of the consular depositions written by the members of the council and orated at the plenary sessions. The transcriptions of these carefully constructed position pieces offer a fascinating insight into the specific interests and passions of the individual counselors and together illuminate the construction of a national cultural identity during the most oppressive years of the military dictatorship.

In addition to the proceedings of the meetings published in *Cultura* and *Boletim do Conselho Federal de Cultura*, the council also produced a quarterly publication entitled the *Revista Brasileira de Cultura*, intended to disseminate the work of the counselors to the general public.[62] It also published the comprehensive *Atlas cultural*

FIGURE 1.32.
Cover of *Cultura* 4, no. 39 (September 1970)
Acervo da Fundação Biblioteca Nacional do Brasil

do Brasil along with over thirty additional books authored by individual counselors, addressing particular aspects of national culture.[63] While serving as a member of the Conselho Federal de Cultura, Burle Marx delivered a total of seventeen depositions to the plenary council between 1967 and 1973, each published in *Cultura* or *Boletim do Conselho Federal de Cultura*. In addition, he wrote one longer deposition for the *Revista Brasileira de Cultura*, entitled "Jardim e ecologia" (Garden and Ecology), published in the first issue in July–September 1969.

Burle Marx delivered his last plenary deposition to the Conselho Federal de Cultura in July 1973 and officially stepped down from the position of counselor in 1974 after seven years of service. His departure was timely. The power of the Conselho Federal de Cultura was significantly reduced by the end of 1972 with the approval of the Política Nacional de Cultura (National Culture Policy), which claimed the executive authority of the Conselho Federal de Cultura and reduced it to a purely administrative role. The council's funding authority for cultural programming was transferred in 1974 to the Programa de Ação Cultural (Cultural Action Program), established by the minister of education and culture, Jarbas Passarinho, at the end of his tenure. Resources were distributed to newly created entities such as the Fundação Nacional de Artes (National Foundation for the Arts), which executed its own cultural programming and budget allocation. Though the council would remain active until 1990 when it was formally dissolved, its political influence had been greatly reduced.[64]

Burle Marx approached his role as counselor as a cultural project itself, which provided him with an effective platform for asserting his views on the Brazilian landscape while exhibiting a bold voice of caution against the rapid development and resource exploitation he observed. This series of eighteen depositions is particularly distinctive because of the explicit political and legal character of the texts and the revelation of Burle Marx's little-known affiliation with the military regime in Brazil as a member of the Conselho Federal de Cultura. During the dictatorship, a period driven by policies and theories of economic development, Burle Marx, serving as one of an elite group of advisors to the president of the Republic, responded with a novel ecological and cultural argument for the environmental conservation and preservation of Brazil's natural and cultural landscapes.

FIGURE 2.1.
Headquarters building of the Ministério da Educação e Saúde, Rio de Janeiro, ca. 1945

Arquivo Gustavo Capanema/Fundação Getúlio Vargas, Centro de Pesquisa e Documentação/Fundação Oscar Niemeyer © 2017 Artists Rights Society (ARS), New York/AUTVIS, São Paulo

CHAPTER 2
Forest Narratives

Roberto Burle Marx's earliest work as a landscape architect emerged in parallel with the presidency of Getúlio Vargas in the 1930s. With his earliest projects in the northeastern city of Recife and the capital city of Rio de Janeiro, Burle Marx explored the role of ecology and celebrated the forest biodiversity within Brazil as a key element of Brazilian modernity. He would continue to develop this theme throughout his professional life.

Burle Marx's early plazas are public spaces for the civic engagement of an actively modernizing state, incorporating narratives of exploration and engagement with the hinterlands into an urban context, thereby promoting the notion of their cultural significance and concomitant conservation. Several decades later, Burle Marx would describe the catastrophic loss of Brazilian forests due to irrational exploitation in his impassioned testimonies to the Conselho Federal de Cultura at plenary councils held at the Ministério da Educação e Saúde (Ministry of Education and Health), a building whose plaza and roof gardens he had designed during this period. Often evoking the Código Florestal Brasileiro (Brazilian Forestry Code) in his depositions, Burle Marx stated that these acts of deforestation were in violation of the law.

The Forestry Code, first enacted in 1934, was rewritten twice, once in 1965 by the military regime and again in 2012.[1] The history of this legislation provides fascinating insight into the development of environmentalism in Brazil, reflecting a trajectory of nation building and political maneuvering as well as the defining of national, cultural, and ecological values.

While a young Burle Marx was developing his plaza projects in Recife during the early years of the Vargas administration, the Primeira Conferência Brasileira de Proteção à Natureza (First Brazilian Conference on Nature Protection) was held in Rio de Janeiro. Organized by a group of scientists with the support of the Vargas administration, the conference was held from April 8 to 15, 1934, at the Museu Nacional do Rio de Janeiro, the institution housed in the former imperial palace at the Quinta da Boa Vista.[2] Initiated by the scientist Alberto José Sampaio (1881–1946) and the botanist Frederico Carlos Hoehne (1882–1959), working with the director of the Museu Nacional, Edgar Roquette-Pinto, the conference identified the protection and conservation of nature as an integral part of the positivist cultural, scientific, and economic vision for Vargas's new modern state. As a part of his argument that the conservation of nature and economic development were not mutually exclusive, Sampaio evoked the prescient ideas of Alberto Torres (1865–1917) at the conference, who had first addressed the topic of resource conservation during the República Velha. Sampaio posited both conservation and the rational use of Brazil's natural resources as part of the foundation upon which the new national identity might be established.

Noting the importance of rare and endangered Brazilian plants, participants in the First Brazilian Conference on Nature Protection presented conservation as both an ethical and an aesthetic imperative.[3] The conference opened with a reading of Johann Wolfgang von Goethe's *Aphorisms on Nature* (ca. 1780), and the organizers emphasized the importance of aesthetics in the valuation of the natural world.[4] But the natural world was not simply a beautiful wild garden: it would provide the necessary resources for economically valuable industries.[5] The conference organizers were certainly aware of the polemics of preservation in other countries, particularly in the United States. The debate there was between the preservationist John Muir (1838–1914), who advocated for nature's spiritual value, and the conservationist Gifford Pinchot (1865–1946), who prioritized the sustainable use of natural resources. The Brazilian organizers of the Conference on Nature Protection established a third position, in which the concepts of conservation, protection, and preservation were interchangeable. Utilitarian, scientific, and aesthetic arguments were not differentiated; for the Brazilians, the greater project was the union of nature and nationhood.

The First Brazilian Conference on Nature Protection was successful in many ways, yielding the incorporation of a Forestry Code, Mining Code, and Water Code into the Constitution of 1934 as well as the first steps toward a national park system.[6] Drafted by an elected Constitutional Assembly and ratified by Vargas on July 16, 1934, the Constitution included an article mandating that federal and state governments protect the *belezas naturais* (natural beauties) of Brazil.

FIGURE 2.2.
Museu Nacional, formerly the Paço Imperial, Quinta da Boa Vista, Rio de Janeiro, ca. 1930
Photo by Augusto Malta/Gilberto Ferrez Collection/Instituto Moreira Salles

The first Forestry Code of Brazil of 1934, written by the minister of agriculture, Edmundo Navarro de Andrade, and enacted by Vargas as Decreto No. 23.793, established the concept of protected forests and reserved lands. The code prohibited private landowners from cutting down more than three-quarters of the trees on the forested areas of their property and also forbade the cutting of trees that grew along watercourses, protected watersheds, or provided habitat for rare species. Industries were required to replant trees, but the code did allow a substitution of species—an existing forest might be entirely cleared and then replanted with a new homogenous forest for future industrial use. The Forestry Code stated that forests were part of the common interest of all Brazilians and defined four forest types: productive (open to commercial logging by permit), protective (native forests protecting watersheds, soils, public health, scenery, and rare species), model (meaning replanted forests), and remnant (native forests protected in national, state, and municipal parks).

The Forestry Code was intended to regulate the use of resources, but few oversight mechanisms were provided and enforcement of the legislation was almost impossible. Nor did a conservationist strategy emerge at the federal level beyond some oversight for profitable agricultural products such as Brazilian pine (*Araucaria angustifolia*) or yerba mate (*Ilex paraguariensis*). But the code did provide leverage for a growing movement supporting the conservation of natural heritage sites in Brazil and the establishment of the country's first three national parks.[7]

Vargas considered the creation of national parks to be a particularly nationalist endeavor and was responsible for the establishment of the first three parks in Brazil: Parque Nacional de Itatiaia (Rio de Janeiro) in 1937; Parque Nacional do Iguaçu (Paraná) in 1939; and Parque Nacional da Serra dos Órgãos (Rio de Janeiro), also in 1939. No additional national parks would be established for twenty more years, when three parks were added to the national register under the administration of President Juscelino Kubitschek.

The Vargas administration was not the first, however, to suggest the creation of national parks in Brazil. In 1876, inspired by the creation of Yellowstone National Park in the United States four years earlier by President Ulysses S. Grant, the engineer, politician, and abolitionist André Rebouças (1838–1898) proposed the establishment of two national parks in Brazil. One was located at the Ilha do Bananal, a fluvial island formed by the Rio Araguaia in the state now known as Tocantins, and the other at the Salto de Sete Quedas, the sublime waterfalls along the Rio Paraná at the border between Brazil and Paraguay. At the time, Rebouças wrote: "The current generation can give no greater gift to the generation to come than to reserve intact, free of iron and smoke, the beautiful islands of Araguaia and of Paraná."[8] Indeed, many of the early environmentalist arguments were made by abolitionists such as Rebouças and Joaquim Nabuco, who saw a causal relationship between the predatory practices of slavery and the exploitative devastation of the environment.[9]

The Parque Nacional de Itatiaia, Brazil's first national park, was established a few months before Vargas's launch of the authoritarian Estado Novo's new Constitution of 1937. The Constitution codified a new way of considering nature, revealing profound cultural values. What had formally been described as *bens naturais* (natural assets or gifts of nature) were now categorized as *patrimônio públlica* (public heritage). The selection and designation of the first national parks was made by considering a number of ecological as well as political factors, including aesthetic value, species composition, natural resources, and the strategic state control of territory at historically contested national borders.

Parque Nacional de Itatiaia is part of the Serra da Mantiqueira mountain range, which runs along the western edge of the state of Rio de Janeiro, straddling the border with the state of Minas Gerais. A massif rising to just above 2,800 meters at the Pico das Agulhas Negras, the country's third-highest peak, Itatiaia is undeniably spectacular. The steep gradient encompasses several ecological zones of the *mata atlântica* biome, including high-altitude meadows and rain forests, and provides habitat for many endemic and endangered species of flora and fauna. Since the expeditions of Auguste de Saint-Hilaire in 1822, many naturalists have noted the

FIGURE 2.3.
Ponte do Maromba, Parque Nacional de Itatiaia, Rio de Janeiro, ca. 1927
Acervo Museu do Meio Ambiente/Instituto de Pesquisas Jardim Botânico do Rio de Janeiro

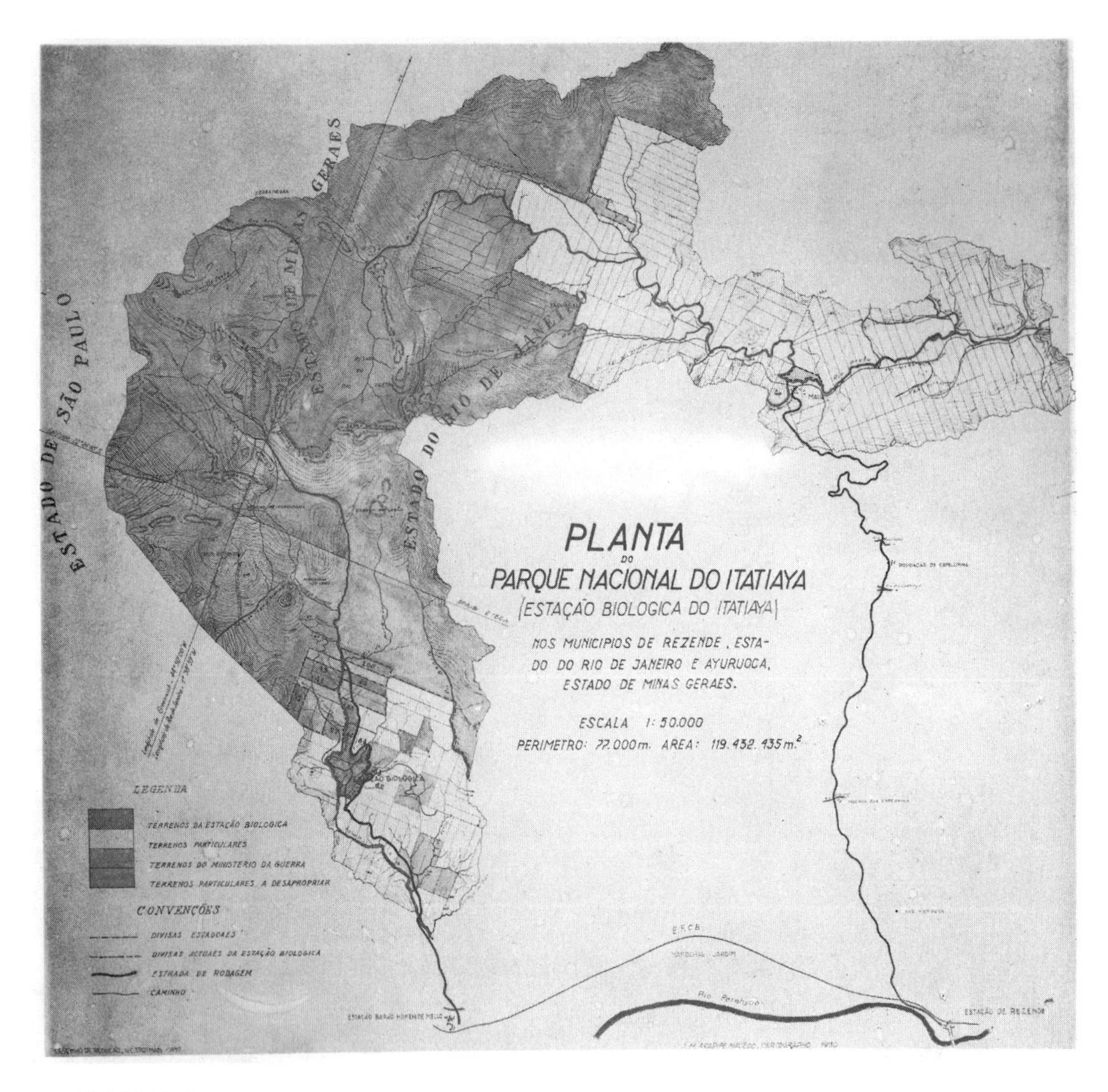

FIGURE 2.4.
Map of the Parque Nacional de Itatiaia, Rio de Janeiro, 1937
Acervo Museu do Meio Ambiente/Instituto de Pesquisas Jardim Botânico do Rio de Janeiro

ecological importance of this region. Auguste François Marie Glaziou led an expedition to the Itatiaia massif in 1872 with Princesa Isabel, the daughter of Emperor Pedro II, later presenting her with a book of the pressed plants that he had collected along their journey.[10] As early as 1913, the botanist Alberto Loefgren and the geographer José Hubmayer argued for the creation of a national park at the Serra da Mantiqueira. In 1914 the government acquired land and established the Reserva Florestal de Itatiaia as an entity of Rio de Janeiro's Jardim Botânico.[11] It became known as the Estação Biológica de Itatiaia in 1927 and was the first territory to be declared a national park (in 1937), with an initial area of approximately 30,000 acres.[12]

Vargas's Estado Novo established two additional national parks in 1939, the Parque Nacional da Serra dos Órgãos and the Parque Nacional do Iguaçu. Beyond the cultural symbolism of patrimonial preservation, natural aesthetics, and, by extension, natural reserves, these territories were considered sites that would support economic development and national security. Parque Nacional da Serra dos Órgãos, encompassing the picturesque mountain range just north of the urban center of Rio de Janeiro, was established in part to protect the headwaters of the rivers flowing into the basin of Guanabara Bay and thereby the city's Acari drinking water system, constructed between 1877 and 1909. The state of Paraná's Parque Nacional do Iguaçu occupied a strategic location at the national border with Paraguay and Argentina and contained the site of a magnificent series of seven waterfalls along the Rio Paraná, the Salto de Sete Quedas at Guaíra.[13] The park's establishment in 1939 was also associated with Vargas's "Marcha para o Oeste" (March to the West), a national campaign intended to open up the farthest reaches of the country to colonization.

After the military coup of 1964, a new Forestry Code, Lei No. 4.771, was promulgated and signed by President Humberto de Castelo Branco on September 15, 1965, superseding the first version from 1934. This new Código Florestal Brasileira

FIGURE 2.5.
Parque Nacional da Serra dos Órgãos, Rio de Janeiro, ca. 1867
Photo by Georges Leuzinger/Instituto Moreira Salles-Leibniz-Institut für Länderkunde, Leipzig agreement

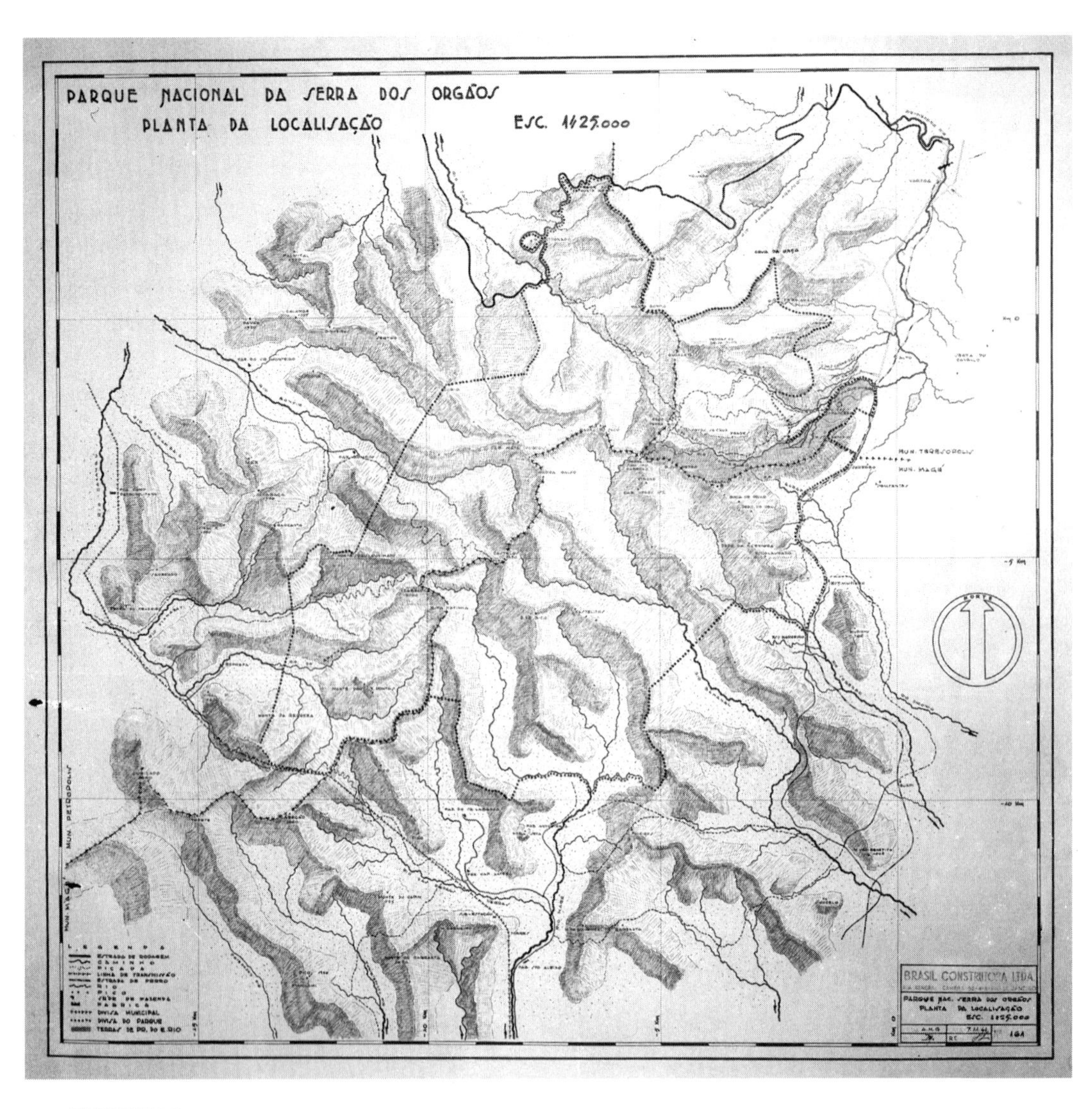

FIGURE 2.6.
Map of the Parque Nacional da Serra dos Órgãos, Rio de Janeiro, 1941
Acervo Museu do Meio Ambiente/Instituto de Pesquisas Jardim Botânico do Rio de Janeiro

included stricter regulations and more enforcement penalties. Its subsequent amendments placed more limits on the rights of private property owners regarding the use of forests and shifted more private forests into state control. The code also required the protection of threatened native plants and animals and established two new legal entities: the Reserva Legal (Legal Reserve) and the Área de Preservação Permanente (Permanent Preservation Area). Legal reserves were defined by region as specific percentages of a property owner's forested lands that were to remain untouched, while Permanent Preservation Areas were forested areas permanently set aside and

FIGURE 2.7.
Salto de Sete Quedas, the seven cataracts of Parque Nacional do Iguaçu, before their inundation by the impoundment of the Usina Hidrelétrica de Itaipu, Paraná, ca. 1971
Photo © Claus Meyer/Tyba Agência Fotográfica

placed under federal ownership. Management plans and government-issued licenses were required before the initiation of forest exploitation in the northeast, northern, and central western regions of the country. But the code had enough loopholes to enable the deforestation of much of Brazil's remaining native forests. In 1967 an independent agency was established, the Instituto Brasileiro de Desenvolvimento Florestal (IBDF: Brazilian Institute for Forestry Development), and made responsible for implementing forestry policy in Brazil. Its focus was clearly on development, however, not conservation.[14]

Through his many depositions to the military regime while a member of the Conselho Federal de Cultura from 1967 until 1974, Burle Marx sought to shift this developmentalist reading of the Forestry Code toward an earlier narrative espoused by Sampaio and Hoehne in the 1930s, addressing the forest as a cultural resource deserving of protection for both ecological and aesthetic reasons. Burle Marx argued that any definition of national culture must include the Brazilian forest (*mata*) and its diversity of flora. The "culture" of the forest, like the legacy of significant colonial or modernist buildings, was to be understood as an aspect of the Brazilian national heritage, deserving both definition and protection. Developed in his earliest work for the plazas of Recife and the Ministério da Educação e Saúde, Burle Marx structured an ecological narrative that brought the forest to the city, evoking an aesthetic appreciation of the unique landscapes of Brazil within the realm of the public garden.

Roberto Burle Marx: Early Public Plazas, 1930s

Plazas of Recife

Burle Marx's earliest public landscape projects, several plazas in the city of Recife in the northeastern state of Pernambuco, reflect his desire for cultural specificity through the use of indigenous tropical plant material. At the age of nineteen, while in Berlin with his father studying music and painting, Burle Marx visited the dramatic glasshouses of the Berlin-Dahlem Botanical Garden, filled with plants from Brazil. In his first testimony to the Conselho Federal de Cultura in 1967, Burle Marx describes being astounded by the wealth of this tropical flora, which he claimed not to have seen in the parks of Rio de Janeiro. Yet native plants had indeed been incorporated in Rio de Janeiro's eighteenth- and nineteenth-century parks by Mestre Valentim, Auguste François Marie Glaziou, Paul Villon, and others. In the early twentieth century Mina Klabin designed gardens of tropical cacti and other native plants in São Paulo to accompany the modernist houses of her husband, the architect Gregori Warchavchik, who would become the professional partner of Lúcio Costa in Rio de Janeiro from 1930 to 1932.

Nevertheless, the Berlin-Dahlem Botanical Garden did have a spectacular collection of Brazilian flora, enriched by the Brazilian plant specimens collected by Carl Friedrich Philipp von Martius (1794–1868) and curated carefully by Heinrich Gustav Adolf Engler (1844–1930). Engler, a German botanist and the garden's director from 1889 through 1921, oversaw the garden's move to Dahlem and the construction of the Große Tropenhaus (Great Tropical Pavilion), the home of the Brazilian plant collection, from 1905 to 1907. Both Martius and Engler were deeply influenced by Alexander von Humboldt (1769–1859), the Prussian naturalist and geographer who traveled extensively in Latin America between 1799 and 1804.[15] Humboldt's work on botany and geography posited that the interrelation of the physical sciences, specifically biology, meteorology, and geology, determined where specific plant species

FIGURE 2.8.
Praça da República, Recife, ca. 1940
Photo by Alexandre Bérzin/Acervo Fundação Joaquim Nabuco/Ministério da Educação/ Governo Federal do Brasil

would grow. From this work came the science of phytogeography, meaning "plant geography," focusing on the geographic distribution of plant species as well as on the factors that governed the composition of entire communities of flora. Engler further developed the notion of phytogeography through his design of the tableaux of world gardens at Berlin-Dahlem, and it was these ecological plant groupings at the Große Tropenhaus that so intrigued Burle Marx in 1928.

In 1934, after an introduction from Lúcio Costa, Burle Marx was appointed as the chief engineer of Recife's Setor de Parques e Jardins (Division of Parks and

FIGURE 2.9.
Das Große Tropenhaus (Great Tropical Pavilion), Berlin-Dahlem Botanical Garden, Berlin, ca. 1910
Archives of the Berlin-Dahlem Botanical Garden and Botanical Museum

Gardens) within the new Diretoria de Arquitetura e Construções (DAC: Office of Architecture and Construction) by the progressive governor of Pernambuco, Carlos de Lima Cavalcanti (1892–1967). The DAC was established the same year by Burle Marx's colleague from the Escola Nacional de Belas Arts, the architect Luiz Nunes (1909–1937). Lima Cavalcanti was particularly interested in the possibilities of social transformation through public works. His support led to the emergence of Recife, the capital of this relatively remote northeastern state, as an unexpected nucleus of early modern architecture in Brazil during an intense period of activity from 1934 to 1937. This was in large part due to Nunes's DAC, despite its interruption in November 1935 under the suspicion of involvement with the Communist movement. Nunes reestablished the agency in 1936 as the Diretoria de Arquitetura e Urbanismo (DAU: Office of Architecture and Urbanism). The office built over thirty projects in less than two years.[16] When Lima Cavalcanti was deposed from power by the incoming Estado Novo in November 1937, the DAU was effectively closed.[17]

The impact of Burle Marx's contributions to Brazilian modernism during this brief period in Recife extended throughout Brazil. As director of the Setor de Parques e Jardins on the DAC team, Burle Marx restored, renovated, and altered over a dozen public plazas during his three years of service. In 1935, writing about his work for the local Recife newspapers *Diário da Tarde* and *Diário da Manhã*, Burle Marx insisted that the modern garden should have three objectives: art, hygiene, and education. Indeed, it was this didactic component, embodied by plant material extracted from Brazil's forests, that Burle Marx embraced with his presentations of tropical plants arrayed in the manner of Engler's phytogeographic tableaux. He wrote: "The immense variety of plants bestowed upon us from our magnificent forests, as well as those exotics that are already entirely adapted to our climate, facilitate our task tremendously. I urge that we begin now to sow, in our parks and gardens, the Brazilian soul."[18]

Joaquim Cardozo (1897–1978), a poet and engineer from Recife who participated as a member of Nunes's DAC team, was impressed by the work of the young Burle Marx. Cardozo gathered a dynamic group of intellectuals around him in Recife, often meeting at the Café Gambrinus or Restaurante Leite. At these discussions, Burle Marx made the acquaintance of the art historian Clarival do Prado Valladares (1918–1938) and the sociologist Gilberto Freyre (1900–1987), both of whom would later serve with him on the Conselho Federal de Cultura. In an interview with the newspaper *Diário da Tarde* in June 1937, Cardozo spoke extensively of the importance and modernity of Burle Marx's garden restorations in Recife, noting particularly two gardens, the Praça de Casa Forte and the Cactário do Largo do Bemfica, now known as the Praça Euclides da Cunha.[19] Indeed, of the many plazas designed by Burle Marx in Recife, the Praça Euclides da Cunha and the Praça de Casa Forte are particularly noteworthy. Praça Euclides da Cunha, completed in 1934, is an elliptical cactarium garden, an aestheticized composition of xerophytic plants drawn from the culturally and botanically rich Brazilian *caatinga* forest ecosystem of the *sertão*, the dry desert interior of northeastern Brazil.[20] The plaza also carries a significant literary reference—it is named for the Brazilian literary figure Euclides da Cunha (1866–1909), the author of the 1902 book *Os sertões*, an epic recounting of the political uprising of the inhabitants of this drought-stricken region in the late nineteenth century.[21] The unusual use of cacti in this public garden, particularly the sculptural mandacaru (*Cereus jamacaru*), evokes the early modern cacti gardens of Mina Klabin as well as the paintings of Tarsila do Amaral.

Praça de Casa Forte, completed in 1935, was conceived as an aquatic garden, a geometrically formal linear park with two rectangular pools and a central round fountain. It is an unusually symmetrical composition for Burle Marx, particularly given the freeform geometries that he later employed. Planted with tropical tree species endemic to the Amazon region, the plaza celebrated forest biodiversity. Its reflecting pools contained a variety of aquatic plants, including the famed *Victoria amazonica* water lilies, native to Brazil and the Amazon basin. Burle Marx did not use Brazilian plants exclusively in this plaza but developed one of the rectilinear ponds with aquatic plants from the Amazon River and the other with aquatic plants of the Nile River, acknowledging the two great rivers of the tropical belt.

FIGURE 2.10.
Praça Euclides da Cunha, with the Clube Internacional do Recife seen beyond, Recife, ca. 1940

Photo by Alexandre Bérzin/ Acervo Fundação Joaquim Nabuco/Ministério da Educação/ Governo Federal do Brasil

FIGURE 2.11.
Roberto Burle Marx, ink and pencil perspective of Praça Euclides da Cunha, Recife, 1934

© Sítio Roberto Burle Marx/ IPHAN

FIGURE 2.12.
Praça de Casa Forte, Recife, with reflecting pool and aquatic plants foregrounding the Colégio da Sagrada Família and Matriz de Casa Forte, Recife, 1938
Photo by Benício Whatley Dias/Acervo Fundação Joaquim Nabuco/Ministério da Educação/Governo Federal do Brasil

FIGURE 2.13.
Roberto Burle Marx, ink and pencil perspective of Praça de Casa Forte, Recife, 1935
© Sítio Roberto Burle Marx/IPHAN

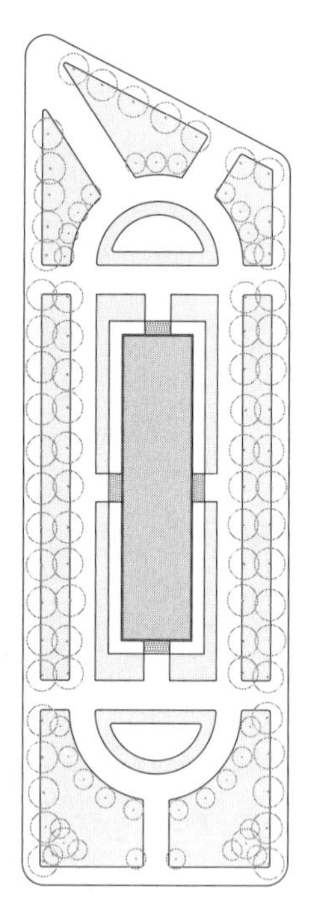

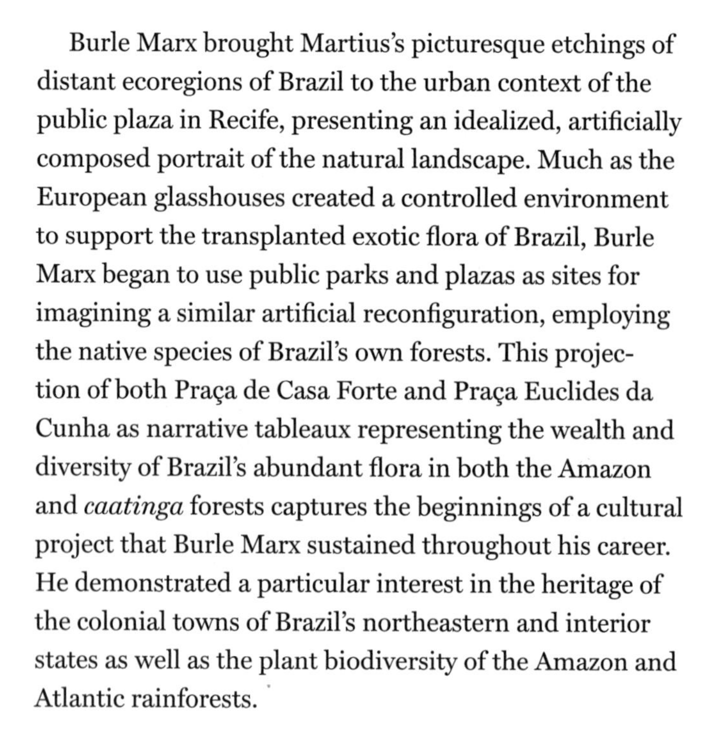

Burle Marx brought Martius's picturesque etchings of distant ecoregions of Brazil to the urban context of the public plaza in Recife, presenting an idealized, artificially composed portrait of the natural landscape. Much as the European glasshouses created a controlled environment to support the transplanted exotic flora of Brazil, Burle Marx began to use public parks and plazas as sites for imagining a similar artificial reconfiguration, employing the native species of Brazil's own forests. This projection of both Praça de Casa Forte and Praça Euclides da Cunha as narrative tableaux representing the wealth and diversity of Brazil's abundant flora in both the Amazon and *caatinga* forests captures the beginnings of a cultural project that Burle Marx sustained throughout his career. He demonstrated a particular interest in the heritage of the colonial towns of Brazil's northeastern and interior states as well as the plant biodiversity of the Amazon and Atlantic rainforests.

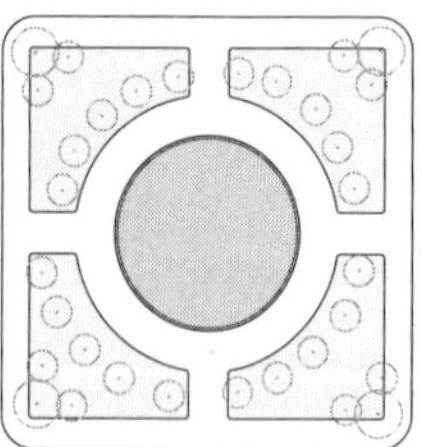

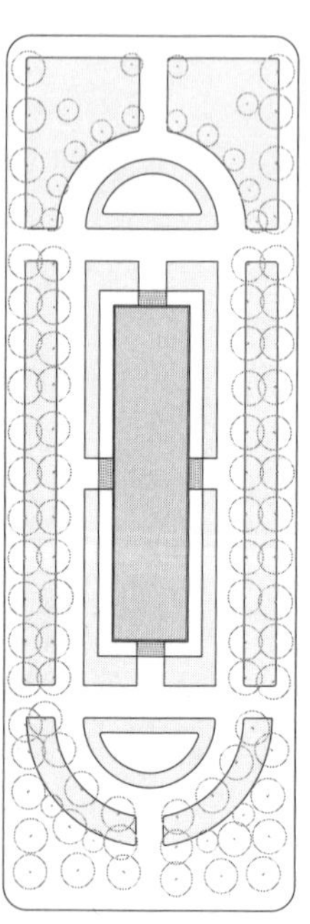

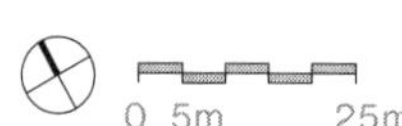

FIGURE 2.14.
Roberto Burle Marx, Praça de Casa Forte, Recife, 1935

Drawing by Catherine Seavitt Nordenson

FIGURE 2.15.
Carl Friedrich Philipp von Martius, *Silva aestu aphylla, quam dicunt caa-tingá* (Leafless desert forest, called the *caatinga*), from *Flora brasiliensis*, ca. 1840–1906
Acervo da Fundação Biblioteca Nacional do Brasil

FIGURE 2.16.
Carl Friedrich Philipp von Martius, *Silva in ripa fluvii Amazonum* (Forests along the Amazon River), from *Flora brasiliensis*, ca. 1840–1906
Acervo da Fundação Biblioteca Nacional do Brasil

Gardens of the Ministério da Educação e Saúde

Burle Marx returned from Recife to Rio de Janeiro after the coup of 1937, when Vargas repositioned his presidency as the authoritarian Estado Novo dictatorial regime. At the invitation of Lúcio Costa, Burle Marx would begin work on the plaza landscapes for the Ministério da Educação e Saúde, a project whose planning was initiated in 1934 during the more liberal years of Vargas's presidency. Vargas had established the new ministry in his first year of government and in 1934 had appointed the forward-thinking intellectual Gustavo Capanema (1900–1985) as minister of education. In 1935 Capanema launched a national competition for a new headquarters building for the ministry in Rio de Janeiro, on the site of the razed Morro do Castelo. Flattened in 1922 because it was perceived as an insalubrious topographic impediment for a newly modernizing city, the area was redeveloped as the Esplanada do Castelo by the French urban planner Donat-Alfred Agache between 1927 and 1930 and then designated as a Federal District for the new ministry buildings. Dissatisfied with the conservative results of the competition, selected by a jury of Brazilian architects, Capanema rejected the winning scheme and appointed Costa to develop a new scheme for the building. Costa in turn gathered a team composed of the young architects Oscar Niemeyer, Affonso Eduardo Reidy, Carlos Leão, Jorge Moreira, and Ernani Vasconcellos. On Costa's advice, Capanema invited the Swiss architect Charles-Édouard Jeanneret (1887–1965), known as Le Corbusier, to come to Brazil from Paris, France, to consult with the team on both the ministry headquarters building and the new Universidade do Brasil (University of Brazil).

Le Corbusier arrived in Rio de Janeiro for a month-long stay in July 1936.[22] He reviewed the Brazilian team's first scheme for the ministry building and as a critique drew up a counterproposal scheme for an alternate waterfront site on Guanabara Bay that he preferred, a narrow linear eight-story slab on pilotis. His perspectival view of the building's site included the landscape at its entrance, with a sketch of one lone vertical royal palm, *Roystonea oleracea*. Just before leaving Brazil, Le Corbusier made another set of sketches for the originally designated ministry site at Castelo. The perspective of his L-shaped scheme, a narrow vertical slab on pilotis perpendicular to a low volume punctuated by the expressive form of the theater, included a double row of ten royal palms that bisected the site. Unlike his first scheme for the bay, which used the views of the urban landscape to capture the tropical spirit of the city, Le Corbusier's sketch here evoked a fragment of an aestheticized forest, the famed double allée of royal palms at Rio de Janeiro's Jardim Botânico.

By 1938, when Burle Marx was contracted by Costa to develop a landscape scheme for the ministry—including the plaza, the minister's private roof terrace, and the tower's roof—the Brazilian architects had developed a new collective architectural solution of their own for the Castelo block, with echoes of Le Corbusier's earlier consultation.[23] Construction began in 1937, but the inauguration of the building

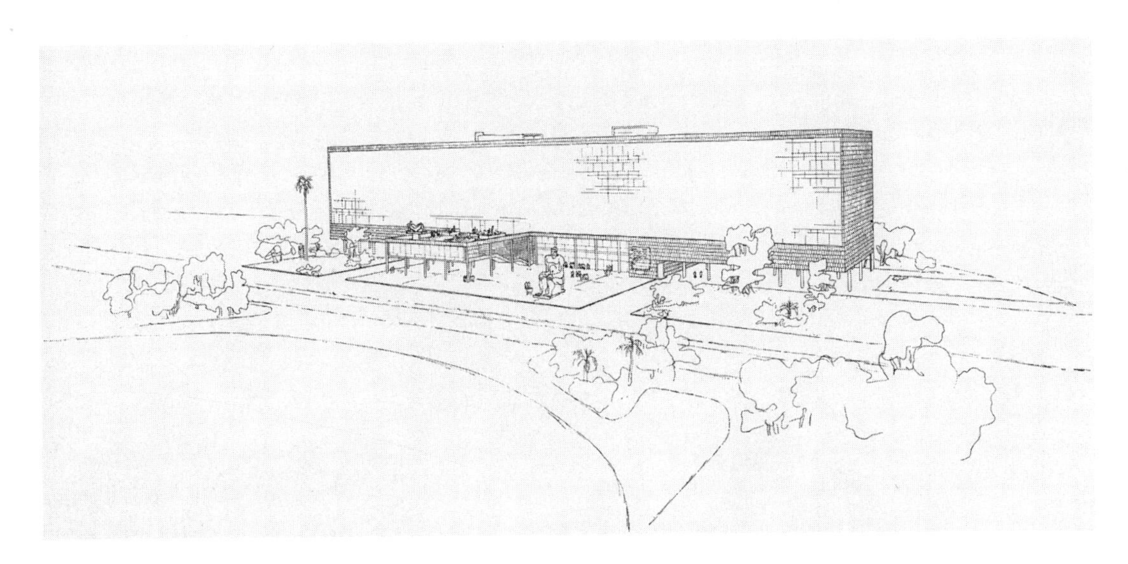

FIGURE 2.17.
Le Corbusier, Ministério da Educação e Saúde, first scheme for the site at Guanabara Bay, Rio de Janeiro, 1936
Fondation Le Corbusier © 2017 Artists Rights Society (ARS), New York/ADAGP, Paris

FIGURE 2.18.
Le Corbusier, Ministério da Educação e Saúde, second scheme for the site at Castelo, Rio de Janeiro, 1936
Acervo Lúcio Costa and Fondation Le Corbusier © 2017 Artists Rights Society (ARS), New York/ADAGP, Paris

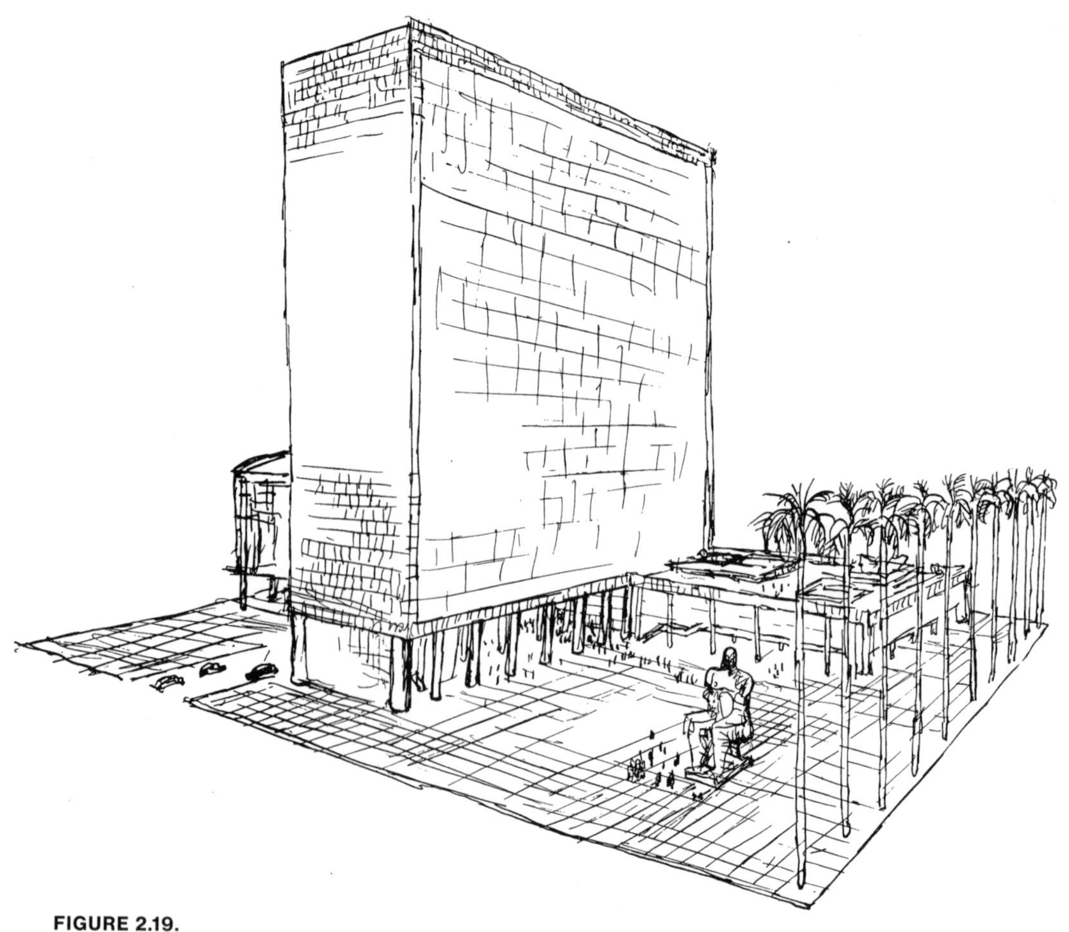

FIGURE 2.19.
Le Corbusier, Ministério da Educação e Saúde, apocryphal scheme of the site at Castelo as developed and built by the Brazilian team of architects, Rio de Janeiro, 1938

would not be held until 1945. A thickened fourteen-story vertical slab was set toward the center of the block, intersected perpendicularly by the low two-story exhibition block and theater to create a T-shaped plan, shaping the public forecourt of the complex through the configuration of the architectural volumes. The façades of the tower were treated appropriately to respond to the specifics of the climate, with the articulation of exterior adjustable *quebra-luz* (sun shades) along the north face of the tower and continuous glazing at the southern façade. With the tower set upon very high columns, the plaza allowed for fluid pedestrian movement across the site. And the plastic geometries of the ministry's architecture were accordingly shaped to receive landscaped roof terraces, sky gardens, and street-level plazas. Burle Marx's design for the minister's private roof terrace garden above the two-story exhibition block and the public plaza at the ground level incorporated amoeboid planting beds lush with tropical species. These forms echoed the nineteenth-century picturesque public parks of both Glaziou in Rio de Janeiro and Paul Villon in Belo Horizonte, serving as a dynamic counterpoint to the neoclassical palace.[24] But in this modernist reenactment, the clean lines of the ministry building provided a three-dimensional palette for the landscape's contrapuntal movement. Planting beds slipped dynamically across the plaza, through the high gallery of columns supporting the tower, and appeared again at the roof of the exhibition hall. The public space of the plaza, with its traditional *pedra portuguesa* paving stones, was shaped by the landscape of Burle Marx's planting beds, enlivened by the painted *azulejo* tiles of Cândido Portinari, and anchored by Bruno Giorgi's monumental statue *Juventude*.[25]

Several years later, in 1944, Burle Marx developed a design for a proposed extension of the ministry's plaza to the south, extending to the Rua Graça Aranha. There his selected palette of plants evoked the Amazonian territories of the farthest reaches of the country through the use of the *Victoria amazonica* water lilies as part of an aquatic garden. Unlike the rectilinear pools of the Praça de Casa Forte in Recife, in this scheme Burle Marx created a sinuous curvilinear lake, wrapped by freeform planting beds, semicircular benches, and a requisite line of royal palms, *Roystonea oleracea*, anchoring the southernmost edge of the site. Though this elaborate proposal was not built, it is a fascinating echo of the garden of the Pavilhão Brasileiro as a tropical extraction from the Amazon, culturally anchored in Brazil's capital city.

FIGURE 2.20.
Paul Villon, Praça da Liberdade, Belo Horizonte, ca. 1910
Acervo do Museu Histórico Abílio Barreto/Fundação Municipal de Cultura

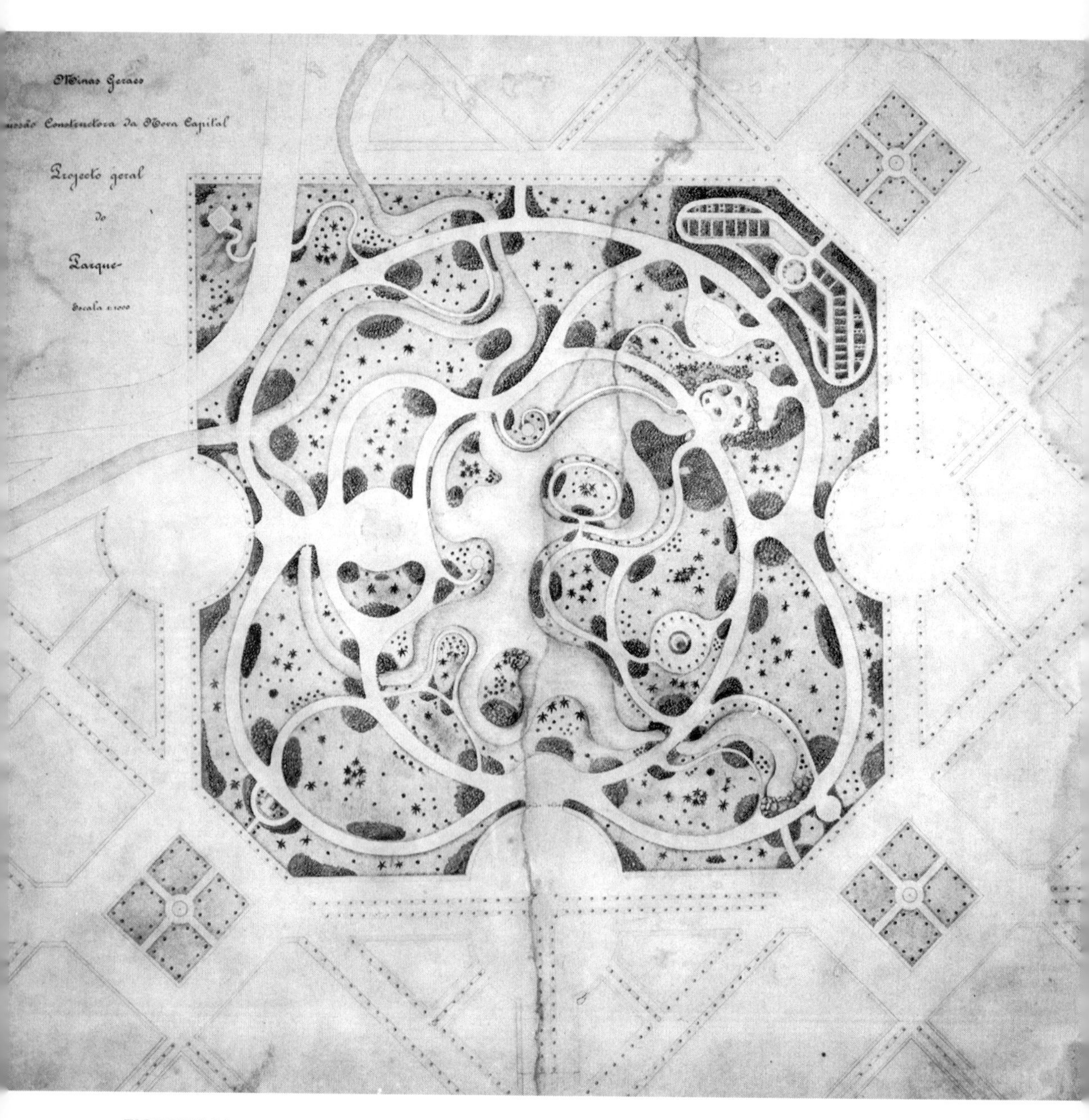

FIGURE 2.21.
Paul Villon, plan of the Parque da Cidade, Belo Horizonte, 1895
Acervo do Museu Histórico Abílio Barreto/Fundação Municipal de Cultura

FIGURE 2.22.
Roberto Burle Marx, gouache plan of the minister's rooftop garden, Ministério da Educação e Saúde, Rio de Janeiro, 1938
© Burle Marx Landscape Design Studio

FIGURE 2.23.
Minister's rooftop garden, Ministério da Educação e Saúde, Rio de Janeiro, 1946
Photo by Marcel Gautherot/Instituto Moreira Salles Collection/Fundação Oscar Niemeyer © 2017 Artists Rights Society (ARS), New York/AUTVIS, São Paulo

FIGURE 2.24.
Mulher (Woman), a 1938–1940 granite sculpture by Adriana Janacópulos at the minister's rooftop garden, Ministério da Educação e Saúde, Rio de Janeiro, ca. 1945
Arquivo Gustavo Capanema/Fundação Getúlio Vargas, Centro de Pesquisa e Documentação/ Fundação Oscar Niemeyer © 2017 Artists Rights Society (ARS), New York/AUTVIS, São Paulo

FIGURE 2.25.
Roberto Burle Marx, perspective view of the proposed southern expansion of the Ministério da Educação e Saúde plaza, Rio de Janeiro, ca. 1944
© Burle Marx Landscape Design Studio

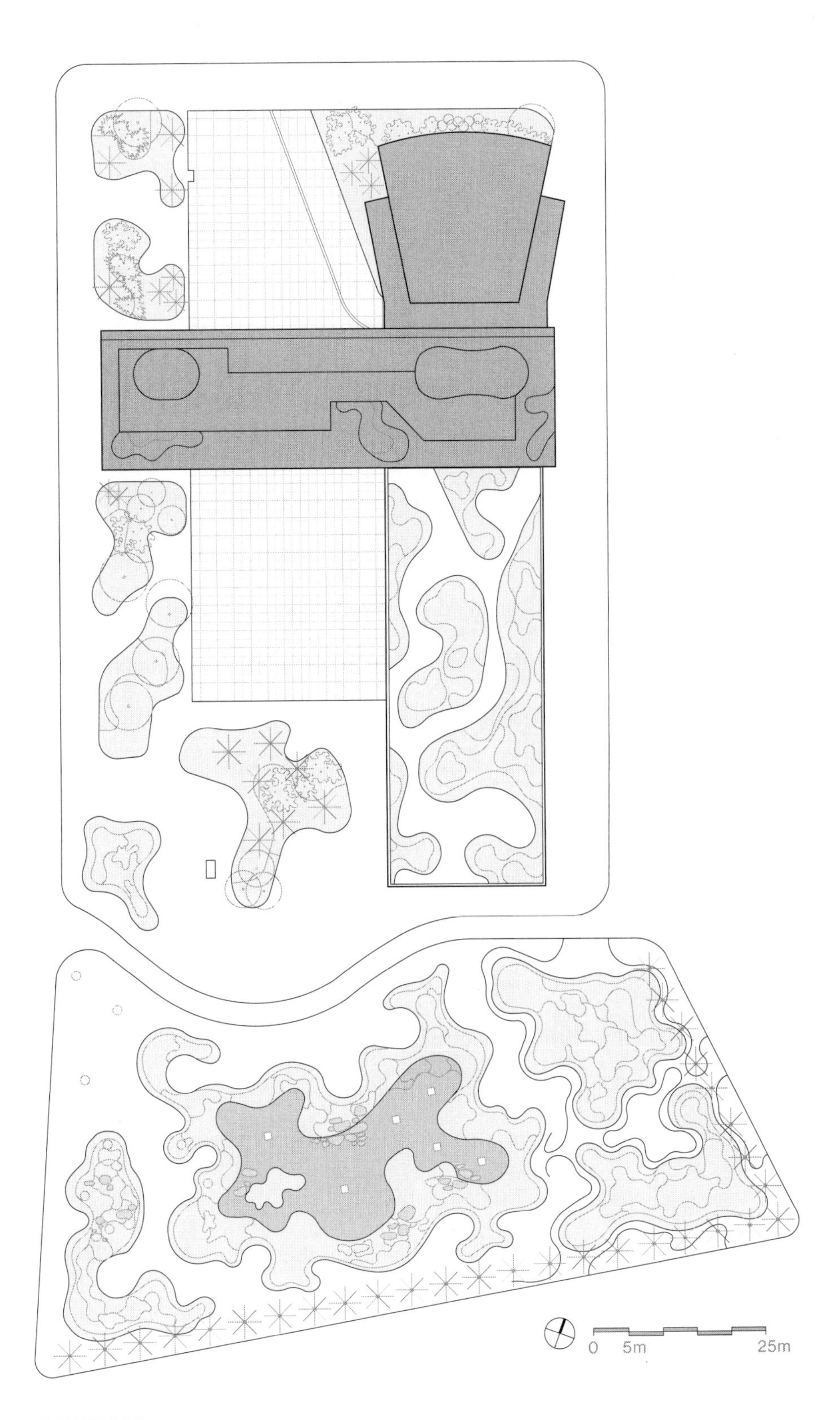

FIGURE 2.26.
Roberto Burle Marx, plaza and rooftop gardens of the Ministério da Educação e Saúde and the garden proposed for the southern expansion of the site, Rio de Janeiro, 1938–1944
Drawing by Catherine Seavitt Nordenson

FIGURE 2.27.
Headquarters building and plaza of the Ministério da Educação e Saúde, Rio de Janeiro, 1955
Photo by Marcel Gautherot/Instituto Moreira Salles Collection/Fundação Oscar Niemeyer © 2017 Artists Rights Society (ARS), New York/AUTVIS, São Paulo

With support from the Vargas regime for both culture (embodied by this new ministry building in Rio de Janeiro) and the aestheticized environment (embraced within the legislation of the Código Florestal), Burle Marx's lush tropical landscapes for the ministry's plaza and roof terraces were deeply impactful. Capanema conceived of his ministry building as a complete work of art, inclusive of its radically new architecture; statuary by Celso Antônio and Bruno Giorgi; interior and exterior murals by Cândido Portinari; and the tropical landscape by Burle Marx. Landscape architecture was embraced as a part of culture, and Burle Marx's contribution was accordingly launched outward to an international audience. Highlighted in the "Brazil Builds" exhibition and catalogue by the Museum of Modern Art in 1943, the building became emblematic of the new Brazilian architecture, with Philip Goodwin, the exhibition's curator, claiming that "Rio can boast of the most beautiful government buildings in the Western Hemisphere."[26]

The completion of the Ministério da Educacão e Saúde took over eight years, from the start of its construction in 1937 until its official inauguration in 1945, with construction delays caused by material shortages due to World War II. National criticism of the project was widespread during its erection—it was seen as embodying a recklessly extravagant use of resources.[27] The building was officially inaugurated on October 3, 1945, a date chosen to mark the fifteenth anniversary of the Revolução de 1930, when Vargas first came to power. A few weeks later, on October 29, 1945, Vargas was deposed from the presidency by a surprise military coup.

In his essay entitled "Testimony of a Carioca Architect: Concrete, Sun, and Vegetation," written to defend the 1948 national landmarking of the Ministério da Educação e Saúde headquarters building by the Serviço do Patrimônio Histórico e Artístico Nacional (SPHAN) to the next administration, Lúcio Costa identified Burle Marx's significant contribution in the development of Brazilian modernism.[28] In his analysis of the materials, landscapes, and atmospheres that defined Brazil's new modern architecture, Costa framed the use of concrete as a Brazilian necessity, not a choice, given the scarcity of steel. In addition to highlighting the plastic inventiveness of Brazilian structural engineers, Costa added two additional significant elements to the Brazilian modernist lexicon: climate and plant material, with "nature itself invited to be a part of the plan."[29] Burle Marx brought Brazilian nature, and the native species of the Brazilian forest, into dialogue with the modern architecture of its cities.

Depositions: Forest Conservation and a Modern Ecology

The idea of the preservation, protection, and celebration of the Brazilian forest as central to a shared Brazilian identity was lost with the rise of the military dictatorship in 1964 and the embrace of a developmentalist theory that encouraged economic growth through resource extraction. Forests provided some of the most easily exploited resources. The new Forestry Code of 1965, which transferred many of the country's forests to state control, made these resources easily accessible.[30] As the military dictatorship pushed the country into the so-called *milagre econômico brasileiro* of the 1970s, the cost was seen in the oppression of democratic values, the exploitation of impoverished populations, and mounting foreign debt. The dictatorship's desire to control and exploit natural resources led to the development of megaprojects with massive impact on the environment, such as the Usina Hidrelétrica de Itaipu (Itaipu Hydroelectric Dam) at the Rio Paraná, the Rodovia Transamazônica and other national highways, the Carajás mining projects in Pará and Maranhão, and the nuclear power plant in Angra dos Reis, Rio de Janeiro.

Yet Burle Marx, as a member of the Conselho Federal de Cultura, boldly addressed environmental and conservation issues, particularly critiquing the regime's emphasis on development at the expense of ecological health. He commented on the unchecked abuses of the new Forestry Code and sought to reinterpret it through an ecological lens. Burle Marx addressed the issue of exploitative reforestation, arguing against the common practice of replacement of native forests with monocultures of commercial timber species. He also highlighted the risk of species extinctions given this practice of commercial overexploitation of forests and the resultant habitat fragmentation. In particular, he noted the unstable climate that was the observable result of deforestation.

In his first consular deposition, "Paisagismo brasiliero" (Brazilian Landscapes), delivered on April 27, 1967, Burle Marx addressed the systemic deforestation that he had personally observed over the course of his career, which had led to the near extinction of several hardwood species and an increase in erosion and mudslides. He cited two recent occurrences in Rio de Janeiro that caused significant loss of life. Invoking a longer time scale by referencing the changing climate and resultant extinctions, Burle Marx conjured the permanent loss of the unique Brazilian species that had come to define the country's forest wealth. His deposition is a call to action, emphasizing the need for the political and financial support necessary for conservation and ecological reforestation.

For Burle Marx, the definition of national culture should include the Brazilian forest and its diversity of flora. That "culture" would be understood as part of the Brazilian national heritage, so it should also be provided ecological protection. These positions were put forth in "Sugestões para preservação dos parques nacionais" (Suggestions for the Preservation of National Parks), published in the August 1967 issue of *Cultura*, and "Conservacionismo florestal" (Forest Conservation), delivered on February 12, 1971. Both depositions insisted on the importance of protecting a diverse set of ecologies through the establishment of new national parks. Burle Marx echoed the views of Wanderbilt Duarte de Barros, the director of Brazil's first national park (Parque Nacional de Itatiaia), who in 1952 argued for new national parks that would capture a wider variety of ecosystems. Burle Marx also insisted on the need to address the urban landscape, through the creation of urban reforestation

FIGURE 2.28. Landslide in the neighborhood of Laranjeiras, resulting in the destruction of two apartment buildings and the death of 132 people, Rio de Janeiro, February 18, 1967

Photo by Ruy Macial/ Fundação Instituto de Geotécnica Geo-Rio

programs, new urban public parks, didactic park program components such as aquariums and amphitheaters, and restoration and preservation strategies for nineteenth-century parks.

Burle Marx's deposition of March 25, 1969, "Política florestal e destruição das florestas" (Forest Politics and the Destruction of Forests), addressed his serious concerns regarding the massive exploitation of *Araucaria angustifolia*, the native Brazilian pine, which provided the finest timber for the manufacture of cellulose for newsprint, as well as various hardwood species. Burle Marx cited several reports quantifying the massive loss of forested areas in Brazil due to economic exploitation and insisted that the government establish and enforce permanent protected reserves as well as robust reforestation programs in order to conserve these forests for future generations.

The specter of extinction was a recent fear; though it was not cited in the first Forestry Code of 1934, by the 1940s the botanist Frederico Carlos Hoehne had developed important research addressing the realities of species extinction in Brazil, the ensuing loss of biodiversity, and the need for conservation. A former member of the Comissão Rondon and an affiliate of the Museu Nacional in Rio de Janeiro, Hoehne worked at the Instituto de Botânica at the Jardim Botânico in São Paulo from 1918 through the end of the 1950s. His studies of native orchid species in the 1940s demonstrated that over three hundred orchid species had become extinct in Brazil due to habitat destruction. For Burle Marx, the documented realities of the near-extinction of multiple species of trees native to Brazil—including the pinheiro da Bocaina (*Podocarpus lambertii*); the quebracho (*Schinopsis lorentzii*), a source of tannin for use in leather tanning; the pau-rosa (*Aniba rosaeodora*), a source of rosewood oil; and the big-leaf mahogany (*Swietenia macrophylla*)—brought a sense of ethical responsibility as well as urgency to the practice of conservation.

Burle Marx's depositions as a member of the Conselho Federal de Cultura established his voice during the early environmental movement with a critique of the state policy of developmentalism that supported resource extraction, road building, and deforestation. He emphasized the need to shift the notion of wilderness preservation toward a contemporary ecology-based strategy of biodiversity conservation. Setting land aside for preservation often resulted in little more than centralized state control of the land, followed by exploratory probing for future resource extraction and economic exploitation. The Forestry Code was typically used as a mechanism for accessing more territory and transforming the forest into an agricultural resource. Burle Marx notes a specific example in his 1971 deposition "Conservacionismo florestal" (Forest Conservation), in which the slopes of a mountainous region are cleared of the existing forest and replanted with a single species, *Pinus*, specifically for commercial timber harvesting. The military regime sought to control, exploit, and profit through natural resource extraction. Burle Marx argued against this position, demanding a reconsideration of the unique ecological wealth of the Brazilian environment as another aspect of the Brazilian modernist identity and indeed of its culture.

Roberto Burle Marx: Depositions

FIGURE 2.29.
Das Große Tropenhaus (Great Tropical Pavilion) with Brazilian palms, Berlin-Dahlem Botanical Garden, Berlin, 1914
Photo by Zander and Labisch/Ullstein Bild via Getty Images

Brazilian Landscapes
April 27, 1967

Delivered to the Plenary Session of the Conselho Federal de Cultura on April 27, 1967. Published as Roberto Burle Marx, "Paisagismo brasileiro" (Brazilian Landscapes), *Cultura: Conselho Federal de Cultura* (Ministério da Educação e Cultura) 1, no. 1 (July 1967): 94–97.

What I intend to speak of here is simply a deposition regarding my work and its relationship to the Brazilian landscape.

When I lived in Germany for two years, brought there by my father in 1928, one of my fascinations was visiting the displays of Brazilian flora thriving in the greenhouses of the Botanical Gardens of Berlin-Dahlem.[31]

This was a wonder to me because I had never seen these plants, which evoked such strong emotions in me, in the gardens and parks of Rio de Janeiro.

Note that the majority of the trees planted in the parks of Brazil are not native. This seems to be a rejection of the plants that grow in our jungles, the trees of our forests, and the palms of our country. In response, I began to create my first gardens in order to advocate for an appreciation of Brazilian flora. I was advised, wisely, by my friend Lúcio Costa.[32]

I am not a chauvinist. However, knowing of the existence of over 5,000 species of trees and more than 50,000 plant species that constitute our native Brazilian flora, I resolved to highlight these plants and our botanical heritage in my work.[33] Yet the Brazilian forest is now being destroyed across the entire country. It is almost impossible to restore a forest's complex biodiversity because of our lack of knowledge in this field. It is thus necessary to protect this unique heritage, despite the great difficulty of such an endeavor, as otherwise little will remain of our flora.

I insist that all Brazilian states should have botanical gardens and, in addition, biological reserves in regions that have unique ecological characteristics. This would protect these areas from the greed of real estate developers. For example, the extremely rich flora of the coastal *restinga* of Jacarepaguá and Camorim is being destroyed because of developers' lack of environmental understanding—they plant exotic trees that are slowly and steadily destroying the environment.[34]

I have traveled through many regions in search of botanical material that might be useful in gardens. Everywhere I go, destruction can be seen and felt.

I was recently in the state of Espírito Santo in the area around the Rio Pancas, an extraordinarily beautiful valley. The mountains that frame this valley resemble the Pão de Açúcar in Rio de Janeiro. Along their slopes flow many small rivulets that then feed the river as it winds through the valley. On these rocky mountain escarpments grows an exquisite and little-known plant.[35] However, *coivara* (using fire to create a clearing in the forest), a practice that we inherited from the Indians, has already destroyed a large part of this plant's habitat. When I visited this region twenty years ago, its appearance was completely different. Very little of this heritage will likely survive. Certainly any other country with a natural landscape like this would be concerned with conserving and protecting it, as if it were a sacred site. And I am citing just one such example, referencing a place that I have passed through many times.

A short time ago I was in southern Bahia. Destruction is seen almost everywhere. I am reminded of a conversation that I had with the botanist Adolpho Ducke, an extraordinary man who dedicated himself to the study of the flora of the Amazon for over fifty years. He stated that this southern region of Bahia was facing a situation similar to that of the Amazon. Because of the extraction of so many understory plants, many rare species of animals have disappeared and now are only known through books of zoology.[36] The same thing has happened with the flora that was studied in the nineteenth century by the naturalist Prince Maximilian of Wied-Neuwied—much has disappeared.[37]

And today, when I embark on *viagens de coleta* in search of material that could serve in the making of my gardens, I see with sorrow and dismay that the destruction is felt wherever one goes. This is a misfortune that seems irreversible, a misfortune that one accepts with melancholy, as if there were no possibility of changing course. If we continue to accept what we are now witnessing, very soon little will remain of this Brazilian flora that is considered one of the richest in the world.

The very idea of the Brazilian garden still rejects Brazilian flora, with a few exceptions. Our gardens make use of exotic plants that are found in all of the tropical zones of the world: *Acalypha*, *Pandanus*, *Spathodea campanulata*, *Cassia siamea*, *Eucalyptus*, *Casuarina*, *Lygodium*, *Terminalia catappa*, and so forth. Meanwhile, the native quaresmeiras, those marvelous members of the Melastomataceae family, are just waiting to be brought to our gardens.[38]

Returning to the topic of the destruction of forests, I would cite the northern region of the state of Espírito Santo, whose floristic reserves are almost depleted. For example, consider a tree species of high economic value that grows in the municipality of Campos, from which it takes its common name, *peroba de Campos* (*Aspidosperma tomentosum*).[39] These stands are already extinct across the entire extent of Espírito Santo, with the exception of the northern regions of that state, the southern regions of the state of Bahia, and the northwestern region of the state of Minas Gerais. The cedar, another tree species known since colonial times, is already extinct in the states of Espírito Santo, Minas Gerais, and Bahia and even in Amazônia along the large rivers. The jacarandá, as well, is no longer extant in the states of Rio de Janeiro and Espírito Santo, and the last survivors are found only in Bahia. On the outskirts of Brasília, another species of jacarandá, the *Machaerium esclerocylum*, is disappearing as well.

In Bahia, we can mention another economically valuable species, *jacarandá-da-bahia* (*Dalbergia nigra*), used extensively in the furniture industry; it is transported directly to the Port of Salvador for export.

Mahogany (*Swietenia macrophylla*), an extremely rare and valuable tree species from the state of Goiás, is almost extinct in the northern region of that state, and this is causing great controversy.[40]

All of these tree species are practically extinct, and this extinction provokes a biotic imbalance that results in a poor distribution of rain. This then becomes the principal reason for torrential precipitation, which in turn provokes flooding, obstructs riverbeds, and strips the soil of the nutrients needed for the cultivation of plants.

This is a state of emergency from the standpoint of reforestation that one finds in the states of Minas Gerais, São Paulo, Rio de Janeiro, Espírito Santo, and Bahia, without even mentioning the Northeast, where very few forested areas remain. About thirty years ago, the forests of the state of Pará sheltered a tree species of high economic value, the pau-rosa (*Aniba rosaeodora* and *Aniba duquerii*). Both these tree species are now on the brink of extinction, overexploited because they produce valuable essential oils. Another example that may be cited are the forests of the state of Minas Gerais. Of the original 215,000 square kilometers of forested area, only a little more than 15,000 square kilometers now remain, and no executive measures are being taken to contain or slow down this destruction. In the state of São Paulo, only 10 percent of the total area of the state is forested. By contrast, in the highly industrialized country of Germany, where living space is tremendously in demand, 20 percent of the land area is forested.

Regarding the recent tragedy that occurred in the mountains of Araras, two very important factors must be taken into consideration: first, the downpours are nothing other than the consequence of an imbalance of nature provoked by the criminal devastation of our forests and woodlands, among other things.[41] Second, the landslides and the collapses that resulted in tragedy are the consequence of a lack of vegetative plant cover on the hillsides, on the roadside shoulders, and in areas where public roads have been carved through the forests. To prevent these accidents from happening again, a minimum requirement is stated by the experts: tree coverage, on the order of 20 percent over the entire region and at every location. In terms of the degree of the importance given to this problem in the rest of the world, suffice it to say that the United States has spent approximately nine billion dollars on the work of conservation.

FIGURE 2.30.
Véu da Noiva waterfall at the Rio Maromba, Parque Nacional de Itatiaia, Rio de Janeiro, ca. 1930
Acervo Museu do Meio Ambiente/Instituto de Pesquisas Jardim Botânico do Rio de Janeiro

Suggestions for the Preservation of National Parks
August 1967

Published as Roberto Burle Marx, "Sugestões para preservação dos parques nacionais" (Suggestions for the Preservation of National Parks), *Cultura: Conselho Federal de Cultura* (Ministério da Educação e Cultura) 1, no. 2 (August 1967): 42–43.

The counselor Roberto Burle Marx, who presented a statement regarding the Brazilian landscape to the Conselho Federal de Cultura, published in the previous volume of *Cultura*, has formulated the following suggestions regarding the subject of the preservation of national parks:

1. Provide for the study and delineation of areas to be preserved, defined, and protected by law as NATIONAL PARKS, in addition to those already existing, in regions threatened by the extinction of biological species, the extraction of minerals, and the potential loss of the characteristic features that provide landscape value.

2. Study and propose legislation for the creation of public parks in cities throughout the country, with adequate planting of trees in relation to both the local surroundings and the adjacent forested areas.

3. Study and propose legislation for the greening of cities and public parks, preventing the improprieties that so often compromise the intended purpose, which is to meet the physical and mental needs of the population as well as to provide an ecological and aesthetic character to the urban realm.

4. Study standards of garden design and parks with a didactic character and purpose, such as aquariums, geological parks, and outdoor acoustic shell amphitheaters, in keeping with the region's demographics and educational needs.

5. Study and propose legislation regarding the reforestation of the areas around cities and of devastated areas, in support of the protection of climate, the security of nearby reservoirs, and the conservation of urban public health.

6. Study the construction of gardens integral to historic architectural and artistic sites, in order to protect these cultural sites while creating better conditions for public visitors.

7. Study the restoration and preservation of gardens and parks dating from the nineteenth century onward, maintaining the character of the original projects while achieving recommended technical upgrades.

8. Study and establish, by means of federal legislation, the protection of the originality of significant works of recently developed landscape architecture, preventing arbitrary alterations and additions that would damage or destroy their artistic value.

9. Study and determine, in conjunction with the counselors serving on the councils of Historic and Artistic Heritage and of Social Sciences, the geographic areas that merit official protection through the creation of national parks and reserves, taking into consideration the reasons already mentioned in the previous items. These areas require collective support and protection in the face of the development of industrial centers, the extraction of natural resources, and the construction of new highways.

10. Study and propose adequate legislation for the protection of natural landscapes, cities, and roadways against the excessive and inappropriate use of advertisement billboards and other damaging works.

Forest Politics and the Destruction of Forests
March 25, 1969

Delivered to the Plenary Session of the Conselho Federal de Cultura on March 25, 1969. Published as Roberto Burle Marx, "Politica florestal e destruição das florestas" (Forest Politics and the Destruction of Forests), *Cultura: Conselho Federal de Cultura* (Ministério da Educação e Cultura) 3, no. 21 (March 1969): 34–41.

Reviewing the document *Carta de Brasília* of the First National Congress of Farming and Ranching advanced by the Ministério da Agricultura under Title III: Forest Policy, I took note of items 1 and 2 of the official statements, cited here:[42]

1.1 "Equatorial, Tropical, and Subtropical Native Forests."
Significantly heterogeneous in their species composition, these forests were dilapidated by selective commercial exploitation and their natural areas diminished by the expansion, often indiscriminate, of agriculture and ranching.

1.2 "*Araucária* Forests."
This largely heterogeneous forest formation has a predominance of *Araucaria angustifolia* in its upper canopy. This native conifer, the *araucária*, provides the finest timber in the world for the manufacture of cellulose for newsprint. These forests have been suffering from the degradation of their canopy mass, a result of the irrational extraction to which they have been subjected.

I shall now make nine brief comments addressing the document *Problemas florestais brasileiros* (Brazilian Forestry Concerns), accomplished with the input of the experts of the Instituto Nacional de Desenvolvimento Agrário (INDA: National Institute of Agrarian Development), the agronomist engineers José Carlos da Costa Martins and Osvaldo José Nery da Fonseca, interwoven with my own "on-site" observations made during my travels to various regions of the interior of the country collecting botanical material.

1. Forest Area
The forested area of Brazil was estimated to be 5,200,000 square kilometers, approximately 61 percent of the country's total area.

FIGURE 2.31.
Araucárias, Paraná, ca. 1884
Photo by Marc Ferrez/Gilberto Ferrez Collection/Instituto Moreira Salles

TABLE 2.1.
Forested area of the five regions of Brazil

REGION	TERRITORIAL AREA (square kilometers)		AREA OF REMAINING FOREST (square kilometers)	
	Total area	Percentage in relation to Brazil	Total area	Percentage in relation to Brazil
North	3,574,000	41.98	2,731,000	32.08
Northeast	970,000	11.39	131,000	1.54
East	1,261,000	14.81	134,000	1.57
South	825,000	9.69	143,000	1.68
Central-West	1,884,000	22.13	384,000	4.49
TOTAL	8,514,000	100.00	3,523,000	41.36

By 1960 this forested area was reduced to 3,500,000 square kilometers or 41 percent of the country's total area.

Of this 41 percent, we can observe from table 2.1 that the North and Central-West Regions have the greatest percentage of forested area (36.57 percent), while the rest of the country has just 4.79 percent. Thus 78 percent of Brazilian forests are located in the North Region of the Amazon basin.

It is interesting that the greatest economic investments in the sector of forest exploitation are made in the South Region, whose forested area is just 1.68 percent of Brazil's total area. This, as we know, is because the South Region includes the *araucária* forests in the states of Paraná and Santa Catarina. Therefore it is important to have a policy of protection and reforestation in the South Region.

In the North Region of the Amazon basin, due to its ecologic conditions, the forest is almost completely reliant on the equilibrium of soils and plants. The region's exploitation will result in serious problems and grave consequences to the soil and climate.

2. Economic Outlook

From an economic point of view, statistics from 1962 establish timber as the fourth-largest Brazilian export, after coffee, textiles, and minerals, with a total value of 70 million dollars. In turn, the lumber industry claims approximately 7.4 percent of Brazilian manufacturing production, a contribution of 5.2 percent of national sales.

3. Forest Destruction

Completed surveys indicate that 300,000 square kilometers of forest are destroyed annually.

In the last forty-two years, the deforested areas of Brazil have reached an initial figure of 1,451,137 square kilometers.

Excluding the territory of the Amazon forest, the forest loss in other regions has been calculated at 691,000 square kilometers, distributed like this:

Northeast Region	160,000 km^2
East Region	244,000 km^2
South Region	104,000 km^2
Central-West Region	183,000 km^2
TOTAL	691,000 km^2

In the case of the Brazilian pine, the *araucária* (*Araucaria angustifolia*), the outlook is truly catastrophic, considering that it is the most important species in exported timber, as indicated in table 2.2.

TABLE 2.2.
Araucaria angustifolia species of the South Region of Brazil

STATE	Number of *Araucaria angustifolia* species existing in 1949	Number of *Araucaria angustifolia* species extracted, 1950–1960	Remaining number of *Araucaria angustifolia* species
Paraná	60,062,000	10,318,000	49,744,000
Santa Catarina	34,208,000	11,265,000	22,943,000
Rio Grande do Sul	5,050,000	2,110,500	2,939,500

We see that after ten years of irrational exploitation, from 1950 to 1960, around 24 percent of our existing *araucária* reserves were cut down for use as timber. This does not include wood used for mechanical and cellulose wood pulp. We must also take into consideration the fact that clandestine tree cutting, and the supplying of "trunks" to Argentina and Paraguay, likely increases the total area of extracted timber by 10 percent. Destruction by fire, such as the recent massive accidental forest fire in Paraná, and the clearing of forests with fire in order to create agricultural lands have significantly increased the estimated percentages of deforested areas. Yet any deforestation occurring in *araucária* forests is now prohibited by the recent Forestry Code (Código Florestal, Lei 4.771, November 15, 1965, article 16, letter C).[43]

TABLE 2.3.
Forest data for the state of Paraná, 1949

Total area	Forested area	Tropical broadleaf forest	Tropical coniferous forest (*Araucaria angustifolia*)
201,277 km^2	176,737 km^2	100,457 km^2	76,280 km^2

TABLE 2.4.
Forest data for the state of Paraná, 1960

STATE OF PARANÁ	Tropical broadleaf forest	Tropical coniferous forest (*Araucaria angustifolia*)
Deforested area	58,840 km^2	53,348 km^2
Remaining forested area	41,617 km^2	22,932 km^2

Today these remaining forest areas are significantly reduced, likely to less than half of these values, particularly in the case of the *araucária* forest.

The scale of the devastation is around 2,500 hectares (6,200 acres).

It is a calamity. If we take the rate of deforestation and apply this to the years 1960 through 1967, we see that there remain just 8,000 km² of native *araucária* forest in Paraná.

Another serious fact in the state of Paraná is that the tropical broadleaf forest has a high economic value. This forest includes valuable tree species such as the Brazilian walnut, cinnamon, cedar, peroba, pau-marfim (ivorywood), and so forth.

Many of these trees are destroyed by the clearing burns for the establishment of agricultural fields.

4. Forestry Inventories

The forestry inventories being done in Amazônia, for the Serviço Florestal (Forestry Service) of the Ministério da Agricultura and the Food and Agriculture Organization of the United Nations, Forestry Inventory section, are directed by Dr. Dammis Heinsdijk, A. de Miranda Bastos, R. Gachot, and others, noted for their knowledgeable assessment of the forestry wealth of this region.[44] However, these inventories have been essentially paralyzed by the departure of Dr. Heinsdijk, because of a lack of funding and the complete disinterest of the authorities. These experts studied a total area of approximately 19,095,000 hectares (47,185,000 acres) in Amazônia, and here is a summary of their conclusions:

> In fact, it is not only in Amazônia but also in the rest of Brazil and in the majority of tropical forests that the usual process of lumbering exploitation is limited to the extraction of the desired trees, leaving the responsibility for the process of regeneration within the remaining forest to nature. After many years, experience has revealed that that regeneration does not occur on its own; or when it does take place, it is in rare cases or occurs in an unsatisfactory manner. As the trees of these forests have such abundant and dense leaves, sufficient light is not able to pass through them in a manner that would allow for the growth of new seedlings.
>
> Exceptions occur only when, for whatever purpose, clear openings have appeared in the forest. Many experts have noted that in the Amazon the species of trees extracted from the forest for a particular trait do not reappear in the same spot, with the exception of a negligible percentage.
>
> Thus we see, and thus we know, that the regeneration of a forest, once cut, is practically impossible.
>
> Fearing this, the Código Florestal, in article 15, stipulates: "Forest exploitation under an empirical approach is prohibited in primeval forests of the Amazon basin and will only be allowed when in compliance with the technical plans of conduct and management established by an act of Public Authority to be filed within the period of one year."

Currently, all exploitation of timber practiced in the Amazon Basin is strictly outside of the law and is criminal (Código Florestal, Lei 4.771, November 15, 1965, article 15).[45]

5. Proposed Forest Reserves

Considering the current situation in Amazônia, the aforementioned technical team has proposed the creation of three large forest reserves in the region, among others to be studied in the future.

These reserves would define and protect typical forest regions, and for this reason they should be established immediately.

To avoid the complete extinction of mahogany (*Swietenia macrophylla*) and also of cedar (*Cedrela* spp.) and *freijó* (*Cordia goeldiana*), high-value hardwood and softwood species, the team has suggested the creation of the Mahogany Forest Reserve in the state of Goiás. This would be sited along the margins of the Rio Araguaia, between its tributary rivers of San Martinho and Corda.

In addition, the following reserves were suggested:

Caxuaná Forest Reserve—In the state of Pará, region of Xingu.

BR-14 Forest Reserve—In the state of Pará, located between Rio Capim and the BR-14 (Transamazonian Highway).

At this time, none of the necessary steps have been taken to realize the recommendations of these experts' reports.

6. Araucária *Survey*

The same team from the Serviço Florestal of the Ministério da Agricultura has also completed a comprehensive inventory of Brazilian pine (*Araucaria angustifolia*) in Santa Catarina, presenting very important data and conclusions.

The area inventoried was 560,000 hectares (1,380,000 acres) and the conclusions reached are somber, as demonstrated by this statement from the commission: "If adequate measures are not put into place as soon as possible, the present Pilot Inventory will have served only to illustrate with numbers the destiny that awaits the forests of the region we are studying, and, by extension, that of the remaining *araucária* coniferous forests, which are presently the dominant natural resource for the softwood manufacturing industry" (1960).[46]

These measures were not taken, and we know that in Rio Grande do Sul there are no longer *araucária* forests available for economic exploitation. In Santa Catarina only small stands of the trees are left, and in Paraná only 8,000 square kilometers remain. This is the situation![47]

7. Forests of Rio de Janeiro

In the state of Rio de Janeiro, we still find two significant forested areas, both primary and secondary.

One is located in a zone that is difficult to access (the reason for its survival) in the municipalities of Santa Maria Madalena, São Sebastião do Alto, and São Fidélis.

The second is the entire Atlantic coast of the Serra do Mar, from Paraty to Conceição de Macabu, and part of the coast of the state of São Paulo.

This is an area that has been reasonably well conserved until now; but given the demand for wood for firewood and charcoal, these forests have recently been targeted, even in areas that are reserves or parks.

The industries located in the Vale do Paraíba (including the municipalities of Rezende, Barra Mansa, Barra do Piraí) are causing the deforestation of both reserves and production forests of the municipalities of Piraí, Angra dos Reis, and Paraty, particularly along the Atlantic-facing slopes of the Serra do Mar.

The Forestry Code legislation covers this entire region, focusing on the protection of mountain ranges with steep gradients. On these slopes, it is not permitted to cut down trees (Código Florestal, Lei 4.771, November 15, 1965, article 10).[48]

It is not necessary to highlight the importance of preserving these forests; we know that their disappearance will certainly cause the destruction of all of the cities located in the lowland valley plains of the state of Rio de Janeiro, both near and far from the Serra do Mar.

As an example we may cite the recent case of Ponte Coberta, in the Serra das Araras, very close to Rio de Janeiro.[49] Macaé, Cachoeira de Macacu, Magé, Duque de Caxias, Nova Iguaçu, Itaguaí, Rio Bonito, and other cities are also at risk from landslides along the Atlantic-facing slopes of the Serra do Mar.

8. Reforested Area of Brazil

Currently (referencing data through 1964) the reforested area of Brazil is estimated to be around 500,000 hectares (1,240,000 acres), of which 400,000 hectares (1,000,000 acres) are in São Paulo. Yet this is just about 0.001 percent of the total area of forest that has been cut down—nothing, given the size of the country.

9. Reforestation Practices

Some industrial companies, given the possibility of finding themselves without the necessary raw material for their factories (principally the metallurgical industry and paper fabrication mills), are dedicating themselves to reforestation.

However, this is reforestation for industrial ends, forsaking the very important and fundamental goal of the conservation of natural resources.

In Brazil, when one speaks of reforestation, the goal is often simply to furnish wood for industrial purposes. The protection of fresh water sources, soil, flora, and fauna is not taken into consideration.

We know that various species of plants and animals are on a path toward extinction.

In the Serra da Bocaina, a marvelous region and the location of the source of the Rio Paraíba, there is a Brazilian tree species of the genera *Podocarpus*, *Podocarpus lambertii*, the *pinheirinho-bravo* or "pine of Bocaina," whose days are also numbered.[50]

The exotic species of *Eucalyptus* and *Pinus* are always used for reforestation by those who do not understand the advantages of using native species. This type of reforestation has industrial goals rather than the goal of protecting or conserving nature.

Native species with high economic values, such as the quebracho, pau-rosa, mahogany, and so forth, are being systematically destroyed without the least protection.

The quebracho, common in the whole region of the "Chaco," is valued as a source of high-quality tannin.[51]

The species *quebracho colorado* (*Schinopsis balansae*), producing 28 percent tannin, is now only found across the border in the Paraguayan and Argentinian areas of the Chaco region (note that Argentina is now implementing large-scale reforestation projects using the quebracho as the principal species). On the Brazilian side of the border, we only find the *quebracho coronillo* (*Schinopsis lorentzii*), which produces just 18 percent tannin. Because of ongoing exploitation, this species is quickly being extinguished.

Almost all of the tannin imported by Germany originates from quebracho species in Paraguay.

The valuable tree species pau-rosa (Lauraceae), a source of various essential oils used in perfumes, soaps, and other products, is being destroyed in a criminal manner throughout the region of Amazônia, because the extraction of the raw material sacrifices the entire tree.

The legally required replanting that one sees being done by industrial companies has not been executed for several years because of a lack of enforcement by the responsible authorities.

It is interesting to note that all of these species and other resources are rigorously protected by the Forestry Code (Código Florestal, Law 4.771, November 15, 1965).

In Espírito Santo, said to have the richest landscape of hardwoods in Brazil, a small-scale pilot inventory studying the state's forests has been recently completed. The study determined that many different economically valuable species have disappeared, resulting in indescribable devastation. As evidence, one can easily verify that the vast majority of sawmills in Rio de Janeiro, Niterói, and even São Paulo work with logs coming from Espírito Santo.

We know that the *jacarandá-da-bahia* (*Dalbergia nigra*), a tree species once common along the entire coastal region of the state of Bahia, has already disappeared, as these trees were criminally extracted from the forest for exportation as logs.

Much technical research has already been accomplished in Brazil, without the knowledge of the general public or of governmental authorities. However, this is not sufficient to protect our forest reserves or, generally speaking, the soils, the flora, and the fauna.

Mr. President, Esteemed Counselors:

I wish to remain calm, but upon reading the conclusions of the "Seminar Concerning Forestry Development, Agrarian Reform, and Plantation Settlement for Latin American Countries," held in Brasília, November 18 through 25, 1968, sponsored by the Food and Agriculture Organization (FAO) of the United Nations with the collaboration of the Brazilian government, I note that my worry is common among the experts, not only in Brazil, but in all of Latin America. This is the reason why I am calling for the publication of this important document, in order to emphasize its advice and recommendations that the Brazilian authorities designate special protection and permanent preservation for these forested areas. Guidance for this protection is given by law, but the law must be enforced. By enacting this measure, we will be conserving our natural resources for future generations.

FIGURE 2.32.
Forest at the Estação Biológica de Itatiaia, later Parque Nacional de Itatiaia, Rio de Janeiro, ca. 1930
Acervo Museu do Meio Ambiente/Instituto de Pesquisas Jardim Botânico do Rio de Janeiro

Forest Conservation
February 12, 1971

Delivered to the Plenary Session of the Conselho Federal de Cultura on February 12, 1971. Published as Roberto Burle Marx, "Conservacionismo florestal" (Forest Conservation), *Boletim: Conselho Federal de Cultura* (Ministério da Educação e Cultura) 1, no. 2 (April/June 1971): 53–56.

About a month ago I traveled to Belo Horizonte, where I am working on a project for a botanical garden. I took advantage of this occasion to see the Lagoa Santa and the Serra do Cipó again, which I had last visited in 1944 in the company of my great friend and professor, Henrique Lahmeyer de Mello Barreto. On that occasion I was amazed by the floral spectacle. The richness and abundance of species was so great that I had the impression of walking from one surprise to another. The number of *vellozias* was astonishing, as were the *lavoisieras*, exhibiting an obedience to a formal geometric system, with their whorled, overlapping, opposite, alternate leaves, and, from this same family of Melastomataceae, representatives of the genera *Cambessedesia*, *Microlicia*, *Leandra*, and *Miconia*. There were enormous quantities of *Lychnophora*, also known as arnica, and *Paepalanthus* covered entire fields in the region. The *Paepalanthus* is a plant that is now being exported and soon may be extinct, given this indiscriminate exploitation. For me, it was very powerful to discover this flora that grows in sandy and rocky quartzite terrains, dating from the Archean eon.[52] I recall seeing a *Wunderlichia* and a *Sipolisia* that my friend Mello Barreto noted had been discovered by the botanist and scholar Auguste de Saint-Hilaire around the date of 1817. After the passing of these twenty-seven years, I was so disappointed to see that the appearance of the place has changed perceptibly. In the creases and depressions of the terrain, where there had once been large and small trees displaying orchids and other epiphytes, such as the *Tillandsia usneoides*, there now remains nothing or almost nothing. At that time, a cold fog would often descend, sometimes for several days at a time, causing many travelers to feel disoriented and lost. Today, with the lucrative business of burning of wood in order to make charcoal, the increased heat, smoke, and fires have transformed the ecological conditions of the region. From the Serra do Cipó, I continued on my journey to Serro and Conceição do Mato Dentro, in the Serra do Espinhaço. In this region, despite the impoverished soil, the flora is uncommonly rich. Interspersed between these rock formations are *Vellozias*, *Lychnophoras*, *Philodendron adamantinum*, *Kalimeris* with their white flowers, *Barbacenias*, *Coccolobas*, and *Vochysias*. Bromeliads with spectacular coloration attach themselves to the rock formations, worn away by the weather and the wind. Sedimentary and corroded, at times they acquire notable sculptural qualities.

In Serro and Conceição do Mato Dentro I saw churches with very unusual characteristics, creating dramatic moments in the landscape. The clustering of houses presents a marvelous pictorial aspect, not only for their coloration and integration with the topographic landscape but also for their unified architectural characteristics, with their protective eaves and vividly colored window frames and door frames, accentuating their structural function. Many backyards have very old *jabuticabeiras*, a tree commonly found in these historic cities of Minas Gerais.

When one arrives in Diamantina, the spectacle is stupendous. One is surrounded by this extraordinarily interesting *Saxicola* flora, those rock-dwelling plants that are associated with sandstone and quartzite geologic formations. Despite the development around the city, this flora is so unusual and impressive that any sensible person with the capacity of observation will discover a unique world of plants unlike anywhere else.

Even with the interference of extraneous architecture, this city has monuments that have retained their original character given the direction and protection of the Department of National Historic and Artistic Heritage.[53] It is a shame that the governmental authorities have not designated adequate financial support for the maintenance and restoration of additional buildings, as these are truly significant works of Brazilian baroque and rococo architecture.

I continued further on, in the direction of the Vale do Jequitinhonha, where the rocky mountain massif merges with a dramatic sky, and the luminosity of the clouds and intensity of the blue seems to be more powerful than in other places. Every time we stopped, we would encounter plants with extraordinarily unusual forms, and a great number of these were unknown to me. It is worth noting that remnants of a primeval forest still exist in this region.

I am certain that, with the support of the president of this council and my colleagues, we could propose the creation of a national park here that would be a sanctuary not only for fauna but also for the flora that is being horribly devastated. With such a park, the flora would be conserved, and we would be setting the precedent of our cultural advocacy.

I recently learned that France is considering the creation of a Ministry of Natural Resources. It would be an example for the world if we Brazilians were to address, once and for all, the problem of conservation in a more serious, vigorous, and definitive manner. Our actions would also be significant in the realm of cultural conservation. Species that are rare or threatened with extinction deserve to have special care. Preserving them through the creation of such a park is one of the goals of the conservation movement.

During my most recent trip to Curitiba, I was astonished and alarmed by what

I saw on the highway from Curitiba to Paranaguá, particularly along the eastern slopes and escarpments of the mountains where a virgin forest was being cut down for the planting of *Pinus*. Along the highway, next to the mountains, one could see a signboard with the words: "Forestry Techniques, Inc.—Before, an unproductive forest. Now, an area forested with *Pinus*." In this region, almost 19,000 hectares (47,000 acres) of completely virgin forest were cut down and replaced by *Pinus elliotis*. After protests by more clear-sighted people, the devastation extending to the edge of the road was stopped, but deeper in the countryside, as I mentioned, almost 19,000 hectares (47,000 acres) were destroyed. This company buys forested lands at 100.00 cruzeiras per 4.84 hectares (12 acres) and sells them, reforested with *Pinus*, at 1,500.00 cruzeiras per 4.84 hectares. This is a profitable business transaction, but only for that aforementioned company, for these are rocky soils, steep mountain slopes, and so forth, generally unproductive for agriculture. Pines are planted even in places with just ten centimeters of soil above slabs of sandstone. Our only comfort is from isolated initiatives. For example, along the road from Curitiba to Joinville, the engineer-in-charge maintains innumerable trees at the side of the road, beautifying it greatly.

But, returning to my theme, I would like to emphasize that conservation and reforestation with a goal of commercial profit are two completely different things. I am not against the planting of *Pinus*, but I think that this species should only be planted in areas that are already degraded, since that will allow for the restoration of the organic layer, the protection of natural springs, and the prevention of erosion. At the same time, the protection and maintenance of our remaining forests and woodlands must be achieved using all possible resources, and I believe that the most effective manner of achieving this is through the creation of national parks in regions like Diamantina and Serra do Cipó, given the unusual characteristics of the flora that thrives in these areas.

My wish is that the Conselho Federal de Cultura dedicate itself fully to the realization of this project with full support, for if we succeed in creating a Parque Nacional do Vale do Jequitinhonha, we will have taken a very important step toward the development of a true policy of conservation for our country.

In conclusion, I propose that the Conselho Federal de Cultura present to the minister of agriculture the present suggestion of the creation of a national park, with an area of approximately 3,000 hectares (7,400 acres), at the Vale do Jequitinhonha, in the event that this motion of my authorship is approved by the plenary assembly of this council.

FIGURE 3.1.
The colonial town of Ouro Preto seen from the Igreja de São Francisco de Paula, with the mountains of the Serra do Espinhaço beyond, ca. 1949
Photo by Alice Brill/Instituto Moreira Salles Collection

CHAPTER 3

Landscapes of the Baroque Interior

Roberto Burle Marx's public landscape work in the 1940s in the interior state of Minas Gerais was particularly influential on his later large parks. His introduction to the architect Oscar Niemeyer while working on the Ministério da Educacão e Saúde headquarters building in Rio marked the beginning of a rich collaboration, which flourished in Minas Gerais—in both Ouro Preto, the colonial mining town, and Pampulha, a garden suburb of the new state capital of Belo Horizonte. Lúcio Costa nurtured the professional relationship between the two men, particularly through his work in support of the Serviço do Patrimônio Histórico e Artístico Nacional (SPHAN: Department of National Historic and Artistic Heritage), the public agency of the Ministério da Educacão e Saúde that classified and protected the country's historic and artistic cultural patrimony.

Although Getúlio Vargas's 1934 Constitution included an article regarding the government's authority to protect objects of artistic and historic interest as well as the *belezas naturais* (natural beauties) of Brazil, the legal structures for the identification and protection of objects, buildings, and places of cultural and national patrimony were not formalized until just before Vargas's Revolution of 1937. This coup initiated the dictatorial regime of the Estado Novo and led to a subsequent rewriting of the Constitution in 1937. New legislation regarding cultural heritage in Brazil,

Decreto-Lei No. 25, had been prepared just before the coup and was then approved by an executive act of Vargas during the first weeks of the Estado Novo in 1937. This significant decree-law established the state as sponsor of SPHAN, a management agency that would define Brazil's cultural heritage.[1]

Article 148 of the provisional Third Constitution, accepted by Vargas in 1934, included a directive to the federal, state, and municipal authorities to protect objects of artistic and historic interest. In July 1934 the Inspectoria dos Monumentos Nacionais (National Monuments Inspection Service) was established as a restoration service, following Vargas's 1933 designation of Ouro Preto as a national monument, persuaded by his second minister of education, Washington Pires. In 1936 Vargas's third minister of education, Gustavo Capanema, appointed Mário de Andrade, the modernist author of *Macunaíma* and mastermind of the 1922 Semana de Arte Moderna, to develop a preliminary proposal for a new federal agency that would replace the Inspectoria dos Monumentos Nacionais. This agency would be responsible for both classifying and protecting Brazil's historical and artistic heritage. Andrade sought to define these objects of national patrimony as well as the legal mechanism that would establish, administer, and protect them. His proposed law also stated that objects should be categorized and inscribed into one of four national registries, called the *livros do tombo*. The four registries—archaeology and ethnography, history, fine arts, and applied arts—would correspond to four national museums, each displaying a copy of its respective *livro do tombo* along with examples of the works it contained. SPHAN, as the law's regulatory agency would come to be called, would be responsible for the registration of these cultural assets.[2] In this way SPHAN may be considered the direct descendant of the Semana de Arte Moderna, with its emphasis on the importance of Brazilian regional traditions as well as the baroque colonial heritage.

Mário de Andrade's proposal was slated for review by the legislative branch of Congress in 1937, which was dissolved when Vargas seized power with an internal coup on November 10, 1937, initiating the Estado Novo and suspending all pending legislation. Nonetheless, Capanema appealed directly to Vargas to approve the proposed law. Through the decree-law powers granted him by the 1937 Estado Novo Constitution, Vargas signed Decreto-Lei No. 25 on November 30, 1937, establishing SPHAN's legal mechanisms through an executive order. Thus, though SPHAN was developed prior to the establishment of the Estado Novo, it was the Estado Novo that initiated its regulatory powers and the Estado Novo's administration that would determine which assets of the cultural patrimony of Brazil would be worthy of legal protection.

According to Decreto-Lei No. 25, "natural monuments, as well as sites and landscapes that are worthy of conservation and protection because of their remarkable features, endowed by nature or obtained through human industry, are subject to registration."[3] Cultural assets with landscape value are thus identified as both

FIGURE 3.2.
Façade of the eighteenth-century Igreja de Nossa Senhora do Carmo with carvings by Antônio Francisco Lisboa (Aleijadinho), Ouro Preto, ca. 1947
Arquivo Público Mineiro

natural areas and designed places with value attributed to the reconfiguration of nature—these could be interpreted as parks or gardens but also as cities or towns cohesively integrated with their natural environment. Decreto-Lei No. 25 describes the categories of the four *livros do tombo*: the *Livro do tombo arqueológico, etnográfico e paisagístico* (archaeological, ethnographic, and landscape registration book); the *Livro do tombo histórico* (historical registration book); the *Livro do tombo das belas artes* (fine arts registration book); and the *Livro do tombo das artes aplicadas* (applied arts registration book). These categories are similar to the four tribunals that would much later constitute the Conselho Federal de Cultura—arts, letters, humanistic sciences, and national historic and artistic patrimony—and the council's counselors often served as advisors to SPHAN.[4]

Capanema appointed the journalist and lawyer Rodrigo Mello Franco de Andrade as the first director of SPHAN in 1937.[5] In the early years of the Estado Novo, SPHAN focused on the protection of Brazil's seventeenth- and eighteenth-century baroque colonial legacy, particularly the religious and governmental buildings located in the states of Rio de Janeiro, Bahia, Pernambuco, and Minas Gerais. Both Capanema and Mello Franco de Andrade were from Minas Gerais and supported and enhanced the narrative that this interior state was the source of Brazilian culture and even independence.[6] Historically, Minas Gerais had been the first region to challenge Portuguese dominion with the Inconfidência Mineira (Minas Gerais Conspiracy), a failed separatist uprising in 1789 that is still considered the first catalyst of a movement toward an independent Brazil. The town of Ouro Preto had been established

FIGURE 3.3.
Aleijadinho, statue of the prophet Jonas at the Santuário do Bom Jesus de Matosinhos, Congonhas do Campo, ca. 1947
Photo by Marcel Gautherot/Instituto Moreira Salles Collection

as a national monument in 1933 through SPHAN's predecessor, the Inspectoria dos Monumentos Nacionais. But by 1938 an unprecedented six historic urban centers were registered in the *livros do tombo* as patrimonial assets, including Ouro Preto, São João del Rei, and Diamantina—all colonial towns of Minas Gerais. Mello Franco de Andrade expressed the nationalist connection to the colonial baroque in 1936, stating: "The poetry of a Brazilian church of the colonial period is, for us, more moving than the Parthenon. And any statue that Aleijadinho carved into soapstone for the churchyard of Congonhas [do Campo] speaks to our imagination more loudly than Michaelangelo's Moses."[7]

Now compounded by an increasingly valuable cultural positioning, the political force and economic wealth of Minas Gerais during in the Vargas era was supported by the state's mineral resources. Much like the exploitation of Brazil's forests as a natural resource, the extraction of minerals in Minas Gerais was highly attractive, especially given the international demand for iron ore during World War II. Minas Gerais (General Mines, now the name of the state) was the territory where diamonds and gold were extracted for the Portuguese crown in the seventeenth and eighteenth centuries, and a constellation of baroque colonial towns developed in the mountainous region. By the twentieth century this extraction had shifted principally to iron ore. In 1942 Vargas established the Companhia Vale do Rio Doce in Itabira, Minas Gerais, as a public company of the Brazilian federal government. Within seven years, the company was responsible for exporting 80 percent of Brazil's iron ore; by the mid-1970s it was the world's largest exporter of iron ore. This wealth of ore deposits, the greatest concentration in Brazil, was located in what became known as the Quadrilátero Ferrífero (Iron Quadrangle), a 7,500-square kilometer rectangle in central Minas Gerais with the cities of Belo Horizonte, Santa Bárbara, Mariana, and Congonhas at its four corners. These same geological territories rich in industrial resources and minerals such as iron ore, bauxite, and aluminum form some of Brazil's most unique landscapes, providing habitat for rare endemic species.

In addition to its significant protection of the Brazilian colonial baroque heritage in Minas Gerais, SPHAN became a vanguard institution for its unique marriage between cultural conservation and modernism, particularly due to the intellectual contribution of Lúcio Costa. Appointed by Mello Franco de Andrade as a specialized regional research advisor to SPHAN in 1939, Costa was designated national director of the Division of Research and Registration in 1946, a post that he would maintain through 1972. Both an expert on colonial architecture and an active proponent of the modernist movement in Brazil, Costa was responsible for the protection of a number of early modernist buildings through SPHAN registration. For Costa, the preservation of Brazil's colonial heritage was not at the expense of modernism, as indicated by his support of SPHAN's construction of Oscar Niemeyer's modernist Grande Hotel de Ouro Preto in that exemplary city of the baroque heritage of Brazil.[8] The hotel, built in 1942 with SPHAN, state, and municipal funding to support tourism in the

FIGURE 3.4.
View of Oscar Niemeyer's modernist Grande Hotel de Ouro Preto in the context of the colonial town, Ouro Preto, ca. 1940
Arquivo Gustavo Capanema/Fundação Getúlio Vargas, Centro de Pesquisa e Documentação/ Fundação Oscar Niemeyer © 2017 Artists Rights Society (ARS), New York/AUTVIS, São Paulo

midst of the restoration of Ouro Preto, was an elegant linear bar of white-stuccoed concrete emerging from a hillside of the town. Its modern presence among the colonial daub and wattle houses asserted that preservation and modernism were not mutually exclusive—indeed, it demonstrated their compatibility. The Grande Hotel de Ouro Preto, for which Burle Marx designed the steep terraced gardens, was an introduction to the state of Minas Gerais for both Niemeyer and Burle Marx and the stepping stone to their modernist complex of buildings and landscapes at Pampulha, a new garden suburb of Belo Horizonte commissioned by its mayor, Juscelino Kubitschek.

Together, Costa and Mello Franco de Andrade (who would serve as director of SPHAN until his retirement in 1967) shaped a consistent vision of the Brazilian cultural heritage for decades. In 1967 the retired Mello Franco de Andrade was appointed to the inaugural group of counselors of the Conselho Federal de Cultura, leading the Câmara do Patrimônio Histórico e Artístico Nacional (Council of National Historic and Artistic Heritage). Burle Marx, as cultural counselor in the Câmara de Artes, would also evoke his interpretation of SPHAN legislation to consider not only the colonial baroque and early modern buildings but also the significant cultural and ecological landscapes of Minas Gerais and other states.

Roberto Burle Marx: Modern Gardens in Minas Gerais, 1940s

Conjunto da Pampulha

Roberto Burle Marx's first large project in Minas Gerais commenced during Juscelino Kubitschek's early political career as mayor of Belo Horizonte, the capital city of Minas Gerais—an appointed position that he held from 1940 to 1945. Kubitschek would become governor of the state and subsequently the third democratically elected president of the Republic following the fall of the first Vargas regime in 1945, holding office from 1956 to 1961. Kubitschek sought to develop a modernist aesthetic expression of Brazilian culture—a project that would culminate during his presidency with the construction of Brasília, the new Brazilian capital on the high plateau of the country's interior. Kubitschek had been introduced to Oscar Niemeyer nearly a decade earlier by Gustavo Capanema during the launch of the Grande Hotel de Ouro Preto and in 1942 commissioned him to design the social and cultural buildings of the new garden suburb of Pampulha, a few kilometers north of Belo Horizonte. This wealthy district was located near an artificial lake created by the impounding of eight streams, intended to create a water supply reservoir for the city to the south. Niemeyer's commission would include five luxurious modern buildings arrayed around the lake, including the Cassino (casino), Iate Clube (yacht club), Casa do Baile (dance hall), Grande Hotel de Pampulha (Grand Hotel of Pampulha), and Igreja de São Francisco de Assis (St. Francis of Assisi Church), as well as a nearby golf course clubhouse and the personal residence of Kubitschek.[9] These programs

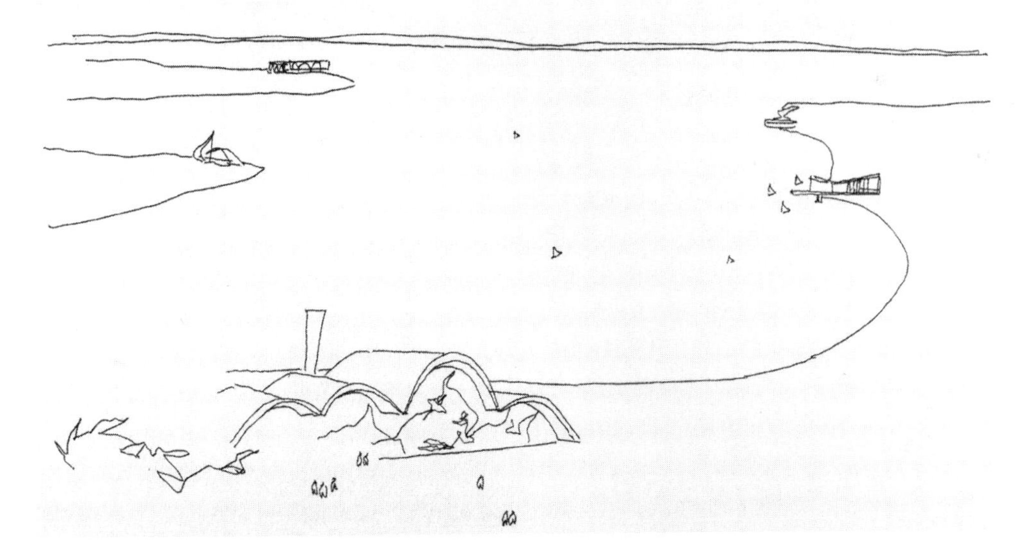

FIGURE 3.5.
Oscar Niemeyer, perspective sketch of the Conjunto da Pampulha showing (*clockwise from foreground*) the Igreja São Francisco de Assis, Grande Hotel, Cassino, Casa do Baile, and Iate Club arrayed in an abstracted landscape, Belo Horizonte, ca. 1942

FIGURE 3.6.
View of the Iate Club and the Cassino seen across the lake, Conjunto da Pampulha, Belo Horizonte, ca. 1943

and buildings embodied both the hedonism and Catholicism of the elite as well as the emergent curvilinear Brazilian modernist style, arguably influenced by the colonial baroque. In 1942 Niemeyer invited Burle Marx to design the landscape gardens of the five lakefront buildings. Their collaboration set a splendid example of the plastic integration of architecture and landscape.

While the Grande Hotel de Pampulha with Burle Marx's proposed rocky lakefront garden was not built beyond its foundations, the rest of the projects were inaugurated in May 1943, with the exception of the church (completed in 1945). Considered the finest buildings of Niemeyer's oeuvre by many critics and prominently featured in the Museum of Modern Art's "Brazil Builds" exhibition in the year of its inauguration, the Conjunto da Pampulha cemented the relationship between Kubitschek and his architect. The politician became an exceptional patron of Niemeyer. As president of Brazil from 1956 to 1961, he would commission Niemeyer to design all of the government buildings for the nation's new capital at Brasília, in accordance with the pilot plan of Lúcio Costa. Niemeyer's great strength was the design of architectonic

FIGURE 3.7.
Canopy at the Casa do Baile, Conjunto da Pampulha, Belo Horizonte, ca. 1960
Arquivo Público Mineiro

complexes, in the sequential interplay of multiple buildings. Burle Marx's important contribution of the integrated landscapes of this early modernist complex at Pampulha was acknowledged by critics including Sigfried Giedion, Bruno Zevi, and Reyner Banham, but he would not complete any projects in Brasília until after the end of Kubitschek's presidency in 1961.[10]

Although the Swiss architect Max Bill would critique Niemeyer's Pampulha buildings a decade later in 1953 as a formally willful and overly expressive architecture that served only the recreational function of pleasure, Costa vehemently defended the significance of Pampulha.[11] The complex certainly reflected the values of the society that commissioned it, but Costa argued that Pampulha was a critical and necessary starting point for Brazilian modernism.[12] Joaquim Cardozo's 1956 "Dois episódios" essay, another veiled response to Bill, noted not only that Pampulha was important to the development of Brazilian modern architecture but also that its buildings sought to achieve a collective social purpose.[13] In the same essay, Cardozo cited the importance of Luiz Nunes's contributions to Brazilian modernism in Recife during the

FIGURE 3.8.
Entrance canopy at the Cassino, Conjunto da Pampulha, Belo Horizonte, ca. 1947
Photo by Marcel Gautherot/Instituto Moreira Salles Collection/Fundação Oscar Niemeyer © 2017 Artists Rights Society (ARS), New York/AUTVIS, São Paulo

mid-1930s and identified Niemeyer's complex of buildings at Pampulha as the second of two episodes in the foundation of Brazilian modernism. In response to Bill's critique of the program, Cardozo suggested that Niemeyer's casino building, closed shortly after its completion because of the national prohibition of gambling in 1946, would be equally useful as a holiday center for students or public workers (it was in fact later transformed into a museum of fine arts). Cardozo especially appreciated Niemeyer's use of curvilinear forms at Pampulha, interpreting this as a masterful technique for achieving lightness, dynamism, and immateriality—a formal strategy employed by Burle Marx as well.

Indeed the Cassino, with its composition based on the complex intersection of planar and curvilinear volumes in both plan and section, provides a rich sequential development of spaces, framed by similar interlocking curves in the forecourt pond and gardens of Burle Marx.[14] The fluid peristyle of the Casa do Baile evokes Niemeyer's later canopy marquee at the Parque do Ibirapuera linking the complex of exhibition buildings and evokes the Ilha dos Amores, the folly island of Glaziou's Quinta da Boa Vista that would figure again in Burle Marx's gardens for Araxá. And the Igreja de São Francisco de Assis, with its beautiful parabolic volumes, received a

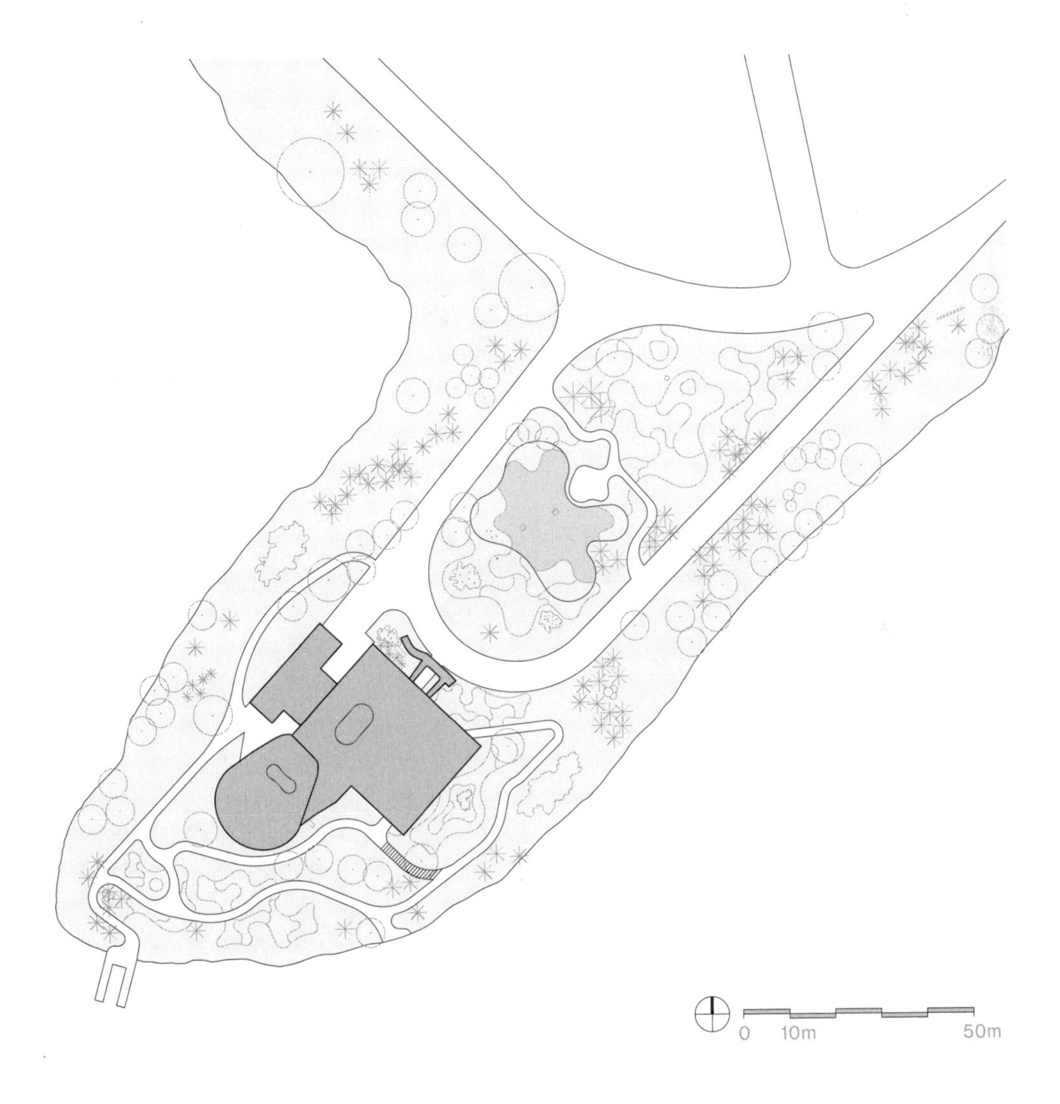

FIGURE 3.9.
Roberto Burle Marx, plan of the Cassino gardens, Conjunto da Pampulha, Belo Horizonte, 1942
Drawing by Catherine Seavitt Nordenson

FIGURE 3.10.
Igreja de São Francisco de Assis, Conjunto da Pampulha, Belo Horizonte, ca. 1947
Photo by Marcel Gautherot/Instituto Moreira Salles Collection/Fundação Oscar Niemeyer © 2017 Artists Rights Society (ARS), New York/AUTVIS, São Paulo

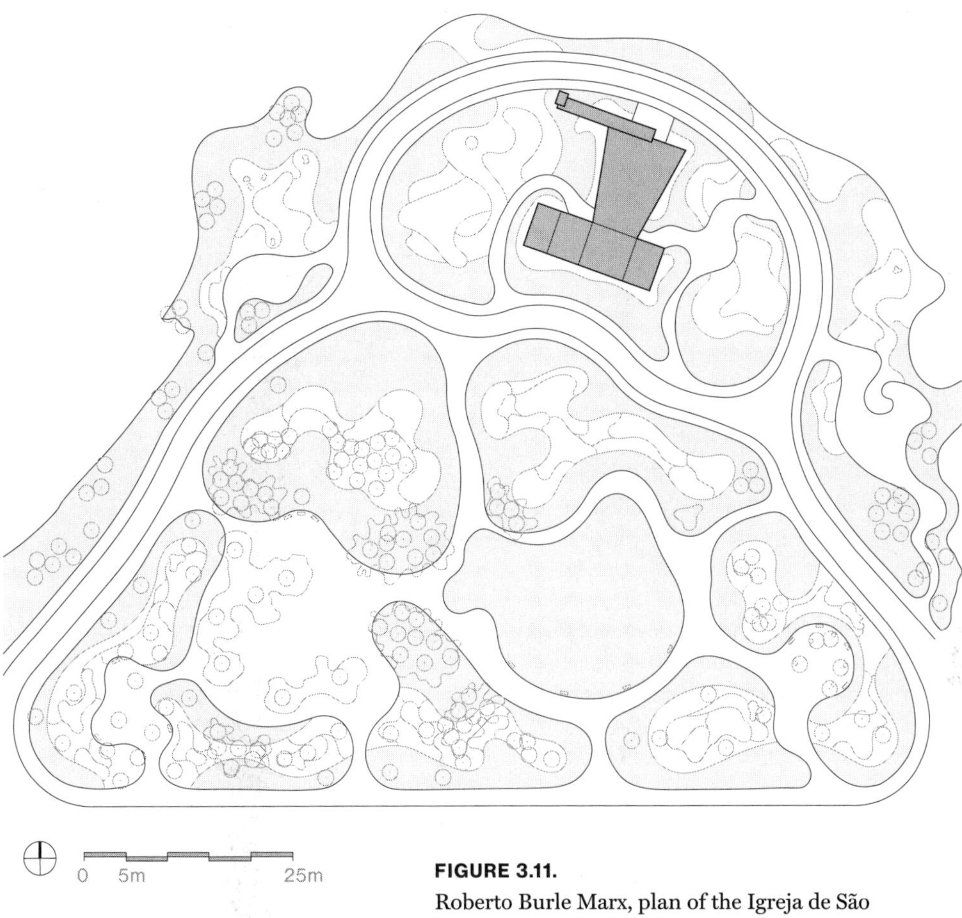

FIGURE 3.11.
Roberto Burle Marx, plan of the Igreja de São Francisco de Assis gardens, Conjunto da Pampulha, Belo Horizonte, 1942

Drawing by Catherine Seavitt Nordenson

luminous exterior *azulejo* tile mural by the painter Cândido Portinari, depicting the life of Saint Francis. This powerful image, deployed across the windowless east façade of four linked catenary arcs, projected outward to Burle Marx's design of the church's gardens and the adjacent (but unexecuted) rose garden.

The Igreja São Francisco de Assis was not consecrated by the Brazilian archbishop for the celebration of religious services until 1959. But it was the first modernist building to be registered for protection by SPHAN, with the support of Lúcio Costa and Rodrigo Mello Franco de Andrade. The building was completed by Niemeyer in 1944. The request in 1947 to inscribe this building in the *livros do tombo* as an object of the national patrimony was motivated by the resistance from the leadership of the Catholic church to consecrate the building as a church, probably due to both its modernist form and the Communist political beliefs of Niemeyer, its architect. But the SPHAN listing was also preventative—it was feared that the building might

FIGURE 3.12.
Roberto Burle Marx, perspective view of the gardens for the Grande Hotel de Pampulha, Conjunto da Pampulha, Belo Horizonte, 1942
© Burle Marx Landscape Design Studio

FIGURE 3.13.
Roberto Burle Marx, plan of the gardens for the Grande Hotel de Pampulha (never built), Conjunto da Pampulha, Belo Horizonte, 1942
Drawing by Catherine Seavitt Nordenson

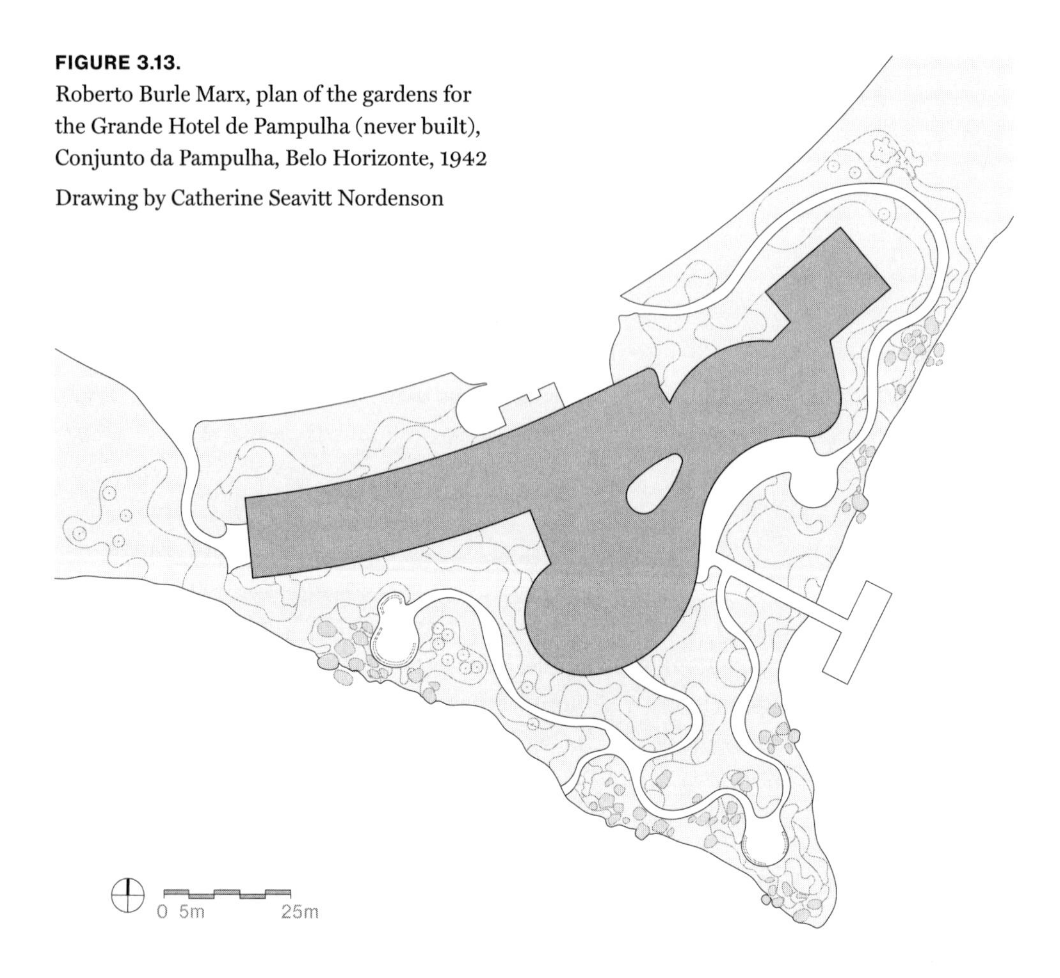

be destroyed by those with opposing ideologies. The church assumed its place, and protection, in the fine arts registry in 1947.

The integration of buildings, gardens, and landscapes at the Conjunto da Pampulha is masterful, reflecting the successful partnership of Niemeyer and Burle Marx. Burle Marx's gardens at Pampulha served as an introduction to the interior state of Minas Gerais and an excellent opportunity for the development of both his curvilinear geometric style and the beginnings of his important collaboration with the botanist Henrique Lahmeyer de Mello Barreto (1892–1962). Mello Barreto accompanied Burle Marx on botanical excursions throughout Minas Gerais, introducing him to the wealth of biodiverse species within the state's mountainous regions, particularly the *cerrado*, Brazil's tropical savanna ecoregion. He emphasized the notion of plant associations—the intertwining of geological features and complex plant communities. Mello Barreto's phytogeographic influence at Pampulha is perhaps most evident in Burle Marx's drawings for the gardens of the Grande Hotel de Pampulha, the only one of the five proposed lakefront buildings that was not executed. Burle Marx evoked a terraced rock garden, with the strong dark forms of the boulders dispersed across the garden as it sloped down to the lake, with philodendrons draping languidly across the walkways.

Parque do Barreiro, Araxá

Just after the inauguration of the Pampulha complex in 1943, Burle Marx was commissioned by Benedito Valadares Ribeiro, the governor of Minas Gerais and a powerful ally of Vargas, to design the gardens of the Parque do Barreiro near Araxá. Located in the western area of the state known as the Triângulo Mineiro (Mining Triangle), Araxá lies in a mountainous region defined by the junction of the Rio Grande and Rio Paranaíba. The village of Barreiro, a few kilometers south of Araxá, had been renowned since the nineteenth century for the medicinal properties of its mineral water springs. Two small hotels constructed in the early twentieth century, serving the tourists attracted by the mineral waters, were located near the site of the future Parque do Barreiro—Hotel Rádio, built in 1919, and Hotel Colombo, inaugurated in 1929.[15] A third establishment, the Grande Hotel de Araxá, was commissioned by Valadares in 1937, a monumental neocolonial hotel and thermal bath complex designed by the architect Luis Signorelli.[16] Burle Marx was tasked with developing a landscape design that would integrate the extensive grounds of the new hotel and bath complex with the sources of the two springs, a new artificial lake, and a public park.

Burle Marx began work on the Parque do Barreiro in 1943. The hotel and its grounds were inaugurated in 1944, although the landscape was not fully completed until 1946. The presence of President Vargas with Governor Valadares at the inauguration was significant and symbolic—the monumental hotel and baths projected an image of vigor and strength. The modernist gardens, which embraced two mineral

FIGURE 3.14.
Roberto Burle Marx, Parque do Barreiro with the Fonte Radioativa in the foreground and the Grande Hotel de Araxá, Minas Gerais, ca. 1945
Arquivo Público Mineiro

sources as well as a recreational sports complex, were intended to reflect the modernity and progress of the federal and state governments. The Grande Hotel de Araxá, with its famed mineral baths, became the site of social, political, and cultural events, bringing an era of cultural splendor to this interior state of Brazil, particularly given the Estado Novo's emphasis on Brazil's mineral wealth and the promise of resource extraction.

For this first large-scale public park commission, Burle Marx worked in close collaboration with botanist Mello Barreto. His intention for the design of Parque do Barreiro was to showcase the rich flora of the diverse phytogeographic regions of Minas Gerais. The landscaping, including an artificial lake, was part of the transformation of this large site that would integrate Signorelli's Grande Hotel de Araxá and the adjacent Balneário, the spa bathhouse. Burle Marx's preliminary design for the park included twenty-five sectors, representative of the various biomes of Minas Gerais and showcasing the native flora of this ecologically diverse region. The plan also included a proposal for a small zoo that would include fauna of Minas Gerais, but this element of the program was eliminated. The formal allée of trees along the northern entrance avenue to the Grande Hotel included typical species from the mountains and plateaus of Minas Gerais, such as the *pinheiro-bravo* (*Pinus pinaster*), and was flanked by gardens with perennial plants from the Serra do Itacolomi.[17]

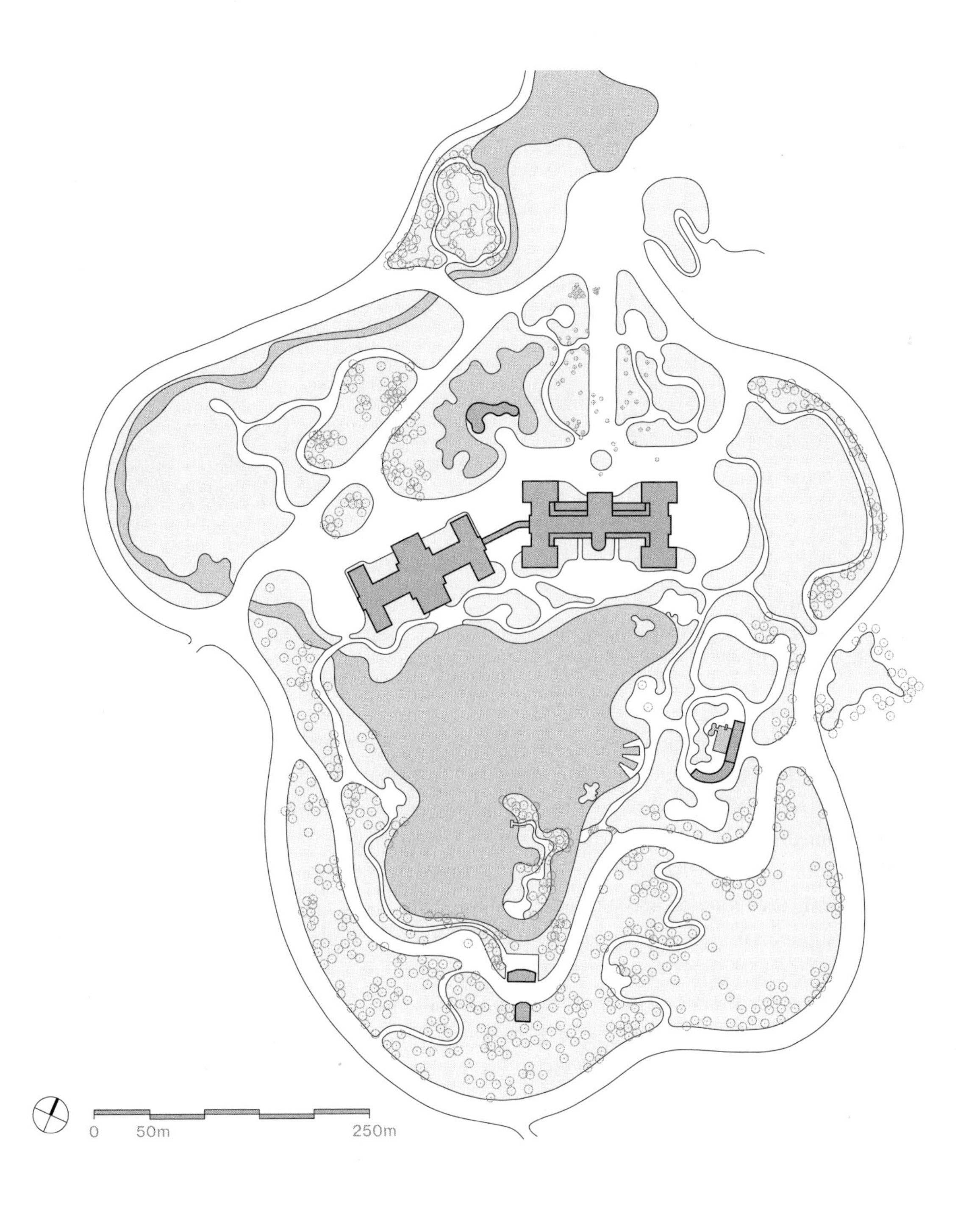

FIGURE 3.15.
Roberto Burle Marx, plan of the Parque do Barreiro, Araxá, 1943
Drawing by Catherine Seavitt Nordenson

FIGURE 3.16.
Roberto Burle Marx, perspective of the Ilha dos Amores at the Parque do Barreiro, Araxá, 1946
© Burle Marx Landscape Design Studio

Species from the calcium-rich geological regions of Minas were planted in the low moist areas of the park, and plants endemic to the quartzite formations of the Serra do Cipó were established in the drier areas.[18] The enormous twin buildings of the Grande Hotel and the Balneário, encircled by a ring road called the Avenida do Contorno, opened up toward the landscaped garden and the new artificial lake to the south, the Grande Lago. Burle Marx shaped the lake as an organic sinuous form, drawing upon his late plaza plans for the Ministério de Educação e Saúde in Rio de Janeiro, but at a much larger scale. The design includes a small island accessible by a footbridge, the Ilha dos Amores. The lake, its folly island, and dominant contrapuntal presence of the neocolonial Grande Hotel recall Glaziou's Quinta da Boa Vista. The southern end of the lake was framed by an ipé forest and the existing structure enclosing the Fonte Dona Beja, one of the sources of the mineral waters believed to have powerful medicinal qualities.[19]

North of the hotel was a smaller lake, the second source of sulfurous waters and mud. This previously had been the site of a small pavilion built in 1932 that housed the pipes that tapped the mineral waters. Burle Marx's reshaping of this northern lake included the implementation of a new pavilion for accessing the sulfurous waters, the Fonte Andrade Júnior. This curvilinear structure was built on a peninsula jutting into the lake, reminiscent of Niemeyer's Casa do Baile at Pampulha. Designed in 1946 by Francisco Bolonha, a young architect and at the time an employee of Burle Marx's office, the pavilion was intended to be an integrated architectonic element of the comprehensive landscape design. Bolonha's design consisted of a thin roof canopy floating on travertine columns, with a glass screen creating an area of partial enclosure to protect the water taps. The pavilion also included a vitrine displaying fossils excavated during the construction of the complex. Burle Marx's *pedra portuguesa* pavement, including patterned images of the prehistoric animals whose fossilized bones had been discovered at the site, moved fluidly across the peninsula and through the pavilion. The fossil motif was also incorporated into Burle Marx's design of the blue-and-white glazed ceramic *azulejo* tiles that wrapped the pavilion's walls.

FIGURE 3.17.
Francisco Bolonha, Fonte Andrade Júnior at the Parque do Barreiro, Araxá, ca. 1946
Photo by Marcel Gautherot/Instituto Moreira Salles Collection

Bolonha's gemlike modernist structure at the Parque do Barreiro, juxtaposed so jarringly with Signorelli's grand neocolonial hotel and bathhouse, illustrated the aesthetic and cultural debate still raging within the Vargas regime between a vision of Brazilian culture defined by the embrace of the neocolonial style and one that reflected a unique national manifestation of the International Style of modern architecture. Although Lúcio Costa did much to protect and valorize the colonial heritage of Brazil, Brazilian modernism as the aesthetic style for a new nationalistic politic was clearly the ascendant contender in the representation of *brasilidade*. Burle Marx's modernist gardens at both Pampulha and Araxá, with their fluid forms and expressive tropical planting palettes, were the ideal counterpoint to this new architecture.

Burle Marx would begin to establish planting schemes in Minas Gerais that addressed entire regions, connecting this approach to his appreciation of the phytogeographic displays of Martius and Engler at Berlin-Dahlem. With the influence of Mello Barreto, he moved beyond his earlier narrative use of plants such as the giant water lily (*Victoria amazonica*) and the dramatic royal palm (*Roystonea oleracea*) as indicators of a particularly Brazilian heritage. Burle Marx now insisted that the individual plant be understood through its association with other plants as well as with the underlying regional geology, and his work at Araxá explored these complex relationships.

Depositions: Notable Natural Landscapes

The progressive political leadership of Minas Gerais in the 1940s embraced a new architectural modernism, but it was also the locus of a developing national preservationist movement that sought to protect Brazil's historic colonial architectural heritage. Burle Marx's professional introduction to the regional landscapes of Minas Gerais through his work at Ouro Preto, Pampulha, and Araxá would significantly influence his later arguments as a member of the Conselho Federal de Cultura for the conservation and preservation of the region's natural and cultural landscapes. Several of his consular statements reflect his interest in the protection and conservation of the natural and cultural landscapes of Brazil, particularly the ecological diversity of the Quadrilátero Ferrífero region of central Minas Gerais. Burle Marx clearly feared this landscape patrimony might be destroyed without a robust system of federal protection, which he insisted should be enacted quickly and with resolve.

Burle Marx addressed the protection of ecological sites at a massive regional scale by adapting the process of landmark registration, codified through SPHAN, to the scale of the regional landscape, arguing that the diverse natural landscapes of Brazil were as much a part of its national patrimony as a baroque church or fountain. He considered the country's environmental assets to be essential aspects of the cultural patrimony of every Brazilian citizen. Drawing upon his earlier experience with the merged architectural and landscape complexes of Pampulha and Araxá, Burle Marx would also invoke this notion of patrimony as part of a nuanced strategy to protect integrated cultural landscapes, both colonial and contemporary.

Lúcio Costa's service as the national director of SPHAN's Division of Research and Registration, reporting to Mello Franco de Andrade and Gustavo Capanema, the minister of education, clearly established a precedent for Burle Marx. Since 1939 Costa had successfully lobbied for the simultaneous conservation of the Portuguese colonial baroque heritage and of Brazil's earliest modernist structures. Years later, Burle Marx's great contribution to the Conselho Federal de Cultura would be the adaptation of these techniques to the protection of the indissoluble cultural and natural landscape, a scope extending well beyond individual objects and buildings.

Like Costa, Burle Marx would address the protection of both historic and contemporary urban parks, arguing that the conservation of cultural heritage should embrace not only the past but also the present. His May 23, 1968, deposition "Parques, jardins, e praças públicas" (Parks, Gardens, and Public Plazas) presented a sweeping history of the arborized public plaza and park, from ancient Greece to nineteenth-century London and Paris to Central Park during the contemporary era of New York City parks commissioner Robert Moses. He addressed the poor maintenance of street trees throughout Brazil and noted the importance of enhancing urban arborization in order to moderate the tropical climate. Lamenting the lack of protection that he perceived at the heritage landscapes of Minas Gerais, Burle Marx described the abuses at the baroque Santuário do Bom Jesus de Matosinhos at the town of Congonhas do Campo, the beautiful colonial pilgrimage complex featuring twelve carved soapstone prophets by the eighteenth-century Brazilian sculptor Antônio Francisco Lisboa, known as Aleijadinho. Burle Marx would revisit this theme of the disfiguration of colonial heritage landscapes in his deposition delivered on August 25, 1969, "Defêsa da paisagem" (Defense of the Landscape). He insisted on the vigilant oversight of local municipal authorities whose actions might result in marring these cultural landscapes and suggested that guidance be provided at the federal level.

Burle Marx could also be complimentary. In his brief deposition delivered on November 28, 1968, "Contribuição cultural" (Cultural Contribution), he reflected admiringly on the extended public service and professional tenacity of Ayrton de Almeida Carvalho, the director of the regional office of historic and artistic patrimony of Recife, Pernambuco. Burle Marx met Carvalho in 1935 as a young landscape architect tasked with the renovation of the public plazas of Recife. Burle Marx lists the numerous restoration projects completed by Carvalho in Recife, notably many baroque colonial churches—one of these, the Capela de Nossa Senhora da Conceição (Chapel of Our Lady of the Conception) in the neighborhood of Jaqueira, included a garden renovation of the church grounds by Burle Marx himself from 1951. Burle Marx also cited the artistic and cultural contributions of the musicologist and critic

FIGURE 3.18.
Jubilee procession at the Santuário do Bom Jesus de Matosinhos, Congonhas do Campo, ca. 1947
Photo by Marcel Gautherot/Instituto Moreira Salles Collection

Ayres de Andrade. Many of the consular addresses were homages to other members of the council or their intellectual peers, but this is the only deposition in which Burle Marx engages the homage as a thematic format.

As a cultural counselor on the Conselho Federal de Cultura, Burle Marx indeed had the power to influence governmental policy. In "Defêsa das reservas naturais" (Defense of Nature Reserves), his deposition delivered on June 27, 1969, Burle Marx cites the edits and comments that he and his fellow counselors submitted for draft sections of the 1969 amendment to the 1967 Constitution. This amendment, developed by the triumvirate of the military junta briefly in power between the presidencies of Castelo Branco and Emílio Garrastazu Médici, made the severely authoritarian Constitution, launched by President Castelo Branco in January 1967, even more repressive regarding civil rights.[20] However, Burle Marx focused his comments on the sections that supported his argument for the protection of natural landscapes. He wrote the following in response to a consular redaction of article 180 of the draft 1969 Constitutional Amendment: "I would just like to clarify my understanding of 'notable natural landscapes' as those that distinguish themselves with the wealth of their species or topographic configuration but also those that provide the ecological conditions to protect neighboring community groups, such as buffering natural springs and providing the recreational resources so important for reducing the stressful and emotional weight of urban life."[21] Put in sharp relief by the context of political repression and human rights abuses in which it was proffered, Burle Marx's comments were radically prescient in explicitly addressing a contemporary notion of the importance of biodiversity as it directly related to human health and well-being.

Roberto Burle Marx: Depositions

Parks, Gardens, and Public Plazas
May 23, 1968

Cultural Contribution
November 28, 1968

Defense of Nature Reserves
June 27, 1969

Defense of the Landscape
August 25, 1969

Parks, Gardens, and Public Plazas
May 23, 1968

Delivered to the Plenary Session of the Conselho Federal de Cultura on May 23, 1968. Published as Roberto Burle Marx, "Parques, jardins e praças públicas" (Parks, Gardens, and Public Plazas), *Cultura: Conselho Federal de Cultura* (Ministério da Educação e Cultura) 2, no. 8 (May 1968): 14–18.

Mr. President, and Fellow Counselors:

The plaza and the public garden have existed since antiquity. In the ancient Greek democracy, plazas were places where philosophers and their students would converse under shade trees. Medieval cities had plazas where both social and political life unfolded, though in spaces so compressed that there was no room for trees. The arborized public plaza reached its apex in the nineteenth century, at the same time that complex urban problems surged. Planted public spaces appeared, such as Hyde Park in England, the Bois de Boulogne in France, and the system of urban parks created by the landscape architect Frederick Law Olmsted for the cities of Chicago, Boston, Philadelphia, and New York. In all of the projects of this period, the problem of vehicular traffic, then taking the form of the horse-drawn tilbury cabs and carriages, was considered in the planning of these parks. The scale of the green space was proportional to the flow of traffic. In New York's Central Park, Olmsted envisioned a division of space for vehicular carriages, equestrians, and pedestrians. This later became one of the basic principles exhorted by Le Corbusier for twentieth-century urban planning. However, a sense of deterioration may be perceived in our parks today, creating the impression that these green spaces are under attack. Recently, Robert Moses, the director of the Parks Department in New York City, wanted to build a parking lot in Central Park, adjacent to an existing restaurant. However, a group of mothers who lived in the surrounding neighborhood organized a protest.[22] When the bulldozers arrived to remove the trees, the mothers encircled the area with their baby carriages. As a result, Moses did not dare proceed with the project, despite his significant political power.

In Brazil, when I attempt to understand urban problems, I observe that the tendency is to reduce the size of green spaces, even while the population density of those same areas is increasing.

FIGURE 3.19.
Parque Halfeld, with tree trunks painted white along the Rua Marechal Deodora, Juiz de Fora, ca. 1950
Acervo Marcelo Lemos

The Jardim Botânico in Rio de Janeiro has been mutilated; one of the lowest acts of piracy perpetrated against this garden was the ceding of its land to the Fábrica Carioca de Tecidos with a 99-year lease.[23] At the end of that period it was to return to the Brazilian government, but the land was inexplicably divided into private lots. We accept these insanities as consummate facts. The Jardim Botânico has also lost all of the area that is today occupied by the Jockey Club.[24] The Passeio Público is getting smaller and smaller. The Quinta da Boa Vista and the Praça da República have had the same misfortune.

At the Praça Cardeal Arcoverde in Copacabana, a new school is under construction, and the existing school has been transformed into a theater. Would it not be better to dispossess other areas rather than replace this public plaza with a school, so that urban parks could continue to serve the purpose for which they were created? Public space is so necessary for this neighborhood, where the population density is perhaps the highest in the world.

During my travels to the interior of the country, I have seen the misfortune that many century-old trees are subjected to the abuse of mayors, who have quite often cut them down. Though these mayors may have good intentions, they do not understand urban problems and use gardening and pruning as a means of political propaganda, demonstrating an exhibitionist efficiency to their constituents.

In Goiás Velho, a plaza filled with large trees with gracious canopies has been transformed into an army of mercury lampposts and benches. These benches have been generously donated by commercial firms, as one can see by the gigantic words of advertisement painted on their backs and seats. We find billboards suspended in strategic places, destroying the panoramic beauty, much like the large illuminated advertisement at Pão de Açúcar in Rio de Janeiro. The few trees that have escaped destruction seem to be wearing white stockings, and as an assemblage these elements create a most depressing spectacle.

In the city of São Paulo, this tree painting demonstrates a paroxysm of bad taste. It is difficult to find a tree that has not been painted, a custom that must have originated in the military barracks with the goal of giving work to lazy, idle soldiers. Similarly, in Juiz de Fora, a once-beautiful plaza has now been transformed into a mass of horrors.

The highest examples of bad taste include concrete bridges imitating tree trunks; sculptures of heroes, politicians, and poets; and poorly pruned trees, trimmed so crudely that one is left with the impression that the parks are in fact the site of a clandestine firewood industry. In other cities, one finds luminous fountains covered in tiles and mosaics that would be more appropriate for a bathroom, making any person of sound judgment tremble.

In cities with severe climate and a punishing sun, there are no trees. In fact, trees are missing in exactly the places where people tend to meet and gather, where shade would appease the heat and reduce the brightness and reflection of sunlight. We know that when trees are planted in an ideal orientation, the heat index is reduced in direct relationship with the increase in canopy. Another curious fact that may be observed is the overwhelming proportion of exotic vegetation planted in gardens and public plazas. To prove this point, it is sufficient to cite trees such as *Spathodea campanulata*, *Ficus religiosa*, *Ficus retusa* "Flamboyant," *Casuarina*, *Amendoeira*, *Lingustrum japonicum*, *Extremosa*, *Acalypha*, *Ixora*, *Agave*, *Croton*, and *Eucalyptus*.[25] The impression is given that we possess nothing of value for planting in a garden and that everything occurring in nature is just weeds. And these weeds are contemptible and should be destroyed.

In the city of Milagres, in the state of Bahia, trees are almost nonexistent. However, our extremely rich native flora continues to challenge the gardens of public plazas, gardens, and parks. By simply visiting the municipal, state, and federal plant nurseries, one can see that the majority of plants being cultivated are exotic.

A governmental agency should be established to oversee gardens, plazas, and public parks, providing reliable guidance in order to avoid the disgraceful abuse of these landscapes that are integrally connected to the beautiful architecture of our cities.

Just as there exist both national and state offices of the Serviço do Patrimônio Histórico e Artístico that have brought extraordinary benefits to all of our cities through their guidance and preservation of buildings that today give such pride to Brazilians, we must create an agency that would similarly advise municipalities regarding the construction and conservation of plazas and parks. This agency would offer opinions and guidance to ensure that the role of public gardens and urban landscapes would be closely linked to the needs of a city and to a strategic and harmonious urban development.

I would like to highlight that making a garden is not just filling up a space with plants, which often makes it difficult for pedestrian circulation. Consider the Piazza San Marco in Venice, where the essential element is a well-balanced space that shapes activities and celebrates architecture, while allowing for the flow of pedestrians. In France, at the public landmarked site of Versailles, there is a law that prohibits any type of construction within a five-kilometer radius around the palace.

In Brazil, it is unfortunate that gardens are truncated with a frightening ease because of unwise political decisions. Plazas are not respected; nor are they considered fundamentally necessary places that are urgently needed. One does not plan for their protection or acknowledge the advantage of those areas designated as places for gathering and strolling, where children might run about freely.

Many people consider themselves capable of resolving problems concerning the landscape. The results are disastrous. For example, Congonhas do Campo has an inappropriate and ridiculous planting scheme, adjacent to the chapels of the Via Crucis. A garden connected to something of such historic importance deserves better treatment from municipal authorities. From this same location, one sees a radio station antenna dominating the skyline, robbing the landscape of its purity, and the prophets that once were silhouetted majestically against an intense blue sky are today interspersed with offensive buildings.

In Rio de Janeiro, because of interference from the Ministério da Aeronáutica (Ministry of Aeronautics), the existing specimens of pau-rei (*Pterygota brasiliensis*) in front of Aeroporto Santos Dumont at Praça Senador Salgado Filho have been heavily pruned. And in an arbitrary act, they have whitewashed the tree trunks and the curbs along the driveway. Ultimately, everything seems to have been done because of an unrestrained desire for the cleanliness and order of the garden.

These things happen because of inadequate knowledge and a lack of coordination.

In 1939 I designed several gardens at Pampulha. After several years had passed, the gardeners wanted to "contribute," adding planting beds in the shape of a moon, stars, and strange animals.[26] This completely disfigured the original project. These acts are perpetrated by gardeners or laypeople who are uninterested in aesthetic issues. They think that to make a garden it is sufficient just to plant some plants, without any specific arrangement or compositional principles.

On the day that the authorities are convinced of the seriousness of my warnings, the first step will have been taken toward ensuring for city dwellers that these places of rest and tranquillity, so necessary for reducing the stresses resulting from the dynamic agitation of life, will remain intact.

I would like to conclude by asserting that the defense of the landscape is part of the protection of historic and artistic monuments. So it appears in the law, but never in practice or in the consciousness of the political governance of innumerable Brazilian municipalities.

FIGURE 3.20.
Roberto Burle Marx, garden of the Capela de Nossa Senhora da Conceição da Jaqueira, Recife, ca. 1955
Photo by Marcel Gautherot/Instituto Moreira Salles Collection

Cultural Contribution
November 28, 1968

Delivered to the Plenary Session of the Conselho Federal de Cultura on November 28, 1968. Published as Roberto Burle Marx, "Contribuição cultural" (Cultural Contribution), *Cultura: Conselho Federal de Cultura* (Ministério da Educação e Cultura) 2, no. 18 (December 1968): 55–56.

Though until now I have only spoken of the errors and outrages in reference to public plazas and parks, as well as the conservation of nature, today I am here to praise the work of two Brazilians who, in my view, are contributing to Brazilian culture in a positive and incisive manner.

The first is an homage to Ayrton de Almeida Carvalho, whom I met in 1935 as a young engineer, and who significantly and effectively supported the construction of the public gardens that I developed for Recife. A man of enthusiastic and passionate character, he entered into the Recife office of Historic and Artistic Heritage. Now, thirty-three years later, he has that same character, with the same passion of youth and a powerful desire to preserve a patrimony that belongs not only to Recife but to all of Brazil.

An extraordinary individual, Carvalho would argue vehemently against those who did not understand the importance of this history and the need for its preservation, including an unenlightened clergy. He addressed questions of preservation, insisting against the alteration of historic monuments. It is particularly easy for these monuments to be disfigured when there is little cultural understanding and support for their preservation.

The impact of Carvalho's work is admirable, honest, and profound. This is an example of devotion to a profession that has no budget for growth. But the churches that I recently visited, in Pernambuco and Paraíba, where the Heritage Department acted through the intervention of this great Brazilian Ayrton de Almeida Carvalho, are a testimony to his significant efforts and desire that these monuments continue to exist as witnesses to a golden period in the history of religious architecture in Brazil.

I offer my respect and my tribute to this great Brazilian.

To illustrate his accomplishments, here is a list of the restoration works in which Carvalho's intervention was the decisive factor in safeguarding our patrimony:

- Complete restoration of the Igreja de São Pedro dos Clérigos, Recife
- Complete restoration of the Capela da Jaqueira, Recife[27]
- Restoration of the Capela de Nossa Senhora das Fronteiras, Pernambuco
- Recovery of all of the carvings and paintings in the Capela Dourada, Recife
- Restoration of the works of art in the interior of the Igreja de Nossa Senhora do Rosário dos Prêtos, Recife
- Recovery of the ruins of the Igreja de Nossa Senhora da Nazaré, Cabo de Santo Agostinho
- Restoration of the Igrejas de São Cosme e Damião e São Francisco, Igarassu
- Partial restoration of the Igreja do Convento de São Francisco, Paraíba
- Partial restoration of the Igreja de São Bento, Paraíba
- Recovery of the ruins of the Casa da Pólvara, Paraíba
- Complete recovery of the Fortaleza dos Reis Magos, Natal

My second homage is offered to the eminent critic and musicologist Ayres de Andrade, who is currently organizing the recitals at the Sala Cecília Meireles.[28] His cultural vision, along with his music school that is mentioned in the program, has a clarity and distinctness of purpose that thrills anyone who loves music. The reason that these recitals have drawn such large audiences, significantly composed of young people, is because Ayres de Andrade, author of the book *Francisco Manuel da Silva e seu tempo*, has organized such splendid programs. It is enough to cite "Encounters with Beethoven" and "Bach." We should strive to always have such competent and zealous individuals working in artistic matters, so that art never fades into the background in Brazil.

I offer my respect and admiration for these men of such dedication, who have significantly contributed to the elevation of Brazilian culture.

Defense of Nature Reserves
June 27, 1969

Delivered to the Plenary Session of the Conselho Federal de Cultura on June 27, 1969. Published as Roberto Burle Marx, "Defêsa das reservas naturais" (Defense of Nature Reserves), *Cultura: Conselho Federal de Cultura* (Ministério da Educação e Cultura) 3, no. 25 (July 1969): 42–44.

I was away from the country when the president of this general council solicited suggestions and information from our individual councils to be proposed to our esteemed minister of education as our contribution to the studies now being undertaken as part of the reform of the Constitution.

However, on June 23 I did receive from the council's Plenary Assembly a mimeographed copy of the amendments and edits to the text that was presented by the Commission of Legislation and Norms and that earned the full approval of the counselors.

Upon reading this, I highlighted the following topics for this commentary:

> Title I, Chapter III, Article 15, Subheading II, Paragraph 1, Item B:[29]
> The governor shall appoint:
> (B) With the prior approval of the president of the Republic, the mayors of municipalities declared by a law proposed by the executive branch to be of interest to *national security*; as well as the mayors of municipalities with assets registered as part of the national historic and artistic heritage, or those that have notable urban ensembles with artistic and historic assets declared by the appropriate section of the federal administration.

COMMENTARY: I enthusiastically applaud the suggested amendment, indicating the authority of state governors to nominate mayors for the municipalities with the most significant artistic and historic monuments and urban ensembles.[30]

If you would permit me, Mr. President, to add my own personal understanding to the description of areas of *national security* and what this might mean in our industrialized civilization today. This is a more complete notion of security than just that of military defense and vigilance. A recent report from the secretary-general of the United Nations indicated the risk to human life because of the impact of pollution in urban and rural areas, rivers, lakes, and forests resulting from their contamination

FIGURE 3.21.
The three members of the Military Junta of 1969 (Aurélio de Lira Tavares, Augusto Rademaker, and Márcio de Sousa e Melo), signing the amendment to the 1967 Constitution of Brazil, Rio de Janeiro, 1969
Centro de Pesquisa e Documentação do Jornal do Brasil

by the chemical derivatives of industrial waste and combustible residues as well as insecticides proposed specifically for use in agriculture and for sanitizing communal and household environments. It was found that the indiscriminate and strongly encouraged use of insecticides, stimulated by consumer advertising campaigns, resulted in mass consumption, leading to the destruction of various species of flora and fauna as well as a profound biological disequilibrium. This has been particularly troubling in countries with small territories, such as the Netherlands and Belgium, and for immense aquatic areas, such as the Great Lakes region straddling Canada and the United States. This can cause scarcity and destruction of natural reservoirs of potable water, including natural springs and the sources of rivers, resulting in risk to human life itself.

With this commentary, I hope to clarify a shift in position. In previous council sessions in which motions were presented to this plenary session, it would seem that my position was drawn solely from my artistic or sentimental interest in the defense of nature.

I wish now to affirm my position in defense of human life and by extension a collective security for communities, provided by the protection of natural resources and the provision of wise planning for urban development and industrial areas.

Similar applause is merited for the edits suggested for the sole paragraph of Title IV, article 180, "Support of culture is a duty of the state":[31]

"Documents, works, and places of historical or artistic value, monuments, and *notable natural landscapes*, as well as archaeological sites, shall be under the special protection of the public authorities."

I would just like to clarify my understanding of *notable natural landscapes* as those that distinguish themselves by the wealth of their species or their topographic configuration but also those that provide the ecological conditions to protect neighboring community groups, such as buffering natural springs and providing the recreational resources so important for reducing the stressful and emotional weight of urban life.

To conclude, allow me to mention my profound gratitude for the suggested edits of Title III, article 162:[32]

"The law will protect nature, defending the sources of fresh water, flora, fauna, and the forestry heritage.
Sole Paragraph: For the reasons above, the Federal Union will create and maintain national parks, forests, and biological reserves."

The edits cited above synthesize in a direct manner all of the comments to the preceding articles and clearly express our position in light of the serious problems that we currently face and that will affect the human species and its integrity, at both a local and global scale.

Please accept, Mr. President, my personal admiration for the wise initiatives that, in the name of this most esteemed council, you have brought to the legislative and executive powers of this country.

FIGURE 3.22.
Santuário do Bom Jesus de Matosinhos, Congonhas do Campo, ca. 1947
Photo by Marcel Gautherot/Instituto Moreira Salles Collection

Defense of the Landscape
August 25, 1969

Delivered to the Plenary Session of the Conselho Federal de Cultura on August 25, 1969. Published as Roberto Burle Marx, “Defêsa da paisagem” (Defense of the Landscape), *Cultura: Conselho Federal de Cultura* (Ministério da Educação e Cultura) 3, no. 27 (September 1969): 21–23.

During a recent excursion to Ouro Preto and Congonhas, including Mariana and Vitória, with the purpose of collecting botanical material, I would like to bring the attention of the council to the following observations: in Congonhas, near the church, there is a wall with a balustrade painted bright blue, exhibitionist and aggressive, and along the Via Sacra booths selling souvenirs.[33] A monstrous edifice of a radio station as well as a hotel disturb the integrity of the complex, where the distinct intention of the seventeenth-century artist Antônio Francisco Lisboa was to give the images of the prophets a stage setting against the sky, always transforming from thick clouds to clear blue, allowing these sculptures to present themselves in a clairvoyant and dramatic manner. We must protect this ideal setting, the original conception of the landscape. It is ruined by the interference of town administrators lacking a humanistic education and thus misunderstanding the importance of these details. This inadvertent mismanagement could interfere with complexes like those of Congonhas and Ouro Preto that exhibit this extremely important moment of our culture.

In Ouro Preto, the municipality has cut down trees from the garden of the Igreja do Carmo, under the pretense that they were dying. If this were the case, they should have been replanted. Near the historic Botanical Garden of Ouro Preto, they mutilated an *araucária* during the Christmas season, decorating it with lights, transforming it into a very tall lamppost that will never again return to its natural grandeur.

I am convinced that in certain cities the town halls should not have these powers of interference, not only in the landscape but also in the urban realm, without first consulting competent and established agencies, such as the State Councils of Culture, the Department of National Historic and Artistic Heritage, and this Federal Council of Culture. Otherwise, with these continued modifications and disfigurations, within a few years almost nothing will remain of the integrity of these historic complexes. Some are landmarked, and others, despite not being legally protected, have all the characteristics of historic treasures, in both their landscape settings and their artistry. In Mariana, the public plaza is maintained by simple gardeners, untrained, who do not understand the purpose of plants. The trees are pruned in an unseemly manner; their trunks are painted white up to a certain height, in the manner of curative surgery; they have installed footlights that provide vulgar and cheap illumination, harmful to the trees; and they have painted the backs of park benches with advertisements for retail stores.

At the Convento da Pena in Vitória, in the state of Espírito Santo, the illumination now obscures the impression of the façade. On top of the balustrade, a canopy supporting neon gas lamps has been installed. A loudspeaker has been attached to the pediment above the entrance, so large that it seems more like a radar instrument. At the church of São João da Barra, located at an unusual site at the mouth of the Rio das Ostras, the façade was renovated and an addition to the walls of the church complex was constructed. Once again, in this example, one senses the interference of people unfamiliar with these challenges. Despite having good intentions, they are incapable of understanding the interaction and connection of this architecture to the landscape. I would be pleased if our learned colleagues on the Commission of Legislation and Norms would consider the wisdom of developing a law that would limit the interventions of mayors and municipal authorities, above all in cities with registered historic monuments or integral urban complexes. This legislation would thus protect these sites from the mutilations and disfigurations that are continually occurring.

Along the verges of the new road that links Mariana to Vitória, trees have been cut down aggressively, with no respect for the flora. First a destructive fire is set, so that the immense bulldozers can more easily plow across the hills, shaping cuts in the terrain more than fifty meters across. Many road cuts could have been avoided if there had been more intelligent planning with respect to the land and the existing flora. Under this predatory mistreatment, the flora will be extinct in a very short time.

Here in Rio, I also worry about what is being done to the slopes of the mountains. It is enough to see the hills of Urca, Babilônia, Corcovado, and Dona Marta, their landscapes scraped and despoiled, with no respect for the existing flora.[34] The Morro dos Cabritos is now propped up with counterfort buttresses unnecessarily painted white, as often occurs with the public works of small-town municipal authorities, perhaps so that they are easily seen by their electorate.

In Barra da Tijuca, a hillside where flora had developed over thousands of years was destroyed, all in the name of the protection of its slopes against landslides.[35] At the Agulha do Inhangá (Needle of Inhangá), a rock formation near the steep street of Ladeira dos Tabajaras in Copacabana, this buttressing has deformed the entire rock which once enchanted the whole region. The *Arecastrum romanzoffisnum* that grew in its fissures was destroyed, as well as all the vegetation that made construction access to its slopes difficult.

In addition, there is news that Corcovado will be reinforced.[36] "Reinforce," in this humorless vocabulary of urbanism, means to destroy, to disfigure, to paint white, to deface the cavities in monumental rocks. This news fills me with apprehensive dread. In a short while we will have a landscape full of adhesive plasters, once the fires have destroyed everything that blooms and thrives. The paper balloons of the festival of São João are encouraged, even publicized.[37] This year I witnessed throughout the region this disastrous habit that, despite its prohibition, is permitted by negligent authorities. The forest fires that often result from these lanterns are massive—they spread out in a disastrous manner, extending over enormous areas. The law is only effective when it is upheld. We must be vigilant and stop these abuses, so that we are able to bequeath to our descendants a future that is less somber and less sterile.

FIGURE 4.1.

Aerial view of Parque do Ibirapuera during the memorial celebrations of the Fourth Centennial of São Paulo, with the obelisk still under construction, São Paulo, July 1954

Arquivo Estadão Conteúdo/Fundação Oscar Niemeyer © 2017 Artists Rights Society (ARS), New York/AUTVIS, São Paulo

CHAPTER 4

Large Parks, Statues, and Disfigurement

Roberto Burle Marx was particularly productive during the 1950s, designing his most significant large-scale urban parks, including the ornamental gardens of the Parque do Ibirapuera, São Paulo (1951–1954); the Parque del Este, Caracas (1956–1961); and the Parque do Flamengo, Rio de Janeiro (1956–1965). These large public parks followed Burle Marx's work on the Parque do Barreiro at Araxá, completed just before Getúlio Vargas's Estado Novo ended in 1945 with a bloodless right-wing military coup. The end of the first Vargas era initiated a somewhat unstable democratic period in Brazil from 1946 to 1964, marked by a return to freely elected presidents and economic and industrial transformation. In 1946 Eurico Gaspar Dutra was the first elected president of this period, but in 1951 Vargas returned to the presidency, winning the election as the candidate of the Brazilian Labor Party. During Vargas's second presidency, Oscar Niemeyer invited Burle Marx to design a series of ornamental gardens for the new Parque do Ibirapuera in São Paulo, an extensive public park and complex of exhibition buildings that would showcase both the agricultural and manufacturing growth of São Paulo, emphasizing the state's rise under Vargas as an industrial powerhouse and celebrating the fourth centennial of the city's founding in 1954. Unfortunately, the ornamental gardens were never executed.

Vargas's ambitious plans for rapid industrialization included the nationalization of resource extraction and the initiation of global trade, exemplified by the 1953 founding of Petrobras, the state-owned oil enterprise, as well as by the modernization of the state-owned mining company that he had created during his first presidency, Companhia Vale do Rio Doce. But inflation was increasing and prices for Brazil's most important export, coffee, were falling. Amid growing popular dissatisfaction, an economic crisis, and political strife—heightened by his bodyguard's failed attempt to assassinate Vargas's chief oppositional critic in Rio de Janeiro, Carlos Lacerda—the president was pressured by the military to resign.[1] He refused. On August 24, 1954, Vargas committed suicide with a gunshot to the heart at the Palácio do Catete, the presidential residence in Rio de Janeiro.

Following Vargas's death, the charismatic Juscelino Kubitschek—former mayor of Belo Horizonte and then governor of Minas Gerais—became the third democratically elected president of the Republic, holding office from 1956 through 1961. Operating with a developmentalist platform similar to that of Vargas, Brazil experienced rapid economic growth during Kubitschek's presidency. He embraced the expansion of the Brazilian interior and campaigned on a project to fulfill the 1891 Brazilian Constitution's directive to transfer the capital to the country's high interior plateau, with the promise of "fifty years of progress in five." This extraordinary phrase captured the vortex of forces that would make Brasília a reality but also acknowledged that the presidential term was limited to five years. Thus Kubitschek set the inauguration date for the new capital on April 21, 1960, the anniversary of the Inconfidência Mineira, the unsuccessful but bold Brazilian separatist movement of 1789. Despite the long-standing Brazilian ambition to create an interior capital, as stated repeatedly in the Brazilian Constitutions of 1891, 1934, and 1946, it took the unflinching drive of a "man from Minas"—the title of *Time Magazine*'s 1960 cover story on Kubitschek—to wrest the political power of the country from the coastal city of Rio de Janeiro and transfer it to the tropical savanna of the Planalto Central.

Lúcio Costa developed a *plano piloto* (master plan) for the new Brazilian capital, winning a national competition with a simple narrative text illustrated with a series of sketches.[2] Kubitschek commissioned Niemeyer as the architect for all of the principal governmental buildings of the plan. Though construction was not fully complete, the new capital was indeed inaugurated on April 21, 1960. Burle Marx, however, did not participate in the planning or construction of Brasília until after the end of the Kubitschek presidency, despite Costa's interest in hiring him as the head of a new Departamento Municipal de Parques e Jardins (Municipal Department of Parks and Gardens) for Brasília.[3] Instead, Burle Marx left the country during Kubitschek's presidency, moving his office to oil-rich Caracas, Venezuela, in 1956, where it flourished. There he completed the 175-acre Parque del Este, a significant shift in scale and program from his previous work. One can merely speculate on what Burle Marx's work at the urban scale for Brasília might have been.

Burle Marx returned to Brazil in the early 1960s. Under Carlos Lacerda

FIGURE 4.2.
Aerial view of Parque del Este, looking north toward the mountains of Parque Nacional El Ávila, ca. 1961
© Burle Marx Landscape Design Studio

(1914–1977), now governor of the Estado da Guanabara, he joined the initiative to reinvent the city after it lost its stature as the capital of Brazil. His masterful design for the Parque do Flamengo, a landfill and parkway along Rio's Guanabara Bay, transforming it into a grand waterfront park, was completed just as the democratic period was collapsing. High inflation and popular discontent were coupled with the institutional crises of rapid presidential succession after the subsequent brief

FIGURE 4.3.
Aerial view of Parque do Flamengo, looking north toward central Rio de Janeiro along the axis of Avenida Rio Branco, Rio de Janeiro, ca. 1964
Acervo Arquivo Geral da Cidade do Rio de Janeiro

presidency and resignation of Jânio Quadros in 1961, followed by the rise of his vice-president, João Goulart. These factors, along with the support of the United States government, driven by cold war Communist fearmongering in the Western Hemisphere, led to the successful Brazilian military coup in Rio de Janeiro on March 31, 1964, and the establishment of Gen. Humberto de Alencar Castelo Branco as president. The military dictatorship would last for twenty-one years, with the most oppressive human rights abuses occurring between 1968 and 1974.

But, before this dark time, each of Burle Marx's three large metropolitan parks reflected the political programming of public space for Latin America's rapidly urbanizing cities. The opening of the Parque do Ibirapuera commemorated the fourth centennial of the founding of São Paulo in 1554 and established an architecturally articulated celebration of art, agriculture, and industry in that state. Likewise, the inauguration of Parque do Flamengo celebrated the fourth centennial of the founding of Rio de Janeiro in 1565 and provided an opportunity for that city to redefine itself after the loss of its historic position as the country's capital when the federal government moved to Brasília in 1960. In Caracas, Venezuela, the 1961 inauguration of the Parque del Este was intended to demonstrate the goodwill of the new democratically elected president of Venezuela, Rómulo Betancourt, following the deposition of the dictator Marcos Pérez Jiménez only three years earlier.

In addition to being a statement on the power of dynamic public space, Burle Marx's work for these parks presents another political posture that is particularly modern through the presentation of an ecological didactic. For Burle Marx, progress and modernity connoted a nationalist vision of the wealth of natural resources in Brazil, yet it was to be distinguished from the developmentalism of resource extraction more common at the time. Burle Marx's public parks supported environmental protection and enhancement through an approach that highlighted the country's unique ecologies and phytogeographic regions. For him, "resource extraction" was the designed transfer of complex associations of native species of plants found in the forests and hinterlands of Brazil to the public parks and plazas of the rapidly growing urban centers of Rio de Janeiro and São Paulo. Burle Marx saw the recomposition of the complexities of the natural world in the public spaces of the city as an educational strategy for the urban citizen. More than just employing aesthetic composition, Burle Marx shaped the social aspect of the urban public garden—an approach that he called the "ecological garden." This composition of a displaced nature within the urban public realm, along with parallel programmatic functions that provided spaces for pleasure and recreation, would serve as a means to educate the public. And these ecological gardens would establish an environmentalist foundation for both cultural and botanical stewardship. But they were also still sorely in need of governmental protection from abusive disfiguration, as Burle Marx would later insist during his years as cultural counselor.

Roberto Burle Marx: Metropolitan Parks, 1950s

Parque do Ibirapuera

In 1953 Oscar Niemeyer and his team invited Burle Marx to participate in the transformation of a São Paulo municipal eucalyptus tree nursery into the 400-acre Parque do Ibirapuera.[4] This project included a general landscape plan previously executed by Octávio Augusto Teixeira Mendes and Niemeyer's complex of buildings for the celebrations marking the Fourth Centennial of the city's founding, to be held on August 21, 1954.[5] Suggestions to transform the site into a public park had been

FIGURE 4.4.
Victor Brecheret, *Monumento às bandeiras* at the entrance to the Parque do Ibirapuera, São Paulo, ca. 1967
Photo by Marcel Gautherot/Instituto Moreira Salles Collection

made for over twenty years; as early as 1936 a massive granite statue by the sculptor Victor Brecheret was commissioned to be erected at the edge of the eucalyptus plantation to mark the entrance of the future Parque do Ibirapuera. Entitled the *Monumento às bandeiras*, the 45-meter long monumental composition represented the seventeenth-century *bandeirantes* (Portuguese explorers). Native Brazilians, Africans, and Europeans portaging an enormous canoe follow two men on horses, a Portuguese adventurer and his native Brazilian guide. Departing São Paulo to explore the interior of the country in search of wealth and riches, the *bandeirantes* are symbolically claiming the vast hinterland for Brazil.

For Parque do Ibirapuera, Burle Marx developed a sequence of fourteen ornamental gardens as a complement to Niemeyer's complex of buildings and Teixeira Mendes's landscape plan, previously developed in 1951. The buildings, completed in 1954, included the Palácio das Indústrias (Palace of Industries), Palácio das Nações (Palace of Nations), Palácio dos Estados (Palace of States), Palácio da Agricultura (Palace of Agriculture), Palácio das Exposições or Planetário (Exhibitions Palace or Planetarium), and Auditório (Auditorium; though a part of the initial master plan, this building was not built until 2003), as well as a large serpentine roof canopy extending over a continuous connective esplanade. In addition to being a site for the celebrations of the Fourth Centennial of the city of São Paulo in 1954, Niemeyer's Palácio das Indústrias building would become the new home of the recently inaugurated Bienal de São Paulo. Initiated in 1951, the Bienal is the second-oldest art biennial in the world, modeled after the original Biennale di Venezia that began in 1895, and draws a large international crowd. Niemeyer's suite of buildings was finally completed after numerous modifications and delays. Burle Marx's designs for a magnificent sequence of abstract gardens within the park's landscape, exhibiting the diverse plant species of the state of São Paulo within a series of fountain plazas, were not executed, however, because of a lack of funds. Yet this project remained especially important to Burle Marx, who described these gardens as representing the culmination of twenty years of his work "as a practical gardener and as a landscape painter-architect."[6]

FIGURE 4.5.
Oscar Niemeyer, site model of the Parque do Ibirapuera, ca. 1953
Fundação Oscar Niemeyer © 2017 Artists Rights Society (ARS), New York/AUTVIS, São Paulo

FIGURE 4.6.
Inauguration of the Parque do Ibirapuera, with Niemeyer's serpentine canopy and esplanade foregrounding the eucalyptus grove beyond, São Paulo, 1954

The ornamental gardens for Ibirapuera were well represented by a series of painted gouaches shown at the second Bienal in 1953 and at a 1954 exhibition at the Pan-American Union, "Landscape Architecture in Brazil: Roberto Burle Marx," organized by the Smithsonian Institute in Washington, DC. In fact, his Ibirapuera garden designs were largely responsible for the launch of his international reputation. The 1953 Bienal de São Paulo brought many important European visitors and critics—including Max Bill, Walter Gropius, and Ernesto Rogers—to the Parque do Ibirapuera to experience the new Brazilian modern architecture firsthand. Burle Marx's 1948 private garden for the Fazenda Marambaia, the residence of Odette Monteiro in Petrópolis, received a prize at the Bienal. Several European critics also visited his tropical garden designs in Rio de Janeiro. In contrast to Max Bill's scathing assessment of the new Brazilian modern architecture—proffered at the 1953 Bienal—as willful and irresponsible, Burle Marx was generally lauded as an innovative modernist garden designer and talented muralist.

Reflecting Burle Marx's knowledge of traditional Mediterranean courtyard

FIGURE 4.7.
Roberto Burle Marx, plan of the ornamental gardens for the Parque do Ibirapuera, São Paulo, 1953
Drawing by Catherine Seavitt Nordenson

gardens, his unbuilt ornamental gardens at Ibirapuera were to be linked both to the architectural complex and to each other through a sequential promenade. Using both contemporary and traditional building materials as a foil for the textures of predominantly Brazilian plants, the designs were exceptional for both their ingenious use of water and their abstractly patterned surfaces. Both *azulejo* glazed tiles and *pedra portuguesa* mosaic pavements were incorporated into the plans.[7] Asymmetrical geometric patterning predominated the colored ground surfaces and walls, and hidden fountains projected vertical jets of water. Like the early plazas of Recife, these ecological gardens highlighted native wildflowers from the São Paulo countryside, aquatic plants from the Amazon, native orchids, and saxifragaceous plants growing among a composition of rocks.[8]

Burle Marx's chromatic floral surfaces were often complemented by vertical sculptures of granite or wire and accented with rows of majestic imperial palms. One of the most inventive of these ornamental gardens, the Suspended Path Garden, included the unexecuted design of an elevated switchback pathway that would have led the visitor above the level of the parterre, presenting a series of transforming views of both the patterned ground surfaces and Burle Marx's large totem-like wire sculptures. The Geometric Garden included abstractly patterned hardscapes paved

FIGURE 4.8.
Roberto Burle Marx, gouache perspective of the Suspended Path Garden, Parque do Ibirapuera, São Paulo, 1953

FIGURE 4.9.
Roberto Burle Marx, wire sculpture prototypes for the Suspended Path Garden, Parque do Ibirapuera, installed at a Rio de Janeiro beach, ca. 1955
Photo by Marcel Gautherot/Instituto Moreira Salles Collection

with black, white, and red *pedra portuguesa*. The horizontal patterning was punctuated with rectilinear pools, colorful planting beds, and vertical granite totems. The entire complex was conceived as a dynamic, cinematic promenade that would give each visitor a series of unique temporal experiences as well as introduce the general public to the wealth of both regional and national Brazilian flora.

Burle Marx's reinterpretation of the courtyard garden, exemplified in this series of outdoor garden rooms for the Parque do Ibirapuera, brought intimate spaces into the public realm. A dynamic sense of movement around the gardens' asymmetric water features established a cinematic series of continually transforming views. Burle Marx developed the gardens three-dimensionally, creating a sense of enclosure through the

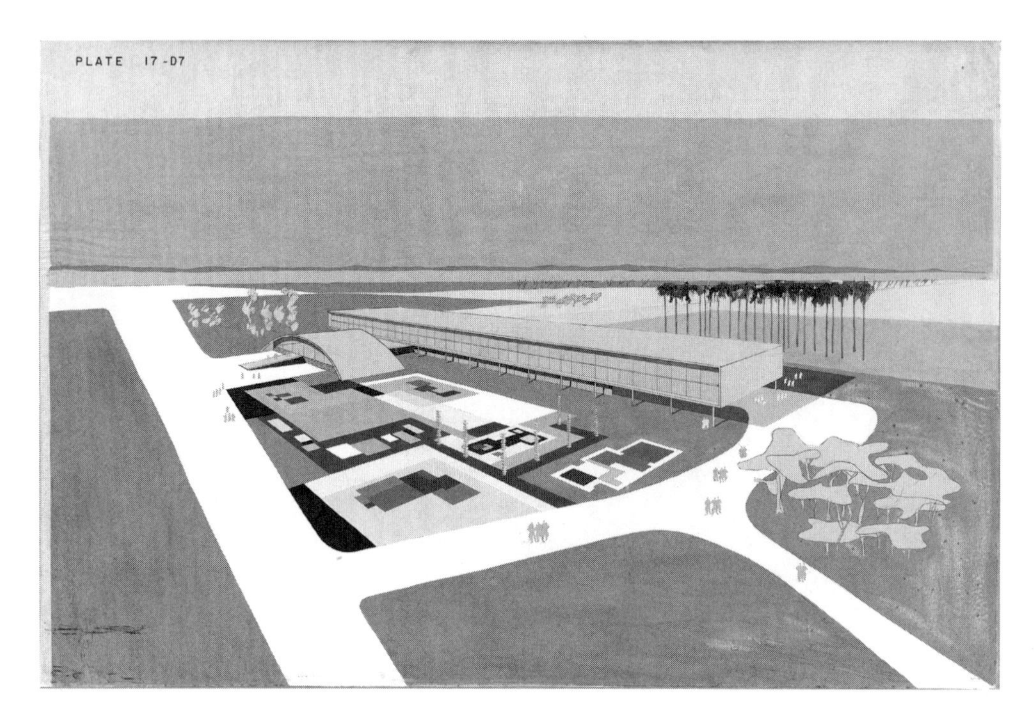

FIGURE 4.10.
Roberto Burle Marx, gouache perspective of the Geometric Garden, Parque do Ibirapuera, São Paulo, 1953

manipulation of the vertical dimension—the fields of palms, the volumetric planters, the sculptural elements in stone and wire, and the vertical jets of water. All of these elements had layered edge conditions, providing a sense of enclosure while maintaining visual connections to the sequence of gardens, the free-flowing marquee, and the architecture. The loss of these gardens in 1954 was likely a great disappointment for Burle Marx, but many of the nascent ideas explored there would inform his later work.

Parque del Este

After the suicide of Getúlio Vargas in 1954, democratic elections were established. The charismatic Juscelino Kubitschek subsequently rose to the Brazilian presidency in 1956. Meanwhile, international acclaim for Burle Marx's work continued. Despite Lúcio Costa's interest in hiring him as the landscape architect for the construction of Kubitschek's new federal capital, a place that Costa envisioned as a garden city, Burle Marx chose not to participate with Costa and Niemeyer in the development and construction of Brasília during Kubitschek's presidency.[9]

Instead, several significant client commissions led Burle Marx to leave Brazil and

FIGURE 4.11.
Roberto Burle Marx, plan of Parque del Este, Caracas, Venezuela, 1961
Drawing by Catherine Seavitt Nordenson

establish an office in Caracas, Venezuela, from 1956 to 1961.[10] There he received several commissions from the military dictator then in power, Marcos Pérez Jiménez, including the 1956 commission for the landscape design of the planned 1960 "Exposición Internacional de Caracas" (International Exposition of Caracas), intended to showcase the newly oil-rich nation's industry, commerce, and culture but also the wealth and diversity of Venezuelan flora and fauna. The exposition project was abandoned after the fall of Pérez Jiménez's dictatorship in 1958, but one-third of the enormous site was nevertheless designated as public parkland, the 200-acre Parque del Este. The entire landscaping project was entrusted to Burle Marx. It was inaugurated in 1961 with the support of the newly elected president Rómulo Betancourt as the model project of Venezuela's new democracy.

The grounds of the former San José coffee plantation and a former military airport in Caracas were initially selected as the site for the Exposición Internacional as part of Pérez Jiménez's nationalist agenda. In 1956, at the recommendation of Carlos Guinand, an architect and president of the advisory board for the exposition, Burle Marx was contracted to design the landscape of a small portion of this extensive complex as a Venezuelan zoobotanical garden.[11] After the collapse of the dictatorship, intensive lobbying by Guinand and others reenvisioned the project as the public Parque del Este, and Burle Marx began work on a new comprehensive landscape plan for the park. The design consisted of three main spaces: an open zone with a large lake and views northward to the mountains of the newly designated Parque Nacional

FIGURE 4.12.
Parque del Este, view of the lake and royal palms, Caracas, Venezuela, ca. 1961
Archivo El Nacional

FIGURE 4.13.
Parque del Este, with the mountains of Parque Nacional El Ávila beyond, Caracas, Venezuela, 1979
Archivo El Nacional

FIGURE 4.14.
Roberto Burle Marx, perspective view of the red-walled courtyard garden at Parque del Este, Caracas, Venezuela, 1961

El Ávila; a tree-canopied zone with a series of ecologically organized gardens; and a formal entrance with a sequence of walled patio gardens and terraces.

During the initial design phase, Burle Marx took several field excursions to the interior of Venezuela with the project's botanist, Leandro Aristeguieta. On these trips to the El Dorado forest, the Canaima plateau, the Maracaibo basin, and the Orinoco River delta, Burle Marx and Aristeguieta selected representative plants, which were then transplanted into prepared earthen beds in the expedition truck and acclimatized at a nursery on the park's grounds.[12] The ecological gardens included a desert garden, an aquatic garden, a tropical forest, a palmetum, an arboretum, a small zoological garden, and a lake. The sequence of outdoor garden rooms, Los Pátios, drew from the tradition of Arab-Iberian courtyards. At the first patio, walls lined with blue- and yellow-glazed tiles acted as a geometric foil to cascading fountains and varied plant textures. The second patio, with curvilinear paths and benches, had red-glazed tile walls contrasting with white-leaved plants. The third patio opened outward to a large lawn and terrace with an array of circular planting beds and a vertical fountain with a cascading water curtain. Burle Marx attempted to demonstrate the wealth of Venezuelan flora at this urban public garden, with compositional ideas explored earlier in Brazil. But he also began to introduce other exotic species from the tropical belt as well, from Brazil, Africa, and India, adding to the richness and diversity of his constructed ecological compositions.

Parque do Flamengo

Upon his return to Brazil in 1961, Burle Marx was appointed by the governor of the Estado da Guanabara, Carlos Lacerda, to an advisory work group to coordinate the continuation of the urban landfill project along Rio's Guanabara Bay, the Parque do Flamengo.[13] Burle Marx was familiar with the *aterro* (landfill) project, known colloquially as "the fill," having worked on its earliest phases at Praça Senador Salgado Filho, the public gateway plaza to the city from the new central terminal building of the Aeroporto Santos Dumont in 1947, a plaza showcasing native trees and other flora from across the country to international and domestic visitors arriving by air. In 1954 he initiated work on the gardens for the Museu de Arte Moderna (MAM: Museum of Modern Art), a project by the architect Affonso Eduardo Reidy (1909–1964).[14] As a key member of the work group for the Parque do Flamengo, Burle Marx would continue to develop the landscape design of this wide strip of landfill as an arborized parkway along Guanabara Bay. The new parkway would extend from the Aeroporto Santos Dumont and the MAM at the city's center through the bayside neighborhood of Flamengo to the new tunnels accessing the southern residential zones at Botofogo Bay.

This waterfront park, considered one of Burle Marx's finest projects, was executed at the same time when he was designing two botanical gardens that were not

FIGURE 4.15.
Landfill construction at Parque do Flamengo, Rio de Janeiro, ca. 1956
Acervo Arquivo Geral da Cidade do Rio de Janeiro

FIGURE 4.16.
Roberto Burle Marx, Praça Senador Salgado Filho at the Aeroporto Santos Dumont, Rio de Janeiro, ca. 1950
Photo by Hélio Santos/Acervo Arquivo Geral da Cidade do Rio de Janeiro

constructed: the Parque Zoobotânico in Brasília and the Jardim Botânico in São Paulo.[15] Perhaps because of this simultaneity, the Parque do Flamengo addresses aspects of the modern botanical garden that he had been exploring since his earliest projects in Recife, ultimately culminating in the creation of an artificial nature on a new topography, a landfill poised between the mountains and the sea in Rio de Janeiro.

Reidy, a talented member of Costa's team of young architects during the design of the Ministério da Educação e Saúde who went on to work as a municipal architect for the city of Rio de Janeiro, began work on the Museu de Arte Moderna in 1954. Its magnificent urban waterfront site was landfill, an extension of the Aterro do Calabouço (Dungeon Landfill) obtained from the Morro do Castelo and placed for the construction of the Aeroporto Santos Dumont and the Praça Senador Salgado Filho. For the museum site, landfill material was obtained from the demolition of a second hill in the historic center, the Morro de Santo Antônio, flattened to construct the new Avenida República do Chile. The soil obtained from the dismantling of the Morro de Santo Antônio was used to continue the landfill along Guanabara Bay. Reidy envisioned the MAM complex as an architectural link connecting the city, the landscape, and the bay. Its horizontal volumetric form, a trapezoidal prism hovering

FIGURE 4.17.
Demolition of the Morro de Santo Antônio with the Aeroporto Santos Dumont at Guanabara Bay seen beyond, Rio de Janeiro, ca. 1955
Acervo Arquivo Geral da Cidade do Rio de Janeiro

FIGURE 4.18.
Construction of the landfill for the Parque do Flamengo, Rio de Janeiro, ca. 1956
Acervo Arquivo Geral da Cidade do Rio de Janeiro

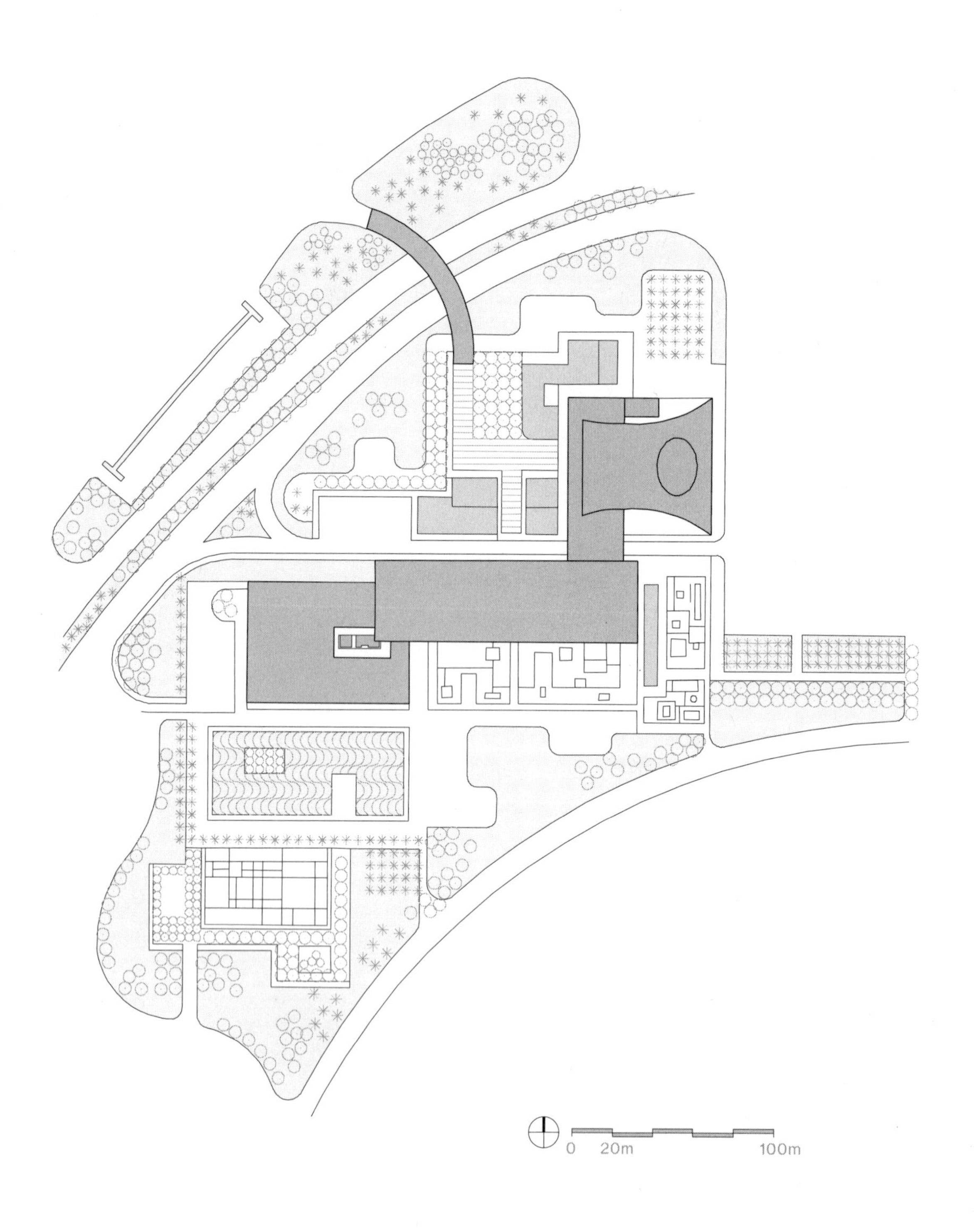

FIGURE 4.19.
Roberto Burle Marx, gardens of the Museu de Arte Moderna, Parque do Flamengo, Rio de Janeiro, 1956
Drawing by Catherine Seavitt Nordenson

FIGURE 4.20.
Gardens of the Museu de Arte Moderna, Parque do Flamengo, Rio de Janeiro, ca. 1970
Photo by Marcel Gautherot/Instituto Moreira Salles Collection

FIGURE 4.21.
Wave motif garden lawn with imperial palms at the Museu de Arte Moderna, Parque do Flamengo, Rio de Janeiro, ca. 1968
Photo by Alair Gomes/Acervo da Fundação Biblioteca Nacional do Brasil

above the ground plane, was suspended by a series of concrete frames, offering vistas both northward toward the urban skyline of downtown Rio de Janeiro and southward across the undulating shoreline of Guanabara Bay to the magnificent Pão de Açúcar (Sugarloaf Mountain)—an international symbol of the city.

Burle Marx completed the garden plan for the MAM in March 1956, just prior to his departure for Caracas. The geometric character of the project is striking in comparison to his earlier work, responding to the architectonic rhythms of the building while echoing the character of the geometric ornamental gardens of Parque do Ibirapuera in São Paulo and foreshadowing the pátios of the Parque del Este in Caracas. The sinuous forms of Burle Marx's earlier plans have been subdued into the undulating geometric curves of the two species of grass planted in a large rectangular field at the museum's southern gardens, a witty interpretation of the traditional wave pattern of black-and-white *pedra portuguesa* pavement of the Copacabana beachfront sidewalk. Here the two types of grasses produce two tones and textures of the green waves, and the carpet is anchored at its southern edge by a row of vertical imperial palms.[16]

The museum complex, including the suspended museum volume, an art school and restaurant, and a theater, is approached from the city via a pedestrian bridge crossing the new parkway, landing gracefully in the museum's northern gardens. A plaza paved with the black-and-white wave motif in *pedra portuguesa*, adjacent to a grove of geometrically planted trees, leads to the museum building and slips below its suspended volume toward Guanabara Bay. At the southern gardens, Burle Marx deployed large round stones and vertical granite monoliths in rectilinear arrangements. The roof garden terrace of the restaurant, above the low rectangular volume housing the art school, echoes the geometries of the ground plane at a more intimate scale. The art school and restaurant of the Museu de Arte Moderna were inaugurated in January 1958. The main part of the museum itself was not fully completed until

FIGURE 4.22.
Southern gardens of the Museu de Arte Moderna, Parque do Flamengo, Rio de Janeiro, ca. 1970
Photo by Marcel Gautherot/Instituto Moreira Salles Collection

1967, three years after Reidy's death, when it opened its first exhibition.[17] Burle Marx's gardens for the MAM were completed in 1960, anchoring the landfill that would soon be completed as the Parque do Flamengo.

Lacerda, elected governor of the Estado da Guanabara in 1960 upon the transfer of the capital from Rio de Janeiro to the newly inaugurated Brasília, won based on a campaign of addressing the city's chronic problems of housing and transportation. His proposal for an express traffic artery along the continuous linear strip of new landfill at Guanabara Bay would link the city center through the neighborhoods of Flamengo to Botafogo and the Túnel do Pasmado and Túnel do Leme. These tunnels, passing through the Morro do Pasmado and the Morro da Babilônia, created a direct connection to the southern residential zone of Copacabana. This continuation of the earlier landfill project extended southward from the MAM, creating an additional 296 acres of land along the bay. Sourced from the same earth from the Morro de Santo Antônio, the project was initiated in 1957 and was called the Aterro do Flamengo—"the fill." In 1961 Lacerda appointed an advisory Grupo de Trabalho (Work Group) to be led by Maria Carlota (Lota) de Macedo Soares (1910–1967), a self-educated urban planner. Macedo Soares in turn formed an advisory and design team that would work with the city's public administrative groups to develop and

FIGURE 4.23.
The Grupo de Trabalho at the field office for the Parque do Flamengo (*left to right*): Roberto Burle Marx, Maria Augusta Leão da Costa Ribeiro, Maria Carlota de Macedo Soares, and Jorge Machado Moreira, Rio de Janeiro, ca. 1964
Centro de Pesquisa e Documentação do Jornal do Brasil

build a new park along the landfill to buffer the presence of the high-speed traffic artery.[18] The Grupo de Trabalho gathered by Macedo Soares consisted of urban planners, architects, engineers, and botanists. Its mission was to develop a public park, the Parque do Flamengo, to benefit the residents of the city.[19] Burle Marx was entrusted with the design and implementation of the park's landscape.

The Parque do Flamengo would be Burle Marx's last commissioned public project before the military coup of 1964 and is arguably his finest and most comprehensive work. The transformation of this landfill into an urban waterfront park and beach created much-needed open space for the rapidly growing population of Rio de Janeiro, particularly the residents of the adjacent neighborhood of Flamengo. Burle Marx's waterfront design is connected back to the city by a series of pedestrian bridges and underpasses, designed by Reidy, that allow for safe passage across the express parkway to the linear extension of the gardens, museum, monuments, and playing fields, as well as a 1,500-meter long artificial beach with panoramic views of the Pão de Açúcar and the mountains across Guanabara Bay. The most prominent of the bridges, the Viaduto Paulo Bittencourt, launches the pedestrian across the parkway along a horizontal and vertical curve, landing gracefully at the northern gardens of the Museu de Arte Moderna.

FIGURE 4.24.
Roberto Burle Marx, perspective drawing for the Parque do Flamengo, Rio de Janeiro, 1961
© Burle Marx Landscape Design Studio

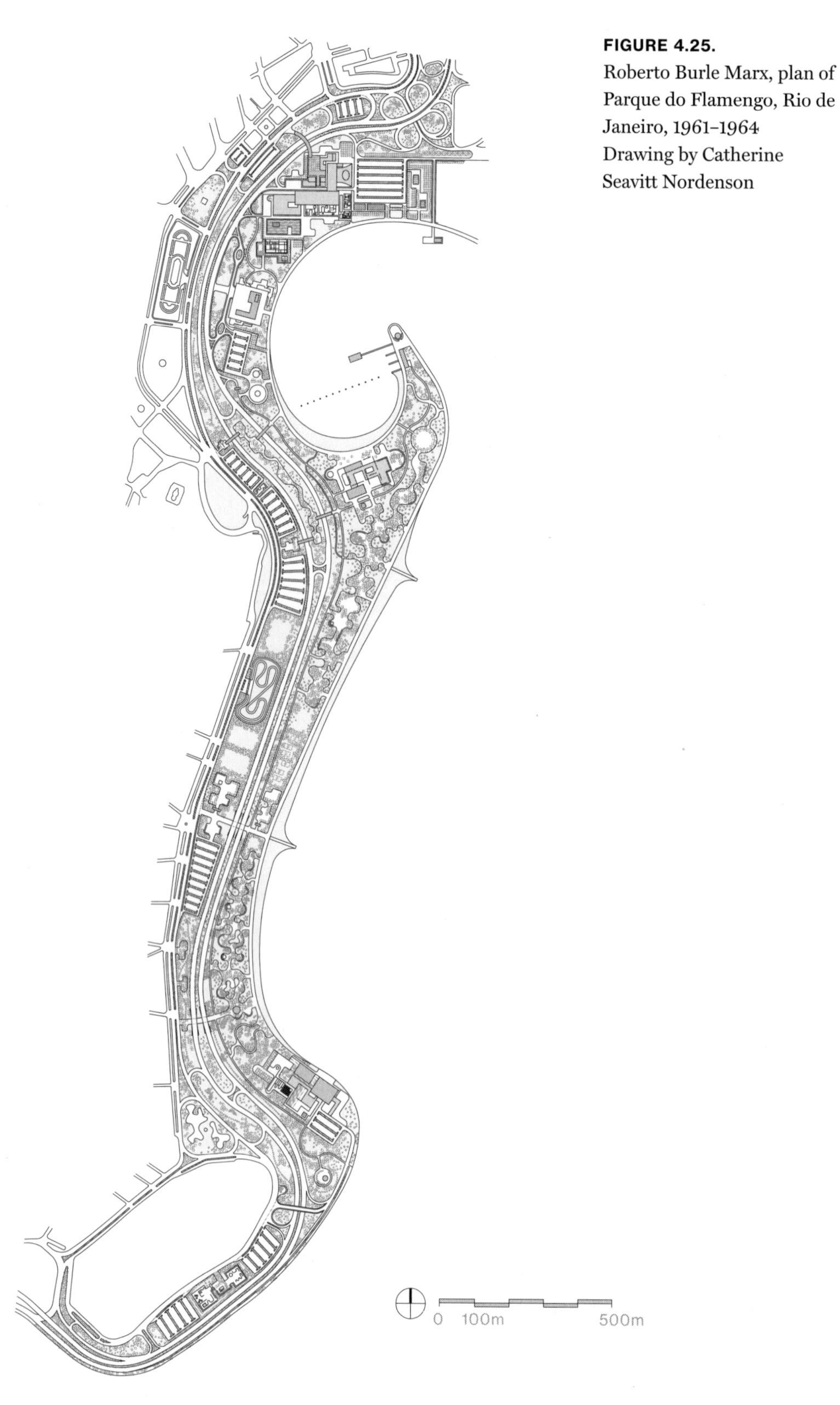

FIGURE 4.25.
Roberto Burle Marx, plan of Parque do Flamengo, Rio de Janeiro, 1961–1964
Drawing by Catherine Seavitt Nordenson

FIGURE 4.26.
Pedestrian bridge with the Outeiro da Glória beyond, Parque do Flamengo, Rio de Janeiro, ca. 1966
Photo by Marcel Gautherot/Instituto Moreira Salles Collection

Once complete, the newly landscaped landfill was seen as enhancing the existing natural beauty of Rio de Janeiro. In 1964 Clarival do Prado Valladares, Burle Marx's colleague from Recife, wrote of this exceptional quality in his journal *Cadernos Brasileiros*: "The landfill project of Glória and Flamengo will establish for Rio de Janeiro a most definitive work of constructed landscape. Rarely has landscape architecture been confronted with a more significant situation, for, in this case, the built landscape is being presented as the foreground to an exceptionally monumental natural landscape."[20]

Burle Marx's *arborização* (afforestation) of this new terrain reclaimed from the sea included more than two hundred different species of trees and fifty species of

FIGURE 4.27.
Aerial view of Parque do Flamengo, Rio de Janeiro, ca. 1964
Photo by Marcel Gautherot/Instituto Moreira Salles Collection

palms, most native to Brazil, but including selected tropical exotics. The planting plan, developed in consultation with the botanist Luiz Emygdio de Mello Filho, was carefully choreographed to present continuous blossoming of the various flowering trees throughout the year.[21] This didactic presentation of "nature" was in fact highly artificial—it is not a graft of an existing environment but rather a rich ecological tableau of species that would otherwise never occur together. The Parque do Flamengo has become a botanical treasury of both native and exotic trees and palms, species that perhaps one day will no longer exist in their natural habitat. This new nature, a waterfront park for urban residents revealed at high speed through the windshields of a burgeoning middle class heading to the wealthy southern zones of the city, was the culmination of Burle Marx's development of the cultural project as a designed landscape.

Parque do Flamengo was officially inaugurated in March 1965, on the four hundredth anniversary of the founding of the city of Rio de Janeiro. Although construction was still ongoing, Governor Lacerda, with articulate support from Macedo Soares, submitted a proposal to SPHAN to have the park landmarked as part of Brazil's historic and artistic heritage. The request was successful, with support from both Paulo Thedim Barreto, head of SPHAN's Art Section, and Lúcio Costa, director of the Division of Research and Registration. A statement by SPHAN council member Paulo Santos acknowledged that the partnership of Reidy and Burle Marx had created a landscape of extraordinary beauty for the city of Rio de Janeiro. On July 28, 1965, the Parque do Flamengo, listed as a garden and park, would become the thirty-ninth inscription in the *Livro do tombo arqueológico, etnográfico e paisagístico* (National Registry for Archaeological, Ethnographic, and Landscape Assets). This was the first example of the use of SPHAN and the process of landmark registration as a preventative protective measure for an urban landscape. Macedo Soares and others argued that the Parque do Flamengo should be protected against the risk of real estate speculation. Legally designating the park as a cultural landscape asset, including the buildings by Reidy and others, precluded real estate development and thus protected the future of this novel landscape.

Burle Marx conceived and constructed the Parque do Flamengo as a didactic landscape for the urban citizen. This idea was nascent in his early projects in Recife, but at Flamengo he further developed this expression of the ecological garden that would engage citizens in the stewardship of a particularly Brazilian heritage: its wealth and diversity of native flora. "The garden of today is for the man of tomorrow," wrote Burle Marx in 1970. He further emphasized this social act of stewardship, stating that "to preserve plant species through the composition of gardens is a way of protecting future generations from an extreme solitude."[22] With the knowledge of a Brazilian botanical heritage gleaned from this constructed nature, he hoped that the public would insist on the protection of its forests and other natural areas from exploitation and destruction.

FIGURE 4.28. Cable cars ascending the Pão de Açúcar mountain, Rio de Janeiro, 1992 Arquivo Estadão Conteúdo

Depositions: On Urban Disfiguration and the Public Park

Burle Marx's insistence on the importance of urban public spaces as didactic and expressive landscapes of Brazilian heritage is clearly voiced in several of his depositions for the Conselho Federal de Cultura. He felt strongly that these public spaces should be protected and not exploited for commercial gain. Burle Marx expressed his frustration with what he saw as the disfiguration of urban public parks and plazas, and his scorn was often directed at municipal politicians whom he viewed as ill-informed or misguided. His critical assessment of the overuse of statuary in Rio de Janeiro is one of his most acerbic yet witty appeals to the plenary council of the Conselho Federal de Cultura. The deposition "Estátuas em jardins" (Statues in Gardens) describes the misuse of commemorative and nostalgic figurative statuary in the city's public spaces and the lack of any civic cultural meaning in these installations. Sculpture, he believed, should serve as a compositional tool to create order,

FIGURE 4.29.
Concrete erosion control pillars completed by the Instituto de Geotécnica in the late 1960s at the Morro do Cantagalo, with the Edifício Gemini seen in the foreground, Lagoa, Rio de Janeiro, 2014
Photo © Robert Polidori

sequence, and focus—not as a manifestation of bad taste. Burle Marx spoke of other kinds of disfiguration as well: the abundance of crude commercial advertisements in public spaces, the overuse of mercury lamppost illumination, the destruction of trees associated with historic cultural sites, and the commercialization of religious pilgrimage sites. In "Paisagem sacrificada" (Sacrificed Landscape), "Preservação de condições paisagísticas" (Preservation of Landscape Conditions), and "Áreas verdes" (Green Spaces), he states his opposition to current developments in Rio de Janeiro that would affect the integrity of his own recently inaugurated and landmarked Parque do Flamengo. These include a proposal for a monumental 35-meter high sculptural composition commemorating the fourth centennial of Rio de Janeiro; proposals to remove full-grown trees to provide space for the carnival parades to march through the park, a kind of urban deforestation; and the proposal for the construction of an enormous hotel on the top of the Morro do Pasmado at the southern end of the park, a granite hill that was to have remained a preserved landscape.

Burle Marx also viewed the embrace of the public park by elected officials as a self-serving means of celebrating their own governance. Several depositions cited such examples in both the small municipalities of Minas Gerais and the urban center of Rio de Janeiro. He often described urban parks and plazas as cultural heritage sites, not only in the baroque colonial cities but also in the city of Rio de Janeiro. He called for protective landmark status for these sites through SPHAN, as had been successfully achieved for the Parque do Flamengo. In the deposition "Conjunto paisagistico" (Landscape Complex) in 1973, for example, Burle Marx argues that the complex of the Pão de Açúcar and the Morro de Urca should be landmarked, in order to prevent further exploitative commercial development by the Companhia Caminho Aéreo Pão de Açúcar (Sugarloaf Mountain Airway Company). Strongly supported by his fellow counselor Gilberto Freyre, Burle Marx's appeal was successful. The Complexo do Pão de Açúcar achieved landmark status as a cultural landscape that same year.

Burle Marx considered the engineered reinforcement of the granite hills throughout Rio de Janeiro—white grids of concrete armatures and buttresses—to be a defacement of the landscape's natural forms. In some ways, he claimed, this was equivalent to the transformation of an otherwise sublime geologic feature into a grotesque statue. Accordingly, as counselor he insisted on the need for federal laws to prohibit what he saw as the irreverent alteration of historic sites and landscape complexes by unwitting municipal leaders and even insensitive geotechnical engineers. Burle Marx clearly noted that protective legal measures should take into account the contextual situation of these cultural landscapes. He consistently argued that it was not just the buildings themselves that should be designated as national historic and artistic cultural monuments but their adjacent and surrounding landscapes as well—these were indeed aspects of Brazilian heritage.

Roberto Burle Marx: Depositions

FIGURE 4.30.
Street photographer (*lambe-lambe*), Rio de Janeiro, ca. 1967
Photo by Marcel Gautherot/Instituto Moreira Salles Collection

Statues in Gardens
August 29, 1968

Delivered to the Plenary Session of the Conselho Federal de Cultura on August 29, 1968. Published as Roberto Burle Marx, "Estátuas em jardins" (Statues in Gardens), *Cultura: Conselho Federal de Cultura* (Ministério da Educação e Cultura) 2, no. 14 (August 1968): 23–26.

Mr. President and Fellow Counselors:

I would like to make a statement regarding the use of statues in our cities, and, above all, those placed in public plazas, parks, and gardens.

A great majority of our statues do not achieve the level of artistic quality that they should. However, they continue to proliferate and multiply. Today Rio de Janeiro is a city that has been "bust-ified." The directors of the Department of Parks and Gardens, seduced by skillful sculptors, have inappropriately and randomly filled up public spaces with statues, using no aesthetic criteria for their decisions.[23] A sculpted *herma* was meaningful in ancient Greece; however, today's parodies of heads on pedestals seem ridiculous. They are tasteless; it is impossible to justify their placement in our public parks. Is it not enough to perpetuate the names of great heroes with the names of streets, plazas, and even cities? Must we accept these horrifying stone heads, just because their actual owners were indeed meritorious? When Michelangelo created the Medici tomb, he was not preoccupied with similitude but with the quality of his sculpture.

In Rio de Janeiro, just compare the original design by the urban planner Donat-Alfred Agache for the Praça Paris with the current situation.[24] A huge number of busts have sprouted up around the four original *hermas* representing the four seasons, such that the garden has completely lost its earlier judicious use of sculptural elements. Add to this the mutilation of the flowerbeds and the lawn, which were intended to act in contrast to the volumes of the trees and shrubs. One can clearly feel the interference of poorly trained gardeners, lacking sufficient knowledge and sensibility.

Statues do not complement gardens—that is, when they are used in a purely sentimental manner. This problem occurs at Botafogo, at the Praça Marechal Floriano, and at the Passeio Público; in fact, it is a problem in the majority of plazas in this city.

Of course there are exceptional public spaces that merit large statues, but unfortunately they often result in truly carnivalesque compositions. I do not object to the allegorical floats that are made specifically for Carnival, for these are created for the ephemeral duration of a single night, filled with noise, colors, and lights. By contrast, we are obliged to put up with this statuary for an entire lifetime.

A sculptural ensemble erected at Cinelândia, a pompous allegory of poor quality and frankly bad taste, is topped off by pigeons.[25] This has transformed a well-meaning intention for a commemorative sculpture into a ridiculous note at the very center of our city.

These sculptures might be compared with the *lambe-lambe* street photographers who frequent our public parks and plazas.[26] These photographers transform the plazas into charming backdrops for portraits, but their work does not attain the artistic level of today's significant photographers.

It is curious that here in Rio statues go walking. They roam around neighborhoods, often abandoning the locations for which they were originally intended. This is the case of a notable work by Rodolfo Bernadelli originally found at the Largo do Machado.[27] This equestrian statue was perfectly proportioned for this plaza and its surrounding buildings, beautifully scaled to the observer, to the passersby, who could contemplate its bas-reliefs and details. But in 1949 the statue was transferred without any visual or spatial logic to the plaza in front of a gigantic edifice, where it now appears completely out of proportion. In the Passeio Público is a bronze bust of an author who appears to have a millstone around her neck.[28] These particular examples, in which the intention was to create a respectful homage, have instead resulted in complete caricature.

The sculpture of Saint Sebastian, in Praça Baden Powell, has today been effectively transformed into an altar for practitioners of Macumba.[29] There are also examples in which statues are removed from cemeteries and then used in public parks. This is the case with the memorial statuary for the victims of the Intentona of 1935 that was moved from the cemetery of São João Batista to the Praia Vermelha at the base of Pão de Açúcar.[30] Often of questionable artistic merit, these are monuments that would certainly be better off at the places for which they were intended. Since there seems to be such a need to exalt and visualize so many heroes and prominent public figures, and since there are certainly so many more to come, perhaps it would be wise to create a public park in the manner of a necropolis, with allées of busts and statues of lesser artistic interest. I believe that relatives, admirers, and pious souls would thus be able to envelope themselves with a greater sentimental feeling, as this grouping of sculptures would be more powerful than if each statue were isolated.

Cities such as Brasília, Rio de Janeiro, and others have restrictions and laws governing building construction. Yet the only concern of their mayors is to erect statues. Recently the Praça de Atibaia was renovated while the façade of its adjacent church was being restored and restuccoed. In front of the church, a luminous fountain was constructed in the manner of a checkerboard and covered with bathroom tiles. A tailor's dummy in stone was offered as a sculptural feature.

During the period in which I was the director of parks and gardens in Recife, I had the urge to assess, demolish, and remove the statues that did not rise to the level of greatness that corresponded with the actual heroes. This was the case with the monument to the heroes of Casa Forte and Admiral Cochrane.[31] The latter had the unusual situation of having a military field cap screwed into the statue after the fact, by official decree. Today I return to this same subject, to propose judicious and sensible regulations that might restrain this type of abuse.

Sculptures in gardens and parks should be carefully considered given the spaces for which they are created, with a goal of attaining the appropriate dimension and proportion. Many sculptures are carved from white marble; this brightness contrasts with the green masses of the trees, potentially creating rhythmic patterns. When well-composed, the use of sculpture to create order and suggest movement through space helps to emphasize certain focal points, such as reflecting pools. Sculpture might also be used to call attention to important places. Together, the volumes and masses of plants, water, and sculpture form a balanced composition so holistic that, if one were to extract a single element, this balance would be destroyed. Such sculptures may be seen in isolation, yet the most important factor is the beauty of the entire ensemble.

Unfortunately, it seems that a concern for public parks and for the natural landscape itself is missing in our country. Even those with a limited capacity of observation can see the obvious offenses committed at Pão de Açúcar. One company has erected a large illuminated advertising billboard. Another provocation is an enormous billboard announcing the time of day. To crown this off with a luminous halo of poor taste, governmental authorities have painted all of the recently constructed public erosion control works with bright white paint. This leaves an impression of gigantic strips of adhesive tape, accentuating the wounds provoked by deforestation and heavy rains.[32] The value of this commendable government work should not be highlighted in this way, for it will both exacerbate a misunderstanding of the problems impacting our landscapes and invert our aesthetic sensibility.

The examples are interminable. The statue of Quintino Bocaiúva at the Lagoa Rodrigo de Freitas has an awful spatial placement, in addition to a lack of artistic value. The statue of Mahatma Gandhi, one of the great figures of humanity, looks like a poor caricature of a comic.

It is alarming that there is not just a glorification of the "post mortem" dead but also of the living, particularly concerning the presidents of the Republic. Many sculptors function as veritable factories. Their studios are warehouses for the hindquarters and heads of horses, the legs and shoulders of soldiers—all ready to be used in the production of future equestrian statues. These are modified by particular specifications; military stripes and medals are added or taken away in accordance with the hero's rank.

At times, the motives for these statuary tributes seem to compromise our society's intelligence. In Praça Saens Peña is a statue of the "Radio-Ginasta," honoring the work of a radio-broadcast exercise pioneer.[33] On Avenida Vieira Souto one finds a monument to a king who visited us once.[34] And there are countless statues given to us by foreign consulates, seemingly sympathetic to this impulse to deface our city.

The charity of the rich is also credited in statuary. At the beginning of this century, an expensive statue of a generous lady was made "for the poor of Botafogo," according to the tourist guide *Guia Rex*.[35]

Inside the Municipal Theater, busts appear in inappropriate places, with no relationship to the architecture.[36] I do not negate the merit of these tributes. But we must point out the impropriety of statuary with no artistic merit. A respectful tribute is perpetuated by statuary that achieves a high level of artistic excellence. One does not venerate a name by deforming it with a poorly sited, banal statue.

In France, the placement of inappropriate busts in the gardens of Versailles or the Tuileries would never be permitted. We must make decisions based on the logic that sculpture must have intrinsic artistic qualities beyond cheap sentimentality. Sculpture is intended for public space—it must serve and benefit everyone. We must end the practice by which an exemplar of bad taste is elevated and mistaken for a work of art. Note that a culture measures itself by its artistic creation—not by commemorative work that perpetuates sentimentality.

Based on these concerns drawn from my recent observations and my professional experience as a landscape architect, I have taken the initiative to bring to this honorable council the suggestion to develop stronger and more restrictive legislation, establishing rules regarding the construction and siting of monuments and statuary, particularly when these are proposed for public parks, streets, and the plazas of public buildings.

Sacrificed Landscape
January 28, 1969

Delivered to the Plenary Session of the Conselho Federal de Cultura on January 28, 1969. Published as Roberto Burle Marx, "Paisagem sacrificada" (Sacrificed Landscape), *Cultura: Conselho Federal de Cultura* (Ministério da Educação e Cultura) 3, no. 19 (January 1969): 51–52.

Yesterday, when counselor Rodrigo de Mello Franco made the serious accusation that the mayor of Ouro Preto was cutting down and destroying trees at the Igreja do Carmo and demolishing houses for the widening of streets to improve traffic for motorists, I did not comment, but I would like to give my complete and total support to the position of our distinguished colleague.

I am of the opinion that there should be a vehement public protest, published in the newspapers, so that this abuse of power will be exposed. I am also of the opinion that all of the sessions of the Conselho Federal de Cultura should be open to journalists, so that they may report on what we are debating and accomplishing.

Ouro Preto is a landmarked city of great universal historic and artistic value, kept intact by the Department of National Historic and Artistic Heritage after a struggle of many years.[37] It is astonishing that this success is now at the mercy of an uncultured mayor who does not understand the importance of this place.

This is not the first time that I have protested against these acts of vandalism. I would be pleased if my suggestions were not forgotten but transformed into reality through the establishment of laws and sanctions. The contribution of the council is to act definitively in response to these abuses, which we have witnessed throughout the country. These incomprehensible and anguishing acts, destroying works of art and indeed the very history of Brazil, have occurred because of a lack of cultural awareness and knowledge of the importance of these monuments.[38]

I hope to make the most of this occasion as I speak before the council today. After having read the *Jornal do Brasil* of January 21, 1969, which reports the construction of an enormous monument honoring the fourth centennial of the city of São Sebastião do Rio de Janeiro, I would like to bring this information to the attention of our honorable counselors, so that these gentlemen are alerted to this proposal for a tasteless monumental and carnivalesque sculptural composition.[39]

Ironically, in this city where the population and the number of automobiles is increasing, it appears to me that the number of monuments is growing proportionally. And it continues like this, over and over, yet another extraneous element proposed for our landscape that is already so compromised. If an immediate stop to these actions is not enacted, our landscapes will be completely sacrificed.

Before this occurs, I want to prevent this from happening in the Parque do Flamengo, the location of the aforementioned monumental sculpture. Nothing more should be built in this park, which has already been registered as a landmark by the Department of National Historic and Artistic Heritage.[40] This sculptural composition has no relationship to the Parque do Flamengo, and its proposed siting is completely arbitrary.

I am not only advocating for the integrity of Parque do Flamengo—I have repeatedly stated that it has already suffered from a series of modifications—but for the dignity of this city. All proposals for sculpture and statuary should be contingent on the approval of the Historic and Artistic Heritage group or of an Arts Council tasked with regulating the appearance of this city that was once one of the most beautiful in the world.

FIGURE 4.31.
The sculptor Flori Gama with a prototype statue of Estácio de Sá, the founder of Rio de Janeiro, proposed for the plaza fronting the Morro da Viúva at Parque do Flamengo, Rio de Janeiro, 1969

Centro de Pesquisa e Documentação do Jornal do Brasil

FIGURE 4.32.
Concrete erosion control structures at the summit of the Agulha do Inhangá, Copacabana, Rio de Janeiro, 2012
Photo © Osmar Carioca

Preservation of Landscape Conditions
September 17, 1970

Delivered to the Plenary Session of the Conselho Federal de Cultura on September 17, 1970. Published as Roberto Burle Marx, "Preservação de condições paisagísticas" (Preservation of Landscape Conditions), *Cultura: Conselho Federal de Cultura* (Ministério da Educação e Cultura) 4, no. 39 (September 1970): 34–36.

I have been traveling for the past three months, visiting a number of countries where I was able to observe the deep respect held for landscapes and gardens. Upon my return to Brazil, I was astonished to learn of a series of governmental decisions that were the very opposite of what I had observed abroad.

I would like to remind you of our session on July 5 [1970], on which occasion I read a copy of a telegram written by the architect Jorge Machado Moreira to the governor of the state, calling for the preservation of the natural landscape conditions at Morro do Pasmado.[41] I had the satisfaction of seeing this council united in support of this appeal, unanimously approving that our own council president address the governor to suggest a reexamination of the project for the construction of a hotel at the referenced location. Shortly after my return from abroad, I became aware of a new call for bids for the sale of the Morro do Pasmado. I confirmed then that, despite the protest of this council and many other groups, our government insists on proceeding with the construction of projects that will deface the landscape character of this city.

We already have several examples of this disfiguration of our landscape, to the point of being unrecognizable. For example, the Agulha do Inhangá has been buttressed with concrete for the purpose of structural reinforcement, rendering it deformed and monstrous.[42]

Another governmental decision that surprised me was the announcement for a submission of bids for the construction of a commercial center at the Lagoa Rodrigo de Freitas, next to the Augusto Frederico Schmidt viaduct. The project encompasses a total area of 100,000 square meters, with construction permitted on 35,000 square meters. It is likely that we will see the same thing that has occurred at the Lagoa with Clube Caiçaras, whose footprint continues to grow conspicuously. In my opinion, these recent governmental actions reflect an attitude of aggression toward our landscape and indeed compromise our culture.

I also read in the newspapers that the government is considering hosting the samba schools' carnival parades at the Parque do Flamengo.[43] It is curious, and at the same time incomprehensible, that such a suggestion would be made. The trees of the park were planted with great effort and expense, and for them to grow to their current state required several years of special care. It is incredible that now, just as the trees are beginning to reach their desired appearance, a proposal is made that is capable of destroying everything within just a few hours of merrymaking.

By contrast with the profoundly lamentable actions occurring here in Brazil, I can cite the deep love for nature that I witnessed, with great happiness and enthusiasm, while on my recent voyage in Great Britain and Greece. In Israel, significant and continuous efforts have been directed at combating that region's aridity, and the results are now being felt across large regions. Where there were once stone quarries destitute of plants, there now are forests. Those in governance perceive with extraordinary clarity that from an ecological point of view the plant can indeed modify the climate.[44]

In countries like Persia, the sidewalks are protected by allées of trees that are planted in linear channel-like depressions that collect water, producing a protective canopy against the inclement heat. In the city of New Delhi, where temperatures can exceed 47 degrees Celsius, I was delighted to see trees planted densely to moderate the harshness of the climate. All the streets were planted with trees that today have dense, leafy canopies.

In Japan, it is poignant to see that the historic gardens have remained intact, despite the population's density, and still delight their visitors. These gardens are highly respected by the Japanese, for they represent a cultural layering of many generations.

In India, I was astonished by the beauty of the Mogul gardens, some dating from the seventeenth century, that continue to complement their surrounding landscapes. Here water is the "leitmotif." Trees may be found that are two hundred, three hundred, and four hundred years old, and these have acquired an extraordinary dignity.

Once again I call for the conservation of the natural and urban landscape. This protection is an expression of our culture, an affirmation that we are worthy of the rich flora that nature has bequeathed upon Brazil.

On our forthcoming Dia da Árvore (Arbor Day), September 21, I hope that the celebrations are not limited to the planting of a tree that is not subsequently maintained. A tree is like a person—it must be cared for continually. Above all, I would like to see more of our many native species planted in our gardens and parks. These are rarely used, and they are being slowly decimated. In no other country have I seen the number of plant species that appear in our native Brazilian flora. However, the number of people who understand this heritage is still very small. It is our responsibility to arouse in our fellow Brazilians the love and respect that our flora deserves.

Landscape Complex
July 7, 1973

Delivered to the Plenary Session of the Conselho Federal de Cultura on July 7, 1973. Published as Roberto Burle Marx, "Conjunto paisagistico" (Landscape Complex), *Boletim: Conselho Federal de Cultura* (Ministério da Educação e Cultura) 3, no. 11 (July/September 1973): 18–19.

Given the responsibility with which I am charged as a member of this esteemed council, and as a professional specialized in the field of landscape architecture, I would like to request the attention of this plenary so that I may present a matter that I find of particular concern.

I have recently observed a number of projects and renovations proposed and realized by the Companhia Caminho Aéreo Pão de Açúcar, resulting in serious alterations and deformations of the hills of the Pão de Açúcar and the Morro da Urca, which, from the point of view of the landscape, form a single complex.[45] Given this esteemed audience of colleagues, it is not necessary to emphasize the international significance of these two locations that together constitute a valuable Brazilian landscape patrimony.

In my capacity as a member of the Conselho Superior de Planejamento Urbano da Guanabara (Superior Council of Urban Planning of Guanabara),[46] I denounced these actions by the Companhia and solicited urgent precautions so that such works would be halted until a master plan of these and other projects was dispatched to the Conselho. The Conselho Superior de Planejamento Urbano, a state agency created for these very situations, would thus be able to evaluate the master plan and issue an opinion.

At the same time, news appeared in the local press concerning the construction of a restaurant with a conspicuous structure on the Pão de Açúcar, disfiguring the appearance and the natural grandeur of this valuable heritage landscape.

We have requested that the Conselho Superior de Planejamento Urbano da Guanabara be immediately provided with additional information about these projects, to ensure that implementation is consistent with our guidance.

Meanwhile it is my responsibility, in my capacity as member of the Conselho Federal de Cultura, to submit to this plenary a petition requesting that the Department of National Historic and Artistic Heritage immediately landmark the site of the hills of Pão de Açúcar and Morro da Urca as well as the unified landscape complex that they form. Its aspect of natural grandeur must be maintained and its authenticity protected through the prevention of any modification of its configuration or any destruction of its botanical elements.[47]

We recognize that we cannot remain silent before such serious offenses are committed against our natural landscape patrimony, certainly when there are state agencies that regulate the conservation of this rich heritage. What we propose is in no way biased against the development of tourism. On the contrary, it supports tourism, as it would provide optimal solutions for both architectural and ecological problems.

For these reasons, I suggest the following action: I recommend that the hills of Pão de Açúcar and Morro da Urca be immediately landmarked by the Department of National Historic and Artistic Heritage, in accordance with the legislation currently in force, and I ask for the endorsement of this plenary session.[48]

FIGURE 4.33.
View of the Pão de Açúcar cable car rising above the Praça General Tibúrcio in Urca to the cable station on the Morro da Urca, Rio de Janeiro, 1972
Arquivo Estadão Conteúdo

FIGURE 4.34.
Carnival street parade celebrations, Rio de Janeiro, ca. 1960
Photo by Marcel Gautherot/Instituto Moreira Salles Collection

Green Spaces
July 11, 1973

Delivered to the Plenary Session of the Conselho Federal de Cultura on July 11, 1973. Published as Roberto Burle Marx, "Áreas verdes" (Green Spaces), *Boletim: Conselho Federal de Cultura* (Ministério da Educação e Cultura) 3, no. 11 (July/September 1973): 28–29.

In today's copy of the *Jornal do Brasil* I read with astonishment and stupefaction a proposal to uproot sixty large-canopied trees along the Avenida Beira Mar so that the carnival parade of samba schools would be able to parade by.

In my view, the suggestion to destroy sixty trees that were planted over sixty years ago for just one day of this parade is madness—indeed, an affront to common sense. If we were to accept this proposal, we would be contributing to the destruction of vegetation in a city that already has a paucity of green spaces and a violently hot summer. This is one of the deliberations occurring within Riotur in which solving one problem creates countless others.[49]

This news article also reports the mad and impudent proposal that after the parade these sixty trees would be replanted in their original locations. Such discussion demonstrates total ignorance. The transplanting of large-canopied adult trees is extremely traumatic, and it is very difficult for a tree to recover. A tree is not a traffic signal that changes at will or in accordance with a sudden demand. It is a living being that must be loved and respected, and we must protect it by whatever means necessary.

One must understand that a garden is not remade in one week. It takes decades for a tree to achieve full maturity.

The Parque do Flamengo, which is a landmarked site, must be defended at all costs, particularly given all of the assaults and attempts at disfiguration that have occurred in recent years. Even now, an idea has been proposed by the extraordinary architect Oscar Niemeyer to build a concert hall along with parking for four thousand automobiles in the park. If accepted, this project would result in the loss of a large area of the park to building construction, setting a dangerous precedent and threatening the integrity of a place that is of inestimable value for a city with few public green spaces. In my opinion, a marvelous solution would be to construct this concert hall in Jacarepaguá, where an admirable master plan developed by Lúcio Costa has designated specific areas for cultural activities.[50]

FIGURE 5.1.
Sítio Santo Antônio da Bica, Barra de Guaratiba, ca. 1976
Photo by Marcel Gautherot/Instituto Moreira Salles Collection

CHAPTER 5

The Scientific Park

Understanding the concept of the botanical garden, both through its colonial European history and in its modernizing, tropical New World context, is critical in order to grasp Roberto Burle Marx's approach to public parks. He understood this typology well and even redefined its limits—during his career, he developed preliminary studies for botanical and zoobotanical gardens in four different states of Brazil. In 1946 he worked with the botanist Henrique Lahmeyer de Mello Barreto on the development of a municipal zoo for Rio de Janeiro, the Jardim Zoológico da Quinta da Boa Vista. Here Burle Marx developed a novel zoobotanical approach to the design of species habitat for both plants and animals. Years later, in 1961, concurrently with the initiation of his work on the Parque do Flamengo in Rio de Janeiro, Burle Marx prepared detailed studies for a transformation of the Jardim Botânico in São Paulo and for a new Parque Zoobotânico in Brasília. And in the early 1970s, during his tenure as a member of the Conselho Federal de Cultura, he began studies for the Jardim Botânico in Belo Horizonte, Minas Gerais. Despite the completion of elaborated proposals for each of these gardens, none were executed.

Burle Marx's own plantation property at the Sítio Santo Antônio da Bica in Barra de Guaratiba, purchased in 1949 with his brother Guilherme Siegfried Marx, was in essence a private experimental botanical garden, consuming his interest until his death in 1994. In 1973 Burle Marx moved his principal place of residence from his home thirty-five miles away in Leme, Rio de Janeiro, to the Sítio, where he would acclimatize and propagate thousands of plants, many of which he collected himself during various expeditions around the country. Housed beneath slatted shade structures, his collections became a valuable nursery for plant materials that he would use in future gardens. Burle Marx's many friendships with botanists, particularly Mello Barreto and Mello Franco, served him well as a plant collector. The notion of the botanical garden as a center of scientific research consumed him for decades, from the time of his visit to the glasshouses of the botanical gardens of Berlin-Dahlem in 1928 through later visits to the Royal Botanic Gardens in Kew, London. In his last published interview, conducted by the landscape architect Conrad Hamerman, he stated: "My atelier is a laboratory—has to be a laboratory. In the final analysis, all of life is an ongoing experiment."[1] Indeed, his conception of public gardens was developed in light of these experiments at the Sítio, and several of his large parks may be interpreted as modernist narratives exploring the possibilities of the botanical garden as didactic public space.

Burle Marx's three most important large public park projects—the unexecuted ornamental gardens of Parque do Ibirapuera as well as the completed Parque del Este and Parque do Flamengo—may be read as variations on the theme of the botanical garden, given the narrative quality of their planting plans. But these public parks do not employ the botanical garden's program of scientific research and plant propagation. Burle Marx engaged in this work of propagation privately at the Sítio Santo Antônio da Bica. Unlike Glaziou, whose significant legacy of plant collecting expeditions in Brazil lives on in the form of a herbarium of 24,000 pressed species in the Muséum National d'Histoire Naturelle in Paris, Burle Marx's heritage is the live plant collection and nursery of over 3,500 species that he established at the Sítio. This 100-acre site, donated to the Brazilian federal government by Burle Marx in 1985, was registered by the Instituto do Patrimônio Histórico e Artístico Nacional in 2000 as a protected site of national historic and artistic heritage.

During his tenure as a member of the Conselho Federal de Cultura, Burle Marx spoke about the historic Jardim Botânico of Rio de Janeiro on several occasions, arguing forcefully for the protection of the garden and its adjacent seedling nursery, the Horto Florestal da Gávea. The botanical garden was established in 1808 by João VI, then the prince regent, upon his arrival in Brazil with the Portuguese court. The garden was conceived as yet another source of profitable colonial exports, acclimatizing and propagating tropical crops such as clove, cinnamon, nutmeg, and even tea that were thriving in other colonial locations. In 1822, upon the return of Dom João VI to Portugal, his son Pedro I declared Brazil's independence and assumed the title of emperor of Brazil. The Jardim Botânico's program was subsequently transformed when the new emperor opened its grounds to the public the same year. Frei Leandro do Sacramento, appointed by Pedro I as the first director of the new botanical garden

FIGURE 5.2.
Philodendron leaves at the Sítio Santo Antônio da Bica, Barra de Guaratiba, ca. 1960
Photo by Marcel Gautherot/Instituto Moreira Salles Collection

from 1824 to 1829, transformed it again from a Jardim de Aclimação (Acclimation Garden) into the Instituto de Estudos Botânicos (Institute for Botanical Studies)—from a source of exploitative export profit to a place of scientific botanical study. By the late nineteenth century the Jardim Botânico had become a nationally renowned research institute for the study of native Brazilian flora. The Jardim currently houses more than 6,500 species of Brazilian and tropical flora and is well known for its magnificent 750-meter allée of more than one hundred royal palms (*Roystonea regia*—propagated from a single *palma mater*, an 1809 gift from Mauritius to Dom João VI) as well as for its pond replete with giant water lilies (*Victoria amazonica*).

Burle Marx emphasized to his fellow counselors that the importance of the Jardim

FIGURE 5.3.
Allée of royal palms at the Jardim Botânico, Rio de Janeiro, 1955
Photo by Marcel Gautherot/Instituto Moreira Salles Collection

FIGURE 5.4.
João Barbosa Rodrigues, director, in his library at the Jardim Botânico do Rio de Janeiro, ca. 1900
Acervo Museu do Meio Ambiente/Instituto de Pesquisas Jardim Botânico do Rio de Janeiro

Botânico as a research center was one of its greatest assets. He believed that the garden's directorship should be held by research scientists in order to uphold this mission best. Like the first directorship of Leandro do Sacramento, the garden's leadership under João Barbosa Rodrigues (1842–1909), between 1890 and 1892 and again from 1903 until 1909, was another transformative period. Burle Marx cites Rodrigues's exemplary directorship, particularly as he augmented the garden's collection of live plants and addressed the necessity of its role in the conservation of native Brazilian species. Rodrigues established a library, a glasshouse, and a herbarium and organized botanical research expeditions to the interior of Brazil, including the significant Comissão Rondon (1907–1915)—journeys that Burle Marx himself emulated with his own plant collection trips.

In 1914 the Jardim Botânico established the Reserva Florestal de Itatiaia as a research annex for the study of the Brazilian highland ecosystem and its rich biodiversity. This research station, renamed the Estação Biológica de Itatiaia in 1927, was at the intersection of the state borders of São Paulo, Minas Gerais, and Rio de

FIGURE 5.5.
Missão Massart at the Reserva Florestal de Itatiaia, ca. 1922
Acervo Museu do Meio Ambiente/Instituto de Pesquisas Jardim Botânico do Rio de Janeiro

Janeiro and became a gathering space for botanists from both São Paulo and Rio de Janeiro. The scientist and physician Antônio Pacheco Leão, director of the garden from 1915 to 1931, strengthened this research vision of the Jardim Botânico, engaging botanists and researchers such as Alberto Loefgren, Adolpho Ducke, João Geraldo Kuhlmann, and Alexandre Brade. Pacheco Leão also sponsored the Belgian botanist Jean Massart's Missão Biológica to Brazil (1922–1923). His successor, Paulo Campos Porto, director of the Jardim Botânico between 1934 and 1938 and again from 1951 until 1961, was another visionary botanist. Campos Porto established the garden's first scientific journal, *Rodriguésia*, with an ambition to disseminate the work of this research institution to a broader international audience. He was the superintendent of the Estação Biológica de Itatiaia from 1929 through 1933 and was particularly active in developing Brazil's policies of environmental conservation. It was his friendship with Gétulio Vargas, along with his early advocacy of nature conservation, that led to the 1937 transformation of the forests and mountains of the garden's Estação Biológica de Itatiaia into Brazil's first national park, Parque Nacional de Itatiaia, under the jurisdiction of the recently established Serviço Florestal.

Burle Marx often focused his consular depositions on what he saw as the degradation of the Jardim Botânico—he urged his fellow counselors to appeal to the federal government for the valorization and protection of this irreplaceable and incredibly valuable national resource. Burle Marx expressed his concern regarding the rapid encroachment of urban development at the garden's perimeter—particularly the impact of federal housing developments at the fringes of the Horto Florestal, a 200-acre sloped woodland area that had been annexed to the Jardim Botânico as a site for seed propagation, seedling growth, and horticultural experimentation. He cited the loss of numerous species within the garden's collection due to a lack of stewardship, leadership, and space. Presenting the garden as a unique cultural heritage site at the council's plenary sessions, Burle Marx insisted that significant action be taken to protect and preserve the Jardim Botânico together with the Horto Florestal da Gávea. In May 1971 Burle Marx's appeal was successful—the 200 acres of the Horto Florestal were integrated with the Jardim Botânico, enlarging its total area to 350 acres. And in December 1973 the Horto Florestal was added to the *livros do tombo* as a protected site and an integral part of the Jardim Botânico.

Roberto Burle Marx: Botanical Gardens, 1960s

Jardim Zoológico da Quinta da Boa Vista

In 1945 the botanist Henrique Lahmeyer de Mello Barreto, with whom Burle Marx had collaborated on the Parque do Barreiro at Araxá, was appointed director of the Jardim Zoológico da Quinta da Boa Vista in Rio de Janeiro. The municipal zoo was to be sited at the grounds of the Palácio de São Cristóvão—the former residence of Dom João VI, Dom Pedro I, and Dom Pedro II—with its picturesque landscape transformed by Glaziou in 1869. After the end of the empire in 1889 and the establishment of the República Velha, the imperial holdings of the Museu Nacional do Rio de Janeiro, the natural history museum established in 1818 by Dom João VI, were transferred from their original building in the Campo de Santana to the former palace at the Quinta da Boa Vista. Its gardens and the museum were opened to the public. During the República Velha, the museum's management was transferred to the Universidade do Brasil.[2] Under Mello Barreto's directorship, the zoological garden was intended to be a part of the museum's scientific program of research, and in 1946 he invited Burle Marx to help with the design of the new zoological garden. Since their earliest collaborations in Pampulha and Araxá, Mello Barreto's role as a mentor to Burle Marx was significant. Burle Marx stated that the botanist provided him with "the character of an actual education," particularly impacting his work on the large-scale botanical and zoological gardens.[3]

Little documentation of Burle Marx's collaborative work on the Jardim Zoológico remains, other than a plan from 1946 and a perspective drawing depicting a view into a rocky forest, including three figures at the edge of a lake. Two large spotted leopards lie at the lake's opposite bank, projecting an idealized harmonious representation of animals and humans in the natural environment. In the original 1946 gouache

FIGURE 5.6.
Auguste François Marie Glaziou, Quinta da Boa Vista, Rio de Janeiro, ca. 1920
Acervo Arquivo Geral da Cidade do Rio de Janeiro

FIGURE 5.7.
Roberto Burle Marx, perspective view of the Jardim Zoológico da Quinta da Boa Vista, Rio de Janeiro, 1946
© Burle Marx Landscape Design Studio

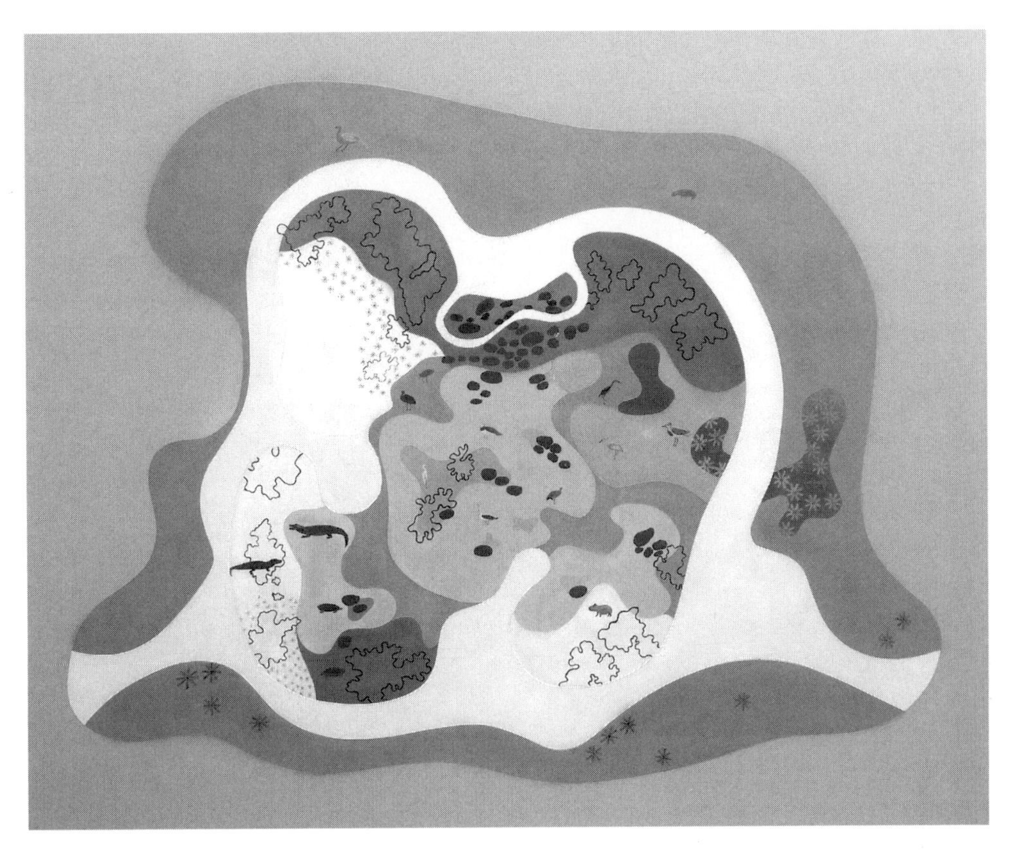

FIGURE 5.8.
Roberto Burle Marx, plan of the Jardim Zoológico da Quinta da Boa Vista, Rio de Janeiro, 1946

plan drawing for the Jardim Zoológico, the animals are drawn as figures on the plan, similar to the mosaics of prehistoric animals that were incorporated into the *calçada portuguesa* pavement at Araxá's Fonte Andrade Júnior. These animals are not represented in cages but within their own natural habitat. With the Parque Zoobotânico, Burle Marx explored ideas of a continuous link between plant and animal habitat with the surrounding geology, confirming what he would write many years later: "In the zoological garden, as we conceive it, it is essential to show this natural reality; that is, the existence of an intimate link between plants, animals, and stones."[4]

Jardim Botânico de São Paulo

Burle Marx's unbuilt project for the transformation of the Jardim Botânico de São Paulo was developed in 1961 at the request of its director, Alcides Ribeiro Teixeira. The Jardim Botânico de São Paulo is located within the state park now known as Parque Estadual das Fontes do Ipiranga and encompasses an area of over 1,280 acres

FIGURE 5.9.
Glasshouses and Jardim de Lineu of the Jardim Botânico de São Paulo, São Paulo, 1961
Arquivo Estadão Conteúdo

within the city's dense urban footprint. The terrain was claimed in 1917 as property of the state of São Paulo in order to protect the source of the Ipiranga stream, which provided drinking water for the adjacent neighborhood. In 1928 the botanist Frederico Carlos Hoehne was invited to develop a botanical garden at the park. Early in his career, Hoehne had been the head gardener at the Museu Nacional in Rio de Janeiro and participated as the field botanist on both the Commisão Rondon (1908–1909) and the Roosevelt-Rondon Scientific Expedition (1913–1914). Since 1918 he had worked at the Seção de Botânica at the Instituto Butantã in São Paulo, studying medicinal plants. Upon the official establishment of the Jardim Botânico de São Paulo in 1938, the Seção de Botânico was transferred to the Parque do Estado and renamed the Instituto de Botânica research station. Hoehne was its director from 1942 until his death in 1959. The Parque do Estado, along with the botanical garden and the Instituto de Botânica, includes a large area of conserved Atlantic rainforest, the Reserva Biológica. The Instituto de Botânica also has two off-site conservation units, representing the state's principal biomes: the *mata atlântica* and the *cerrado*. While director, Hoehne was responsible for developing the garden's orchid collection, now numbering over 20,000 varieties. The Jardim Botânico includes a

FIGURE 5.10.
Historic staircase and monumental gate at the Jardim Botânico de São Paulo, São Paulo, 1956
Photo by Reynaldo Ceppo/Arquivo Estadão Conteúdo

FIGURE 5.11.
Interior of the glasshouse at the Jardim Botânico de São Paulo, São Paulo, 1930
Photo by A. Federmann/Acervo do Instituto de Botânica de São Paulo

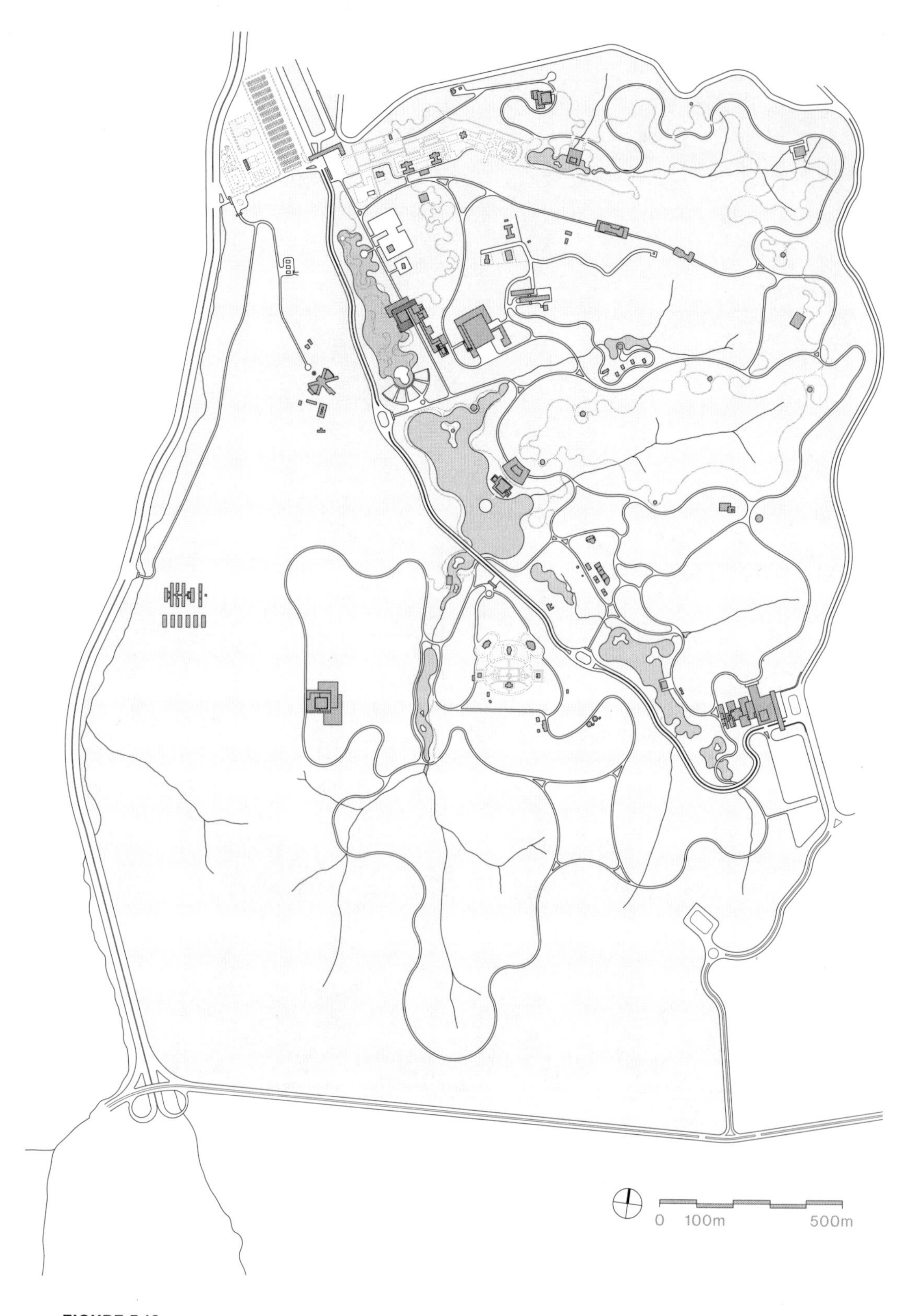

FIGURE 5.12.

Roberto Burle Marx, plan of the Jardim Botânico de São Paulo, São Paulo, 1961
Drawing by Catherine Seavitt Nordenson

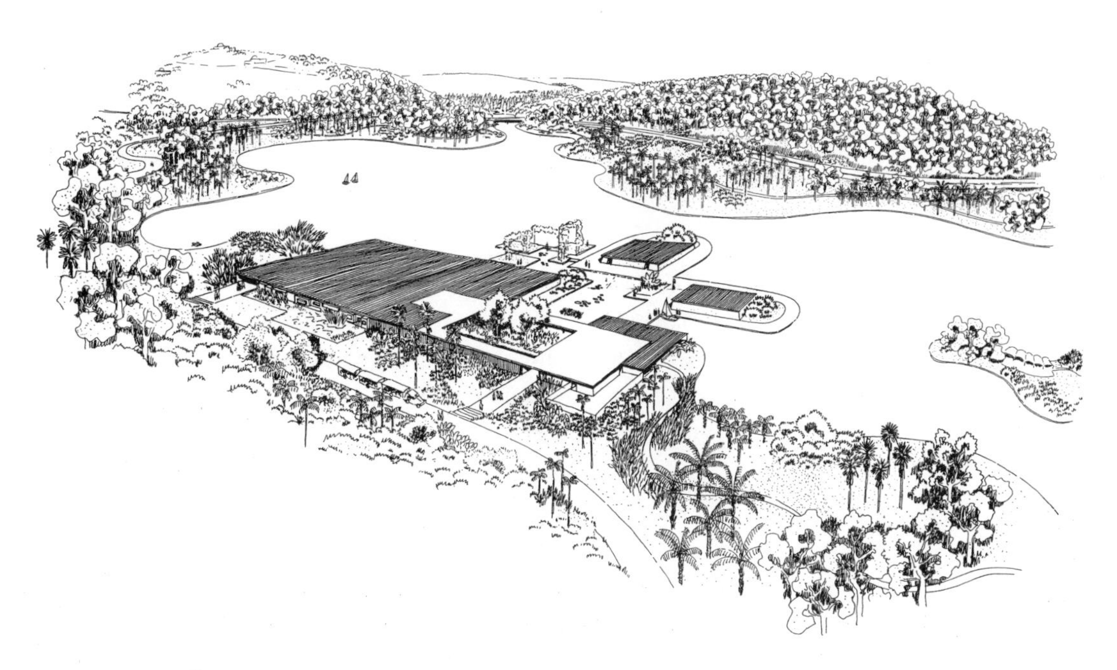

FIGURE 5.13.
Roberto Burle Marx, perspective view of the Jardim Botânico de São Paulo with slatted shade structure, 1961

museum; the Jardim de Lineu, inspired by the botanical garden in Uppsala, Sweden; historic glasshouses built in 1928; and a historic entrance staircase and gate dating from 1894.

The 1961 master plan proposal by Burle Marx included a transformation of the botanical garden, a separate zoological garden, an astronomical observatory, an experimental animal farm, and several other programmatic elements, all distributed around a series of lakes created through the daylighting and damming of the Pirarungáua Creek, a buried tributary of the Ipiranga that once flowed through the northern part of the site. Burle Marx's new programming was organized around the three elements that composed his vision of an ideal botanical garden: the public areas and collections, consisting of gardens, playgrounds, and picnic areas; the ecological gardens, representing the flora of the state of São Paulo; and an area for the Instituto de Botânica, with its historic greenhouses and scientific collections. Internal roads were pushed to the park's perimeter, and didactic pedestrian pathways and a small visitors' train on a looped railway created public connections between the Jardim Botânico and the larger Parque Estadual.[5] Burle Marx understood the botanical garden as primarily a scientific institution, in which the organization of the plant material was the essential aspect of the design. Nevertheless he saw the garden as fulfilling several complex needs: scientific research, ecological preservation, and urban recreation.[6] Burle Marx was particularly interested in the possibilities of engaging the public with this eclectic program, creating new alliances between an ecological urban garden and the presentation of the greater regional landscape.

Parque Zoobotânico de Brasília

Lúcio Costa's 1957 *plano piloto* for the new capital of Brasília indicated locations for separate botanical and zoological gardens. But in 1959 the zoologist João Moojen de Oliveira, appointed by the federal government as the director of the new Departamento de Proteção à Natureza de Brasília (Department of Nature Protection of Brasília), suggested that the two programs be merged, thus creating a zoobotanical garden that would include both plants and animals.[7] The location determined for the Parque Zoobotânico, in consultation with Mello Barreto, was at the end of the southern curved axis of the *plano piloto* at its crossing with the Riacho Fundo stream, one of the sources of the dammed Lago Paranoá.[8] But this was a contested site—the designated territory, over 1,500 acres, included the pioneer settlement of Candangolândia, one of the first pioneer encampments constructed in 1956 to house both the administrative headquarters of the Companhia Urbanizadora da Nova Capital do

FIGURE 5.14.
The pioneer settlement at Candangolândia, site of the proposed Parque Zoobotânico de Brasília, Brasília, ca. 1955
Arquivo Público do Distrito Federal

Brasil (NOVACAP: Urban Development Company of the New Capital of Brazil), the agency responsible for building the new capital city, and the thousands of migrant construction workers and their families who arrived to build the city. The federal government had always considered Candangolândia and other encampments—Núcleo Bandeirante, Vila Planalto, and Vila Paranoá, among others—to be temporary settlements, destined to be torn down after the completion of the new capital. Their residents were expected to relocate to the new peripheral *cidades-satélites* (satellite cities) at a distance of twenty-five kilometers from the *plano piloto* or return to their places of origin. But at Candangolândia as well as other encampments, many residents refused to leave.[9]

Nonetheless, after the end of Kubitschek's presidency in 1961, Burle Marx was commissioned by Moojen de Oliveira, the director of the newly established Fundação Zoobotânica do Distrito Federal (Zoo and Botanical Foundation of the Federal District), to produce a master plan for the zoobotanical park. The plan, which assumed the erasure of the Candangolândia settlement, was never executed; indeed, the neighborhood continues to thrive today.[10] Yet the Parque Zoobotânico remains one of Burle Marx's most important proposals for a scientific public garden and highlights his study of the ecological regions of Brazil's interior. The plan was innovative due to its novel composition of a sequence of *tableaux vivants* including both flora and fauna. Like Martius's detailed etchings illustrating the phytogeographic regions of Brazil, Burle Marx was compelled by the interdependency of plant and animal life and asserted that these associations should be represented and understood in the context of a zoobotanical park. He described this interdependency with a musical metaphor: "I want to insist that nature is a complete symphony, in which the elements are all intimately related—size, form, color, scent, movement, etc. Within this understanding, the plant or animal is no longer only an isolated entity, something to be collected. It is much more: nature is an organization endowed with an immense dose of spontaneous activity, possessing its own *modus vivendi* with the world around it."[11]

The plan for the Parque Zoobotânico was separated into two parts. The smaller area of the Zoarium would contain the animal exhibits along with the educational, research, and administrative aspects of the park—it was sited exactly on the footprint of the Candangolândia settlement. Wrapping the Zoarium was a much larger area with various *ambientes ecológicos* (ecological environments), traversed by two tributaries of the Riacho Fundo stream that were dammed to create a series of small lakes. Burle Marx called for the representation of sixteen ecological regions of Brazil, each with their own particular flora and fauna, including an area devoted to the Amazon forest. In addition, with an acknowledgment of Engler's world gardens at Berlin-Dahlem, it included areas representative of the equatorial zones of North America, Europe, Africa, Asia, and Australia—every continent within the tropical

FIGURE 5.15.

Roberto Burle Marx, site plan of the Parque Zoobotânico de Brasília, 1961
Drawing by Catherine Seavitt Nordenson

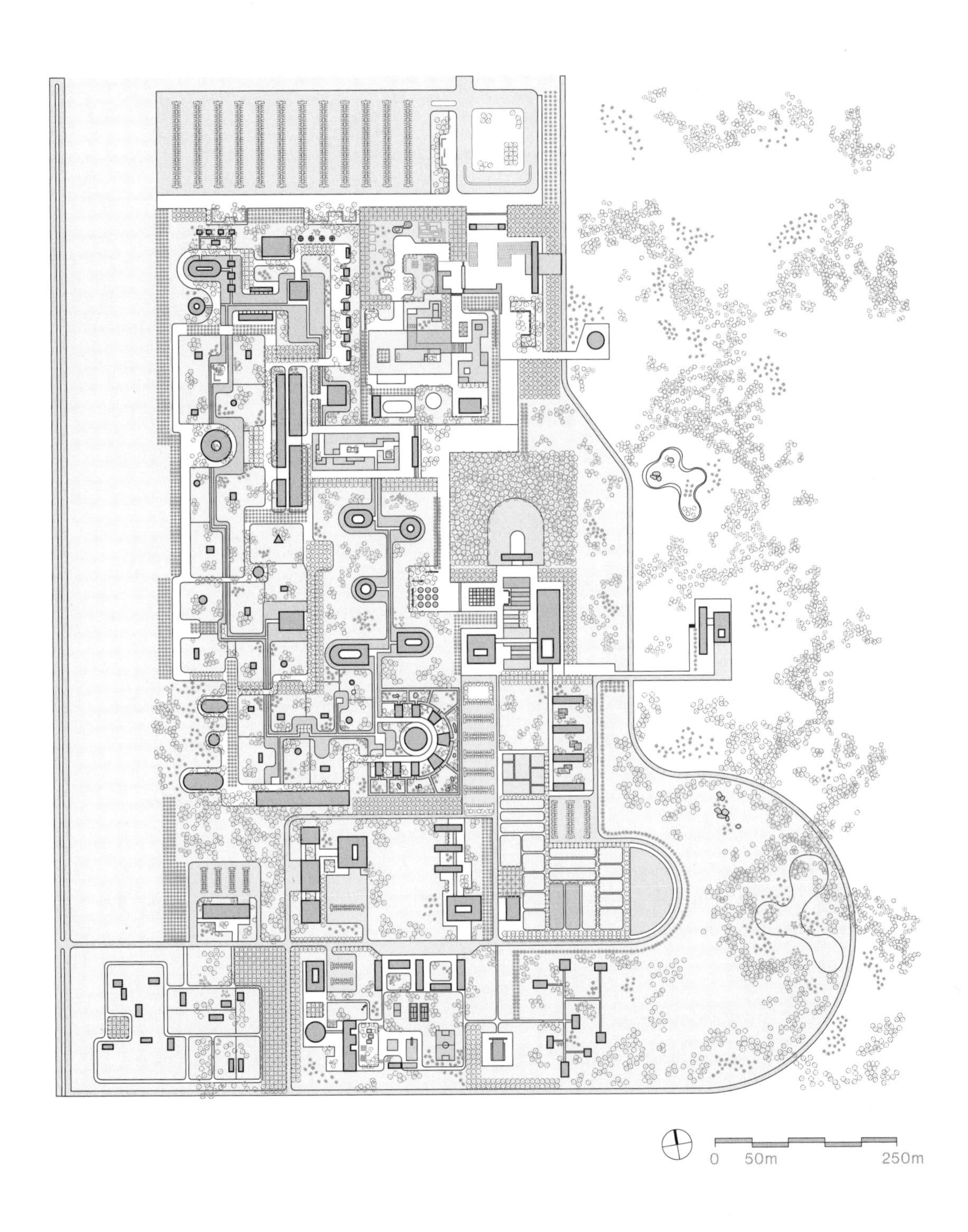

FIGURE 5.16.

Roberto Burle Marx, detailed plan of the Zoarium of the Parque Zoobotânico de Brasília, 1961
Drawing by Catherine Seavitt Nordenson

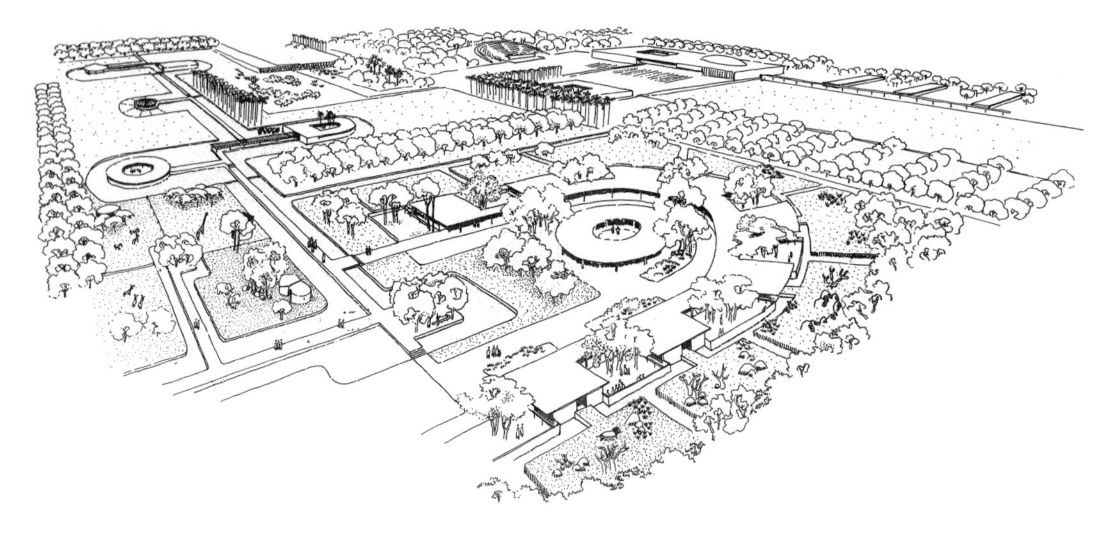

FIGURE 5.17.
Roberto Burle Marx, perspective view of the Parque Zoobotânico de Brasília, 1961

belt was present. Because of the vast size of the zoobotanical garden, a small train was proposed to encircle the park and convey visitors to its full extent.

In 1962 Burle Marx created a series of detailed *Flora* drawings, each representing one of four unique ecological domains of Brazil: *Flora da Amazônia* (Flora of the Amazon Basin), *Flora da caatinga* (Flora of the *Caatinga*), *Flora do granito* (Flora of Granite), and *Flora do calcáreo* (Flora of Limestone). Developed as visual studies for the Parque Zoobotânico of Brasília, these perspectival drawings emphasize the important relationships between regional geology and the diversity of associated plant and animal life. They resonate strongly as contemporary evocations of the etchings of phytographic regions of Brazil created almost 150 years earlier by Martius for his *Flora brasiliensis*. Burle Marx's vision for the Parque Zoobotânico sought to present an urban audience with accessible and compellingly aestheticized grafts of Brazil's diverse ecologies.

Sítio Santo Antônio da Bica, Guaratiba

In 1949 Burle Marx and his younger brother Guilherme Siegfried Marx purchased a former coffee plantation, the Sítio Santo Antônio da Bica, at Barra de Guaratiba, a small village west of the center of Rio de Janeiro. The professional office Burle Marx e Companhia had been established six years earlier, and the plantation site would serve to accommodate the growing plant collection then located at their home in Leme as well as providing space for the establishment of an experimental plant nursery. A stream ran through the large 150-acre property along a steep hillside, and the land

FIGURE 5.18.
Roberto Burle Marx, *Flora da Amazônia*, 1962
© Burle Marx Landscape Design Studio

FIGURE 5.19.
Roberto Burle Marx, *Flora da caatinga*, 1962
© Burle Marx Landscape Design Studio

FIGURE 5.20.
Roberto Burle Marx, site plan of the Sítio Santo Antônio da Bica, Barra de Guaratiba
Drawing by Catherine Seavitt Nordenson

FIGURE 5.21.
Capela de Santo Antônio da Bica, Barra de Guaratiba, ca. 1970
Photo by Alair Gomes/Acervo da Fundação Biblioteca Nacional do Brasil

FIGURE 5.22.
Sítio Santo Antônio da Bica, Barra de Guaratiba, ca. 1949
Photo by Marcel Gautherot/Instituto Moreira Salles Collection

extended from the top of the hill to a flat marshy area below, providing a variety of microclimates. The property also included a small chapel, the Capela de Santo Antônio da Bica, originally dating from the seventeenth century and reconstructed in the late eighteenth century.[12] The chapel was restored by Burle Marx in the 1950s with the help of the architects Lúcio Costa and Carlos Leão, and the existing plantation farmhouse was renovated and enlarged by another of his frequent collaborators, the architect Wit-Olaf Prochnik. In 1963 additional work was completed by the architects Haroldo Barroso and Rubem Breitman on new pavilions to house the kitchens and an outdoor dining area.[13] Over the course of his 45-year ownership of the Sítio, Burle Marx continued to add structures, the last being the rugged brutalist veranda and painting studio constructed by the architect Acácio Gil Borsoi in the early 1990s, built from granite salvaged from nineteenth-century buildings demolished in downtown Rio de Janeiro. The Sítio is a manifold creation of both landscape and buildings, unfolding over time and space, very different from the architectural consistency of Niemeyer's complex of buildings at Pampulha. Similar to the eighteenth-century anglo-chinois *parcs à fabriques*, with their small ornamental follies, the Sitío's pavilions are distributed across this picturesque landscape, presenting stunning views that unfold throughout the sloped site.

The most significant aspect of the Sítio, however, is its development by Burle Marx for almost half a century as an experimental botanical garden. He wrote very little of the Sítio, and there is no reference to this plantation in any of his Conselho Federal de Cultura depositions. In 1973, the date of his last published deposition and the year before he stepped down from the Conselho, Burle Marx moved from the Leme neighborhood of Rio de Janeiro to the Sítio. It was his private garden, the site of a 45-year project of many experiments with the plants obtained from his travels throughout the country. The Sítio became a personal scientific research institution in the tradition of the great botanical gardens, with plants categorized and organized by species.

Burle Marx's extensive collection of plants included representative species of the families of Araceae, Bromeliaceae, Cycadaceae, Heliconiaceae, Marantaceae, Arecaceae, and Velloziaceae. Over 3,500 species of live plants were grown at the Sítio, and many of these were native flora collected by Burle Marx himself during his expeditions throughout the various geographic regions of Brazil. Continuing the long tradition of exploratory naturalist voyages in Brazil, he called these expeditions *viagens de coleta* (collection travels), searching for plants to be propagated at the Sítio for possible use in future garden designs. In 1975 he wrote: "It is necessary to be a good observer. A plant expedition can lose its integrity if it is not accompanied by observations *in loco* of the conditions in which plants are found. One must verify its location, light conditions, type of soil, humidity. It is also necessary to know the appropriate conditions required by each plant."[14] Thirty-seven previously unidentified species were discovered by Burle Marx during these expeditions, and their scientific botanical names include the Latinized *burle-marxii*.

To care for this plant collection at the Sítio, Burle Marx formed new lakes for aquatic species and developed shade structures to emulate the understory conditions of the forest. These extensive open-air shaded greenhouses (an area of almost three acres at the northern edge of the property) were covered with a shading fabric called *sombrite*, stretched across a slatted spanning structure, and were thus called the *sombral*. There are eleven separate *sombrais* clustered into this area. Two were named after Burle Marx's close friends, the Sombral Graziela Barroso and the Sombral Margaret Mee. Barroso was an exceptional Brazilian botanist affiliated with the Jardim Botânico of Rio de Janeiro; Mee was a British painter of botanical specimens from the Amazon rainforest, with a particular interest in bromeliads. Both regularly accompanied Burle Marx on his *coletas* and were frequent guests at the Sítio. The

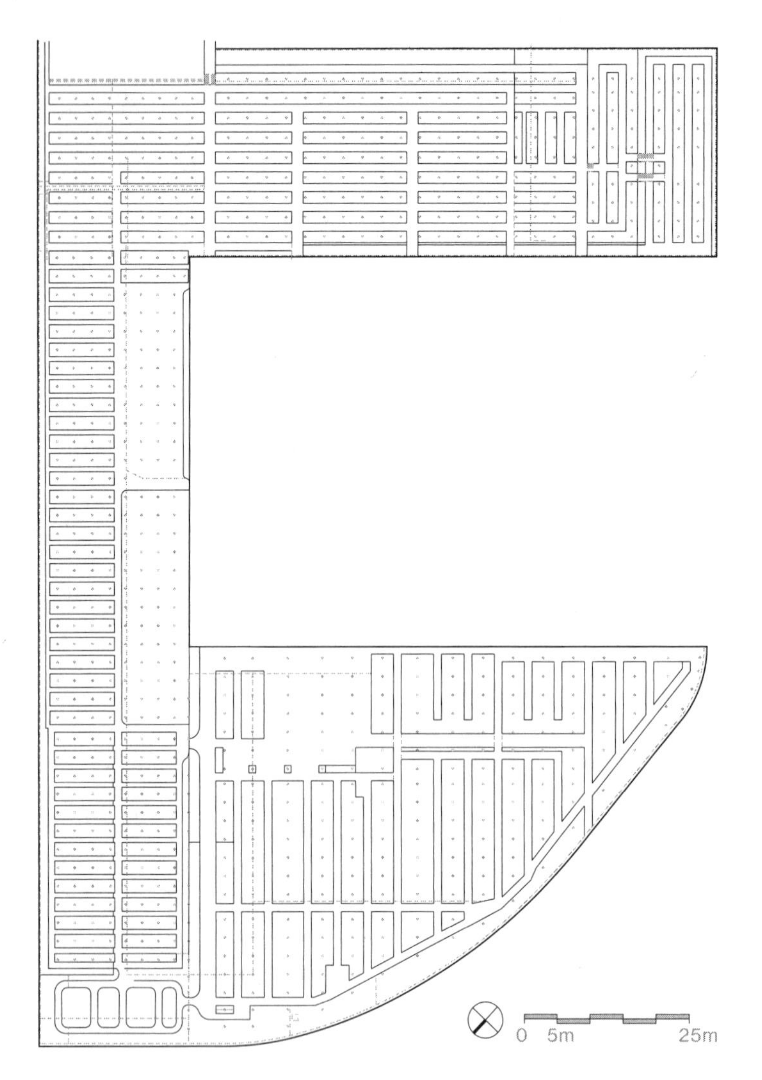

FIGURE 5.23. Roberto Burle Marx, plan of the Sombral Graziela Barroso plant nursery at the Sítio Santo Antônio da Bica, Barra de Guaratiba Drawing by Catherine Seavitt Nordenson

botanists Henrique Lahmeyer de Mello Barreto and Luiz Emygdio de Mello Filho, early collaborators and mentors of Burle Marx, were also regular visitors.

In 1985, just after the end of the 21-year period of the military dictatorship in Brazil, Burle Marx donated the Sítio Santo Antônio da Bica to the federal government's Fundação Nacional Pró-Memória, the executive arm of the Instituto do Patrimônio Histórico e Artístico Nacional (IPHAN). The former plantation site, now renamed the Sítio Roberto Burle Marx, thus became a Brazilian national cultural heritage site and the property of the Brazilian government, although Burle Marx continued to live at the Sítio until his death in 1994. The government was tasked with the responsibility of maintaining the site as a research center for the study of the Brazilian landscape and the conservation of nature as well as conserving its plant collections, buildings, and the objects within them in perpetuity. This responsibility, however, did not prevent the Brazilian Ministério do Exército (Ministry of the Army) from claiming a large portion of the property in 1992, the stretch between the Estrada da Barra de Guaratiba (now known as the Estrada Roberto Burle Marx) and the Canal da Maré, reducing the Sítio's acreage from 150 acres to just over 100 acres. In 2000 the Sítio Roberto Burle Marx was fully registered and landmarked in a new category developed by IPHAN, the *unidade especial* (special unit), as it did not fit neatly into any of the four *livros de tombo*. It is currently one of five such special units in Brazil and is known officially as the Centro Cultural Sítio Roberto Burle Marx.

FIGURE 5.24.
Interior of the sombral plant nursery, Sítio Santo Antônio da Bica, Barra de Guaratiba, ca. 1968
Photo by Marcel Gautherot/Instituto Moreira Salles Collection

Depositions: In Defense of the Botanical Garden

Given the focus of both his public work and his private experiments at the Sítio, it is clear that Burle Marx valued botanical gardens as well as the botanists and scientists who directed these research institutions. The botanical gardens of Brazil, particularly the Jardim Botânico of Rio de Janeiro, were addressed in four of his depositions delivered while a member of the Conselho Federal de Cultura. In "Situação atual do Jardim Botânico" (Current Conditions at the Botanical Garden), delivered in 1968, Burle Marx began with a global view of various botanical gardens and continued by describing the three significant botanical gardens of Brazil—the Jardim Botânico of Rio de Janeiro; the Jardim Botânico de São Paulo, for which he had prepared a renovation plan; and the Parque Zoobotânico de Brasília, an unexecuted project of his own design. He delivered strong support for the Jardim Botânico of Rio de Janeiro in the concise 1968 deposition entitled "Jardim Botânico" (The Botanical Garden of Rio de Janeiro), describing it as a cultural heritage site for Brazil but also as an important part of an international research network for knowledge exchange. He often affirmed his position that the botanical garden in Brazil should be considered an indispensable cultural institution for the promotion and conservation of complex natural ecosystems. He warned that the institution of the Jardim Botânico of Rio de Janeiro was at risk—not only was its area reduced, but its collections were poorly maintained, valuable species were disappearing, and its leadership appeared to have abandoned its scientific mission.

The subsequent deposition "Jardim Botânico e Horto Florestal" (The Botanical Garden and Woodland Nursery), delivered in 1969, appealed for the protection of the Jardim Botânico of Rio de Janeiro and its adjacent forest nursery. Here Burle Marx grappled with a complex social issue that was often at odds with his advocacy of conservation: the encroachment of informal housing settlements into natural areas. As the population of these *favelas* surged in Brazil during the 1960s, the government quickly realized that the national intertwined issues of dramatic income inequality, rural populations migrating to urban centers, and insufficient housing supply required attention. The Banco Nacional de Habitação (BNH: National Housing Bank), established by the military regime in 1964, was developed as a financial entity to address the housing issue through the construction of social housing.[15] Burle Marx comments on two problems that appeared at the Horto Florestal—the presence of informal housing settlements and the ceding by the government of a significant area of the lands belonging to the Horto Florestal for the construction of new social housing as part of the national *favela* removal strategy.[16] These questions of land use, environmental protection, social inequity, informal housing, and displacement raise the challenging ethical issues of social justice, ecological integrity, and resource conservation that are still being debated today.

Burle Marx's last consular deposition addressing the topic of the botanical garden,

"Jardim Botânico de Belo Horizonte" (The Botanical Garden of Belo Horizonte), was delivered in 1970. There he returned to Minas Gerais and the botanical legacy of his mentor, Henrique Lahmeyer de Mello Barreto, discussing the importance of the cultural institution of the botanical garden and referring to one of his then-current projects, a commission to study the possibility of developing a new botanical garden for the Universidade Federal de Minas Gerais. He was thrilled by the prospect of establishing such a garden and exploring the diverse and complex phytogeographic regions of Minas Gerais. Yet he bemoaned again the speculative real estate development occurring at the edges of the territory designated for this garden. Burle Marx insisted that the full extent of the garden be maintained and protected from encroachment, as a reflection of the historically innovative urbanism of the planned city of Belo Horizonte.

Roberto Burle Marx: Depositions

Current Conditions at the Botanical Garden
February 7, 1968

The Botanical Garden of Rio de Janeiro
September 27, 1968

The Botanical Garden and Woodland Nursery
August 26, 1969

The Botanical Garden of Belo Horizonte
May 6, 1970

Current Conditions at the Botanical Garden
February 7, 1968

Delivered to the Plenary Session of the Conselho Federal de Cultura on February 7, 1968. Published as Roberto Burle Marx, "Situacão atual do Jardim Botânico" (Current Conditions at the Botanical Garden), *Cultura: Conselho Federal de Cultura* (Ministério da Educação e Cultura) 2, no. 8 (February 1968): 55–59.

Fellow Counselors:

Having recently traveled to Morocco, France, and England, I have had the occasion to visit the botanical gardens of these countries. While at Kew Gardens, I felt great pleasure upon encountering the Brazilian plants. Some of these plants were sent there by me, while others were cultivated by gardeners and botanists who maintain the high quality of these nurseries and collections.

Currently there are three botanical gardens in Brazil. There should be more, but these institutions lack permanence and longevity. The first is in Rio de Janeiro and the second in São Paulo. In Belo Horizonte, a botanical nursery was established by Henrique Lahmeyer de Mello Barreto at his own expense. He planted young tree shoots and prepared them for transplanting, covering their roots with soil and wrapping them in burlap. Finally, the third botanical garden is in Brasília, where the concept was to reunite the botanical garden with the zoological and geological elements.[17] Unfortunately, due to the administration's lack of continuity, this project remains at square one, on the drawing board. Those responsible for this are the zoobotanical park's directors, who believe themselves capable of resolving problems on their own, when in fact an entire team of botanists, plant pathologists, agronomists, and gardeners is needed. Note that these gardeners should have a certain education—although some of them do have good intentions, they have insufficient knowledge to address issues such as plant culture, plant maintenance, and the process of transplanting and propagating plants. The team should also include zoologists, veterinarians, ecologists, and phytogeographers, all under the direction of landscape architects, who would be entrusted with the aesthetic aspects of the challenge.

The establishment of such a zoobotanical park would involve challenges that could only be resolved by a team, not through the deliberations of a single administrator. Such administrators have so often demonstrated their inability to manage parks.

FIGURE 5.25.

Das Große Tropenhaus (Great Tropical Pavilion) in ruins after World War II, Berlin-Dahlem Botanical Garden, Berlin, 1947

Photo by Roman Vishniac/© Mara Vishniac Kohn, International Center of Photography

I recently visited our Jardim Botânico in Rio de Janeiro, which I do periodically, and this time I had a most melancholy surprise. I looked for the collection of *Philodendrons*, and I discovered these have been almost decimated. The collection of *Begonias*, gathered by Apparício Pereira and Edmundo Pereira, had almost entirely disappeared. The collection of Orchidaceae is also being destroyed, and the Cactaceae, cultivated by the gardeners Otto Voll (recently deceased) and Marchetti, are not protected from the rain and will likely perish.

Tilapias have been introduced into the lake displaying aquatic plants. An herbivore, this African fish is a predator of the flora that is so representative of the lakes and rivers of Brazil. The Nymphaeae and *Victoria regia* will disappear as a result of these fish.[18]

The areas of the garden devoted to plant collections are being significantly reduced. A parking lot is currently being built that will displace part of the collection. At London's Kew Gardens, cars park in the surrounding streets, as the responsible authorities would never have the audacity to mutilate the garden by reducing its area. One has the impression that the scientific and didactic functions of Rio de Janeiro's botanical garden are disappearing and being replaced by the workings of a public garden. Yet until 1962 the Jardim Botânico was as important as its counterparts throughout the world.

Its property area has diminished year by year. Its dimensions during the period of Dom João VI were delimited by a line that departs from the base of the Dois Irmãos mountains, to the Hotel Leblon, extending along the whole beachfront of Leblon, Ipanema, the slopes of the Morro do Cantagalo and Cabritos, the ridge that runs between Botafogo and Copacabana, wrapping around the cove of Urca, all of the beach at Botafogo, continuing past the ridge of Mundo Nóvo, between Botafogo and Laranjeiras, Morro de Dona Marta, the base of Corcovado, extending past the ridge of Sumaré, going further to the Mesa do Imperador, embracing the Parque do Cidade, and closing the circuit again at the base of Dois Irmãos. These were the limits of the area that was acquired by the order of Dom João VI and given to Rodrigo de Freitas in 1808 for the establishment of a gunpowder factory and in its environs an acclimation garden. This garden was first designated as the Real Horto (Royal Nursery), then was transformed into the Real Horto Botânico (Royal Botanical Nursery), and finally became the Jardim Botânico (Botanical Garden).

Dom João VI, upon establishing this acclimation garden, also intuited that the director should be trained and knowledgeable in the realm of living nature, particularly in the field of botany. For this reason, the first appointed director was Serpa Brandão, who came directly from Portugal to fulfill this assignment. It was considered important that the subsequent directors of the Jardim Botânico should be botanical scientists or researchers from an allied discipline. From then onward, tradition dictated that the leadership of the Jardim Botânico would always be entrusted to a well-known scientist. Lamentably, this tradition was broken in recent years.

The specialists that succeeded João Barbosa Rodrigues—Alberto Loefgren, Adolpho Ducke, João Geraldo Kuhlmann, Alexandre Curt Brade, Fernando Romano Milanèz, Carlos Toledo Rizzini, Graziela Maciel Barroso, Armando de Mattos, Apparício Pereira Duarte, and Paulo Occhioni—were jettisoned from the Jardim Botânico. The team of trained gardeners was disbanded, resulting in serious damage to the maintenance of both the live and preserved plant specimens, including the herbarium collection and the preserved fruit collection.

Currently, the garden is being invaded by a series of construction projects that should not be undertaken in this location intended for plants, a place that conserves a rich and underrepresented flora. These projects will reduce an already insufficient space.

When looking specifically for Brazilian plants at the Jardim Botânico, one finds their numbers extremely reduced, in comparison with other exotic plants. There was a period during which Brazilian flora was very well represented, but today almost nothing is left. To illustrate this point, here are the conditions of the few remaining Brazilian collections:

Melastomataceae—Family with more than 1,000 species represented in the Brazilian flora, of which practically none remain at the Jardim Botânico.
Convolvulaceae—Collection semiextinct.
Verbenaceae, of the genus *Clerodendron*—Extinct.
Araceae—Semiextinct, with the remaining ones in a very bad state of cultivation.
Dieffenbachia—In a deplorable state.
Bromeliaceae—Grouped in the middle of a dense forested area, without any identification plaques.
Labiadas—Practically extinct, with only exotic species still existing.
Malpighiaceae—Semiextinct.
Acanthaeceae—In a deplorable state, dying from exhaustion and lack of care.
Amaryllidaceae—Semiextinct.
Genera *Crinum*, *Panacraceum*, and *Aloe*—Also in a state of semiextinction.
Passifloraceae—There are more than three hundred species of *Passiflora* represented in the Brazilian flora. The collection is completely extinct.
Aristolochiaceae—This family has had the same bad luck.
Euphorbiaceae—Only exotic species remain.
Lauraceae—The same situation of semiextinction.
Pteridophyta—A group extremely well represented in the indigenous flora but having the same bad luck as the preceding examples.
Other extinct collections: Oxalidaceae, Gesneriaceae, Amaranthaceae, Ciclantaceae, Scrophulariaceae, short-period Leguminoseae, Commelinaceae, Urticaceae, and Rosaceae.

The Maranthaceae have been abandoned and are dying from a lack of care,

> and the heliconias are in a very bad state. The florae of the *cerrado*, *restinga*, *saxícola*, *gneiss-granitica*, *caatinga*, and *canga ferruginosa* are not represented.

Must we bear witness to this destruction as a hopeless misfortune, without protest? When several of the glasshouses of Kew Gardens were damaged from the bombing during the war, the government prioritized the reconstruction of that institution. The Botanical Garden of Berlin at Dahlem was almost completely destroyed by bombing. Today, a little more than two decades later, it has been completely rebuilt, including what is referred to as the Große Tropenhaus (Great Tropical Pavilion) and the herbarium.

This decadence at the Jardim Botânico has been particularly felt in recent years and now has reached its apex. During my recent visit, I saw workers disposing leaves in the river—in other places, this material would be utilized to make a rich compost for fertilizer. And these workers, who have not been instructed about gardening, were using the identification plaques as dustpans. These plaques, after this improper use, are then returned to the wrong locations, compromising in a comical manner the classification and identification of the many plants in the garden.

I would never have imagined that such incomprehension could reach this level. This can only be a result of the direction given by the garden's current administration.[19]

Along the allée of mangos, trees are dying and are not replaced; the lakes are silting up from erosive rains; numerous exemplary species are missing their identification plaques and are not being cared for properly. The purpose of a botanical garden is not merely to cut grass and sell plants, often relinquishing the exemplary specimens of the collections, but to provide the ideal conditions for study and to serve as a scientific entity. To care for a botanical garden is not to transform it into a public park—its ultimate objective should be scientific research.

Given these observations, I unfortunately must conclude that we are quickly approaching the melancholy end of our Jardim Botânico, or at least its role as a cultural archive for scientific knowledge that it has bequeathed to Brazil for more than one hundred and fifty years.

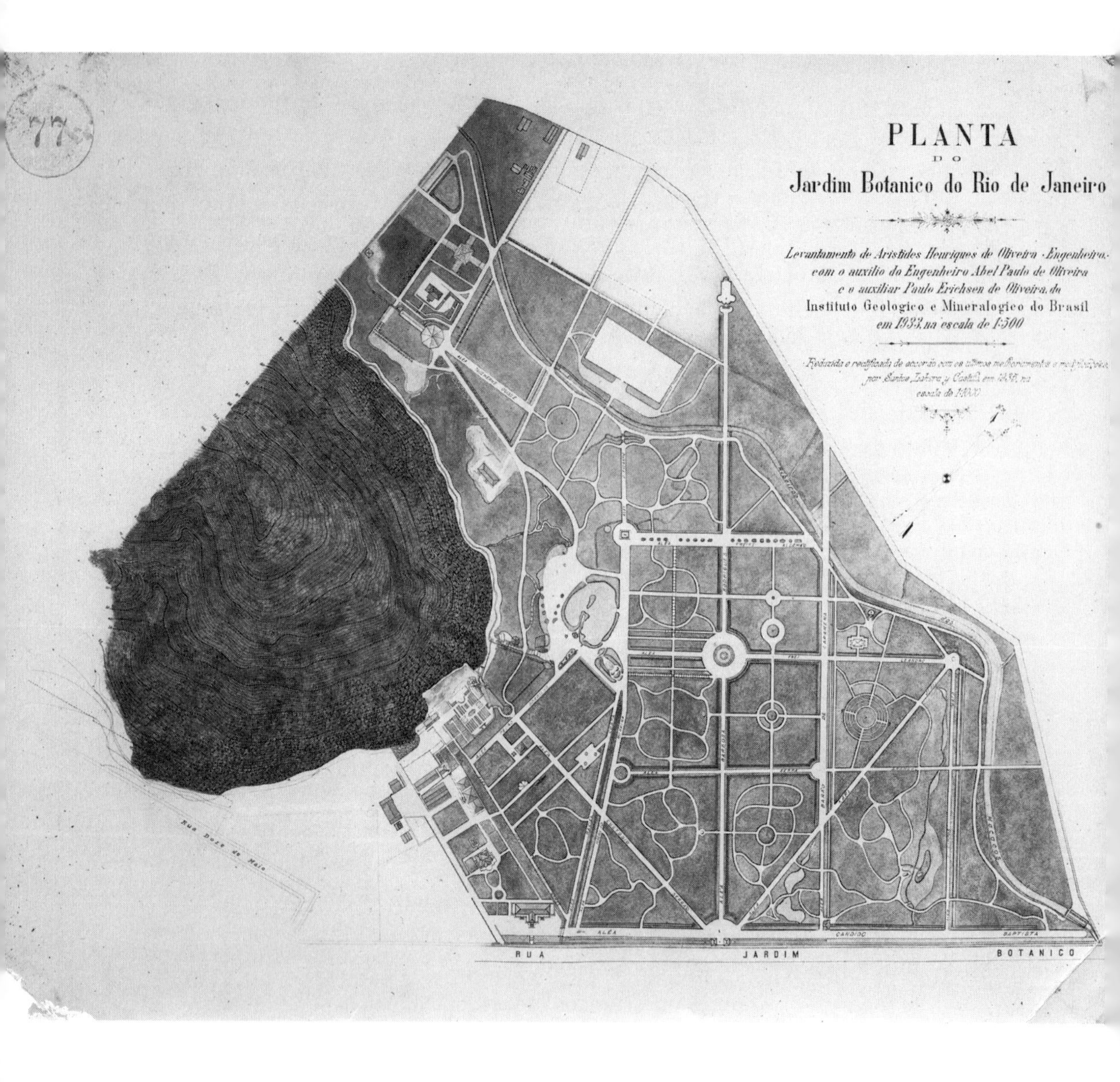

FIGURE 5.26.
Plan of the Jardim Botânico, Rio de Janeiro, 1933
Acervo Museu do Meio Ambiente/Instituto de Pesquisas Jardim Botânico do Rio de Janeiro

The Botanical Garden of Rio de Janeiro
September 27, 1968

Delivered to the Plenary Session of the Conselho Federal de Cultura on September 27, 1968. Published as Roberto Burle Marx, "Jardim Botânico" (The Botanical Garden), *Cultura: Conselho Federal de Cultura* (Ministério da Educação e Cultura) 2, no. 16 (October 1968): 16.

As a member of this plenary session, I have often expressed my personal concern for the incomprehensible loss of our natural reserves and for the offenses that our landscapes and artistic heritage have suffered in the face of continual vandalism. Yet all of my protests, while understood and applauded by my comrades on this eminent plenary assembly, systematically face the indifference and insensitivity of those responsible for public administration.

During the session yesterday, September 26, we heard the public condemnation made by the honorable counselor Djacir Menezes regarding the notice in the morning newspaper of the same day, concerning Decreto No. 62.698, executed on May 14, 1968.[20] Our esteemed president has designated me with the task of presenting a motion regarding this subject.

I do this as an expression of protest and am counting on the necessary help from this plenary assembly to transmit this to the attention of the esteemed president of the Republic, who will certainly understand our obligation to preserve one of our most rare and culturally relevant natural reserves.[21]

Along the same lines, I note the importance of observing the law, given the registration of the Jardim Botânico as a cultural landmark, and thus preventing building construction and alterations at the garden's surrounding areas.

Therefore let it be known to the directors of the Department of National Historic and Artistic Heritage, the entity responsible for the patrimony and defense of all of our historic and artistic holdings, that the Jardim Botânico and its adjacent nursery, the Horto Florestal, constitute exceptional examples of both national and international interest.

FIGURE 5.27.
Entrance to the Horto Florestal from the Jardim Botânico, Rio de Janeiro, 1942
Acervo Museu do Meio Ambiente/Instituto de Pesquisas Jardim Botânico do Rio de Janeiro

The Botanical Garden and Woodland Nursery
August 26, 1969

Delivered to the Plenary Session of the Conselho Federal de Cultura on August 26, 1969. Published as Roberto Burle Marx, "Jardim Botânico e Horto Florestal" (The Botanical Garden and Woodland Nursery), *Cultura: Conselho Federal de Cultura* (Ministério da Educação e Cultura) 3, no. 26 (August 1969): 18–24.

Once again, I am obliged to make use of the deposition to call attention to a topic that is not receiving the scrutiny that it deserves, despite its vital importance in defining the cultural and scientific progress of this nation.

I am referring to the systematic attempts at mutilation that the Jardim Botânico and Horto Florestal have undergone, from both a misdirected woodlands policy and an inability to defend these historically inseparable sites.

Regarding natural resources, it is necessary to understand the choice of legal proceedings and methods of investigation in order to arrive at a clear position on the existing situation as well as the due care expected for their preservation, exploration, and utilization.

It is not enough for experts merely to study the occurrence or distribution of resources. It is necessary to understand the consequences of their use. Within these guidelines, we must defend a strategy for the effective protection of natural resources that includes the policy of permanent preservation. And this demanding task is consistent with initiatives that should be taken to educate and develop a cultural understanding in the BRAZILIAN people. Therefore the biologists, agronomists, foresters, researchers, botanists, and so many other experts linked to the subject of resources should consider the strategy of conservation. These protected nature reserves provide sites for research, aesthetic appreciation, and even tourism.

The administrative organizations that establish standards for buildings, site access, and housing must maintain reasonable distances so that these architectural developments do not disfigure the natural environment. Public areas must not be affected. This includes both the overall landscape and the existing plant cover, whether remnant or secondary. If buildings are to be built, it is important that they be carefully integrated into the landscape, in a manner that does not disfigure the existing conditions.

In addition, it is the responsibility of our public administration to support funding to restore or conserve landscapes, advised by vigilant individuals who understand the importance of protecting these territories.

Often these areas require immediate action because they are being rapidly destroyed, despite being parks of a didactic character, national parks, or protected forests.

Consider the Jardim Botânico: its original area has been subdivided and significantly reduced by shrewd and skillful forces. It is not only recently that the Jardim has suffered such amputation. For example, the entire area now belonging to the Jockey Club was ceded from the Jardim Botânico. This was the area of the garden that sustained valuable collections of plants from the lower Amazon basin and other regions, collected by the eminent botanists Ducke, Kuhlmann, Barbosa Rodrigues, and others. This section of the garden was transferred to the Jockey Club despite vehement protests from the distinguished botanist Pacheco Leão, who was obliged to cede under pressure.

Natural resources must be conserved for future generations, with the goal of perpetuating this patrimony that belongs to an entire nation, not merely to a single group.

The Horto Florestal da Gávea, the forest nursery, consists of a two-hundred acre parcel of land, the natural prolongation of the Jardim Botânico. Having been annexed to the garden long ago, it is included in the published history of the Jardim Botânico. The Horto Florestal had been used for the production of seeds and woodland tree seedlings for the purpose of distribution and sale. The Horto has functioned as a productive nursery since 1910, and seeds for future propagation are drawn from its cuttings. All of the technical activities for which the Horto was intended have not been disrupted until now. From 1933 to 1942 its activities remained under the jurisdiction of the Seção de Silvicultura (Forestry Section) of what was then the Serviço Florestal (Forest Service). In 1942 Decreto No. 9.015 deemed that "the area of the Jardim Botânico shall be enlarged to include the Horto Florestal da Gávea, with its respective installations."[22] Thus the expansion of the Jardim Botânico was assured, an ideal outcome for this overpopulated garden containing more than 30,000 plant species. The Horto Florestal is an integral part of the Jardim Botânico. It is not acceptable for part of its area to be taken away and ceded to the Banco Nacional de Habitação. This act would only address the housing problem and would completely negate the cultural validity of this institution, where a great number of reputable botanists, both Brazilian and foreign, have produced significant scientific work. If the cession of this area is executed, we will see the Jardim Botânico transformed into the backyard of this new housing project, as was stated so effectively by our eminent colleague Pedro Calman.

In 1961 a forty-acre area of the Horto Florestal was pursued ambitiously by the governor of Guanabara in order to develop a "cemetery-park," but his desired goal was not achieved, given the protests of the local neighborhood residents against such an initiative.[23] Such arbitrary land claims violate the very principal and purpose of the Jardim Botânico, a site of scientific and historic heritage. That proposition did not represent the best use of the area of the Horto Florestal, given the incompatibility of its purpose with that suggestion. Nor is it acceptable to install high-voltage electrical towers and other facilities, as suggested by the Ministério de Minas e Energia (Ministry of Mines and Energy), or to resolve the problem of housing with the construction of thirty-two five-story buildings.[24] The Código Florestal (Forestry Code) of 1965 states wisely: "The existing forests of the national territory, and other forms of plant material known to be useful to the lands that they cover, are assets held in the common interest for all the inhabitants of the Nation."[25] As the Jardim Botânico is part of the cultural heritage of this country, it is necessary that this and similar areas be defined and protected once and for all, so that they are not ambitiously pursued by government entities. They do not have the right to ruin an area with a defined use and an unequivocal purpose.

On the other hand, the purpose of the Horto Florestal is to support the propagation of seeds and the reproduction of trees as well as to safeguard the many species that are difficult to propagate or fated for extinction. Its purpose is not merely to establish eucalyptus saplings or Christmas trees.

The work of reforestation, conservation, organization, cleanliness, and improvement in the area of the Horto Florestal—the area added to the Jardim Botânico in 1942 as part of Decreto No. 9.015—aims to achieve ecological and thereby scientific objectives. These actions also address the landscape objectives inherent in the specialized laws of forest development (see Decreto-Lei No. 289, February 28, 1967, article 3, item IV).[26]

The existing woodlands of this area include countless trees, such as the *roxinho*, *cássia*, *angico vermelho*, and others. Their seeds, once propagated, will produce seedlings that are required for a robust plant community. They are indispensable for the expansion of forest ecosystems that protect soil and water. In addition, they reduce the toxic effects of carbon monoxide and the impact of the strong winds produced by storms in this forest complex of the Jardim Botânico, Horto Florestal, and Parque Nacional da Tijuca. This is a region with special ecological characteristics.

Given the fragile conditions at this zone, it is not advisable to build such residential housing, driven by real estate speculation, as this would compromise the health of the forest. Those responsible for enforcing the law must uphold it and defend what are considered "assets of common interest" for all of this country's inhabitants.[27]

In every civilized society, there eventually emerges a desire to conserve the existing forests, to improve their conditions and yield, and to create new woodlands to replace those that are degraded or that are being degraded by damaging agents. It is necessary to manage these forests appropriately so they will not be destroyed. The Jardim Botânico should have an area zoned for future expansion, as there are an enormous number of Brazilian species that are not yet represented in the garden.

As part of the recent reorganization of the Ministério da Agricultura, based on Lei Delegada (Authorized Law) No. 9 of October 11, 1962, the Departamento de Recursos Naturais Renováveis (DRNR: Department of Renewable Natural Resources) was created. At this time, the Serviço Florestal, first established by Decreto-Lei No. 9.821 on December 23, 1938, ceased to exist.

Within this new governmental structure, new studies and preliminary projects under the jurisdiction of the DRNR were authorized by the Ministry of Agriculture in early March 1963. These studies continued for nine consecutive months, finally culminating with the signing of Decreto No. 52.442 into law on September 3, 1963.[28]

Since then, the fragmentation of the Horto Florestal from the Jardim Botânico has become even more evident: the accountable agency, DRNR, has been in charge of this mission since 1965. Its disregard for the forested canopy of the Horto is evident—DRNR has not fulfilled its mission of forest protection. The irresponsibility of this department, along with the move of the DRNR administration to Brasília, does not demonstrate evidence of the respect and responsibility needed for the improvement of forests through constructive work and technological development. It negates the importance of maintenance, protection, and even conservation of the entire complex. It has neglected to protect these woodlands against those that have attempted to destroy, damage, and remove trees. It has permitted penetration into the forest of elements that are not compatible with woodland health and that have impeded the natural regeneration of forest cover and other forms of vegetation, mistreating the plants and mature seed-carrying trees.

It appears that the DRNR has determined that it would be simpler to delegate all responsibility for its work to inexperienced nonprofessionals. Nor has the DRNR leveraged the Código Florestal to establish new forested areas under the protection of permanent preservation. Permission was given for the installation of high-voltage electrical transmission towers in forested areas. Worse yet, an area of restored forest was ceded to the Ministério de Minas e Energia for the construction of the Furnas Hydroelectric Plant.[29] This was permitted without any study examining the potential impacts of this power plant on the surrounding forest. In addition, this transfer of our land and our forestry heritage was done without the corresponding approval and consent of the Ministério da Agricultura, with the claim that this was outside of its jurisdiction of forested areas. It is at the Horto Florestal that one can clearly see the presence of truly impressive examples of a rich environment, from the waterfalls that nourish the Jardim Botânico to the groves of trees that contribute to a heterogeneous, complex, and diverse environment. These are now violated by concrete posts and barbed-wire fences, in contrast with their previous enchanting appearance. With its extension of the Horto Florestal, the Jardim Botânico reaches the Iglésias stream and the Rio dos Macacos and extends along the Rua Pacheco Leão. Here excavations by Furnas for the construction of residential buildings are devastating the banks of the river, in flagrant disregard of the Código Florestal.

Many diverse species are found at the Morro da Margarida, and one can clearly observe a vigorous and successful natural regeneration.[30]

As for the proposed residential complex adjacent to the Horto Florestal at Rua Pacheco Leão, the presence of these buildings will serve as a catalyst for the construction of additional buildings, with the goal of housing the families now living in *favelas* in the vicinity of the Lagoa Rodrigo de Freitas. Such is the difficult and uncertain situation that is currently affecting the forested areas in the vicinity of the Horto.

The Jardim Botânico proper, its adjacent forests, and the areas contiguous with the Parque Nacional da Tijuca and beyond will have their forested areas compromised.

Therefore the public interest in this case, for this region and these green spaces, should be the preservation of the Horto and other forested areas in this zone. These should be protected by the responsible governmental authorities, through the use of "permanent preservation" in accordance with the concepts and principles set forth in the Código Florestal (Lei No. 4.771 of September 15, 1965).

Consequently, the concession of any area of the Horto Florestal, whether small parcels or its entirety of over 200 acres, would constitute a violation of both cultural institutions and history. The relationship of the Jardim Botânico and the Horto Florestal must be considered an indivisible whole, with a combined area of over 340 acres. Like other fragments of the suffering patrimony of the Brazilian forest, this area should be protected, not abused and subjected to devastation and loss.

Places of natural beauty must be preserved for history, as well as their surrounding green spaces, for these serve to unify the landscape. This position is defended by the first article of the Código Florestal, and even outside of our country by the International Convention of the Peoples of the Americas, countersigned by the National Congress (Decreto Legislativo No. 3 of February 13, 1968—article V, no. 1 and no. 2).

The restoration of small deforested areas must be done as part of the necessary work needed to support the recomposition of a forest. This includes the regulation and discipline of land use planning, the establishment of vigilance by qualified personnel, and the organization of a seed bank—these actions are for the benefit of all and support scientific and historical work.

The Jardim Botânico houses a collection of plants from the states of Minas Gerais, Amazonas, Goiás, and beyond. These plants provide a source for the seeds that will enable the survival of species otherwise destined for extinction as well as serving a scientific purpose. The springs within these contiguous terrains at the Jardim Botânico are of extraordinary importance for the park's conservation. They must be protected, and the best technique is to maintain dense vegetation that will in turn protect the sources of these streams. We are fortunate still to have an area with these dimensions—devastation throughout the Estado da Guanabara has vastly modified the landscape, and the destruction of the flora of forests, rock outcrops, and sand dunes has provoked heavy erosion. We must protect the remnant areas of our surviving forest patrimony at all costs.

In view of the above, I announce to this council that, in accordance with the law, I will make a recommendation to the director of the Department of National Historic and Artistic Heritage to consider the protection of the Horto Florestal as an indispensable and integral part of the Jardim Botânico, whose historic patrimony is already registered and protected by law.

This initiative is consistent with the spirit of the law regarding the protection of nature and of water sources recently proposed by the well-informed counsel of the Comissão de Legislação e Normas (Commission of Legislation and Norms). This agency has been selected to advise the legislative body currently tasked with constitutional reform.

The Botanical Garden of Belo Horizonte
May 6, 1970

Delivered to the Plenary Session of the Conselho Federal de Cultura on May 6, 1970. Published as Roberto Burle Marx, "Jardim Botânico de Belo Horizonte" (The Botanical Garden of Belo Horizonte), *Cultura: Conselho Federal de Cultura* (Ministério da Educação e Cultura) 4, no. 35 (May 1970): 36–38.

I was called by Marcello Vasconcellos Coelho, president of the Universidade Federal de Minas Gerais, to study the possibility of establishing a botanical garden at the location of the former Instituto Agronômico.[31] This is a great honor, particularly because this location was once the site of an arboretum established by the now deceased botanist Henrique Lahmeyer de Mello Barreto, an extraordinary scientist who developed an herbarium containing over 30,000 classified species. The arboretum was created through personal sacrifice and exceptional unselfishness. The budget provided was minimal, yet even so this woodland nursery exists because of the great love and dedication of this man. If more funding and support had been available, he would have done even more.

This idea of creating a botanical garden is most commendable, above all in a city whose planning was initiated from a modern urban design. Today, however, the city has been transformed into a true labyrinth destitute of green space—cluttered, disorganized, a place where it is difficult even to imagine a botanical garden.

A botanical garden for our time should be considered not only from an abstract point of view but as a garden poised to reveal the unique flora of the state of Minas Gerais. These include the *saxícola* flora found in rocky formations of gneiss-granite, iron ore, limestone, and sandstone-quartz; flora of the meander belt of the Rio São Francisco; flora of the diverse types of *cerrado*; flora of the Serra do Mar; and flora of the *caatinga*.[32] These ecological aspects must be emphasized, as they will provide us with a more extensive understanding of the region from both a scientific and cultural point of view. However, the terrain established for the garden has been massively reduced—once consisting of three hundred acres, it has now been reduced to an area of one hundred acres.

The lands of the Instituto Agronômico were divided by the governor of the state into four parcels. One hundred acres were transferred by covenant to the Universidade Federal de Minas Gerais for the construction of the Museu de História Natural and the Botanical Garden of Belo Horizonte. Another area of thirty-four acres was ceded by covenant to the Fundação Nacional do Bem Estar do Menor (FUNABEM: National Youth Welfare Foundation), from which a parcel was transferred to the Serviço Nacional de Aprendizagem Industrial (SENAI: National Department of Industrial Training) for the construction of medical offices.[33] In this area, trees are already being cut down. A third area of one hundred and twenty acres was sold to the Caixa Econômica Federal (Federal Savings and Loan Bank: Decreto No. 10.212 of December 30, 1966) for the construction of a housing complex.[34] In this area, the layout of the streets is now partially complete. Finally, the fourth area of forty-five acres was transferred to the Companhia de Urbanização da Serra do Curral (Urban Development Company of the Serra do Curral) for future development into lots. This area is covered with a forest of inestimable value.

Now, in a city that strives to be a pioneering center of civilization, a green space such as this new botanical garden is vital for cultural and educational development. Its importance has been enhanced with the initiative of the rector of the Universidade Federal de Minas Gerais to construct a museum of natural history. The reduction of the available area for the Botanical Garden is criminal. I believe that we must fight to ensure that this entire territory is given exclusively to the university, so that the work initiated by Mello Barreto may be continued in a dignified manner.

One of the neighbors benefiting from the development of this area dared to suggest that additional trees be cut down to allow for direct sunlight on their recently constructed swimming pool. It is curious that certain politicians do not understand that progress is intimately linked to the maintenance of our patrimonial assets. One *mineiro* authority even suggested that the development of the terrain of the former Instituto Agronômico is the "price of progress."[35] By extension, progress is thus the destruction of forest reserves and green spaces.

Today on the radio I heard the suggestion that the carnival parades in Rio de Janeiro should be held in the Parque do Flamengo, in an area of plantings that are still being completed, where the flux of visitors into the park has contributed to the destruction of many recently planted botanical species. The maintenance of this park is challenging enough as it is—if this suggestion were approved, it would mean mass destruction. Such reasoning could only come from someone with no respect for nature and no understanding of the importance of green spaces in our cities.

In Nova Friburgo, a deplorable thing is happening. More than sixteen centenary eucalyptus trees, each approximately three and a half meters in circumference, were cut down in the Praça Getúlio Vargas in order to construct a playground.[36] Measures must be taken to prevent this damage from continuing; the municipality is now cutting down the magnolias planted in the Praça do Suspiro. Once again, it is clear that municipal administrators should not be allowed to make certain decisions without previous consultation with a specialized agency, such as, for example, the Department of National Historic and Artistic Heritage, which would provide advice and direction so that these abuses of authority will not be perpetrated. Brazil has approximately 4,200 municipal districts. It is imperative that every municipality is made aware of its responsibility for the preservation of our forestry heritage and understands that this is necessary not only in rural areas but in urban areas as well.[37] I was in Cabo Frio recently and can attest that the Companhia Nacional de Álcalis is planting an army of *Casuarinas* in unified lines along one of the beaches of Arraial do Cabo. They are also painting the rocks white, spilling their whitewash and lime and polluting water that was once crystalline and transparent but is now milky and opaque. I am noting just a few examples that I have observed recently while traveling in various regions and cities of Brazil.

As for the Botanical Gardens of Belo Horizonte, it is important that the governmental authorities understand that this territory must not be used as speculative real estate to the detriment of our collective interest. I appeal to our president and my fellow counselors so that we may take the necessary precautions to prevent this from continuing. And I also call for the authorities to reconsider the possibility of maintaining this area of the Universidade Federal de Minas Gerais intact so that it may have, in the very near future, a botanical garden that is worthy of the cultural significance for which this state aspires and that it deserves to have.

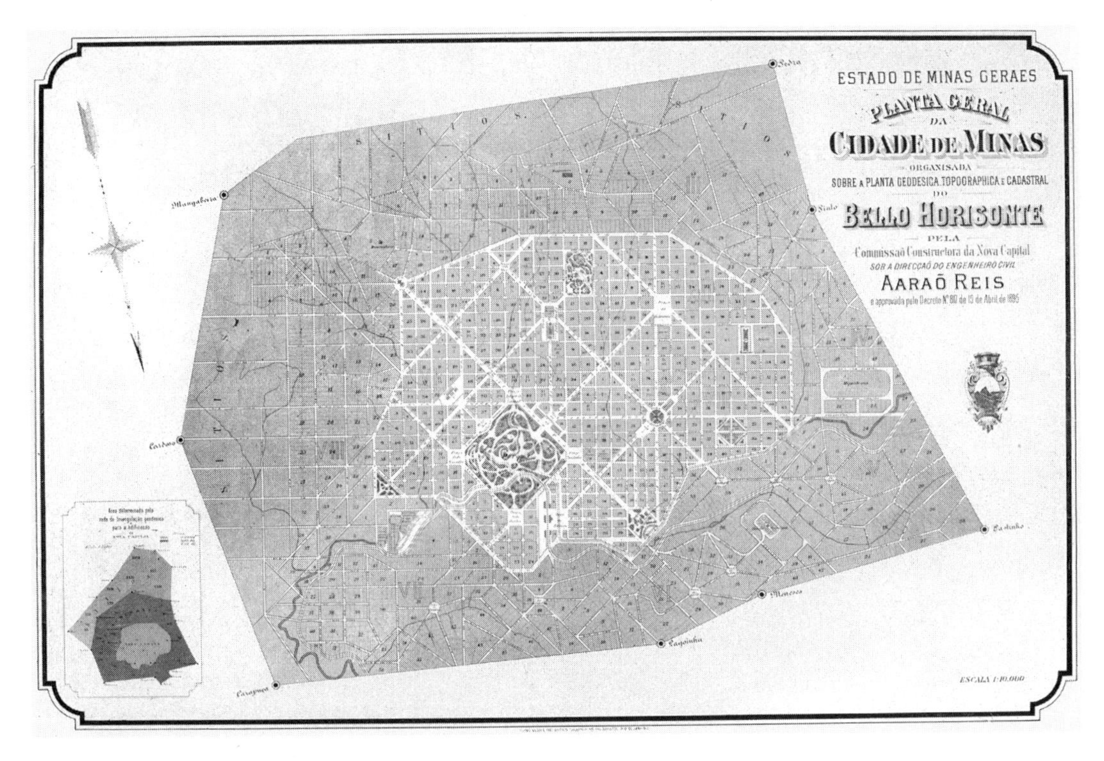

FIGURE 5.28.
Aarão Reis, plan of Belo Horizonte, Minas Gerais, 1895
Acervo do Museu Histórico Abílio Barreto/Fundação Municipal de Cultura

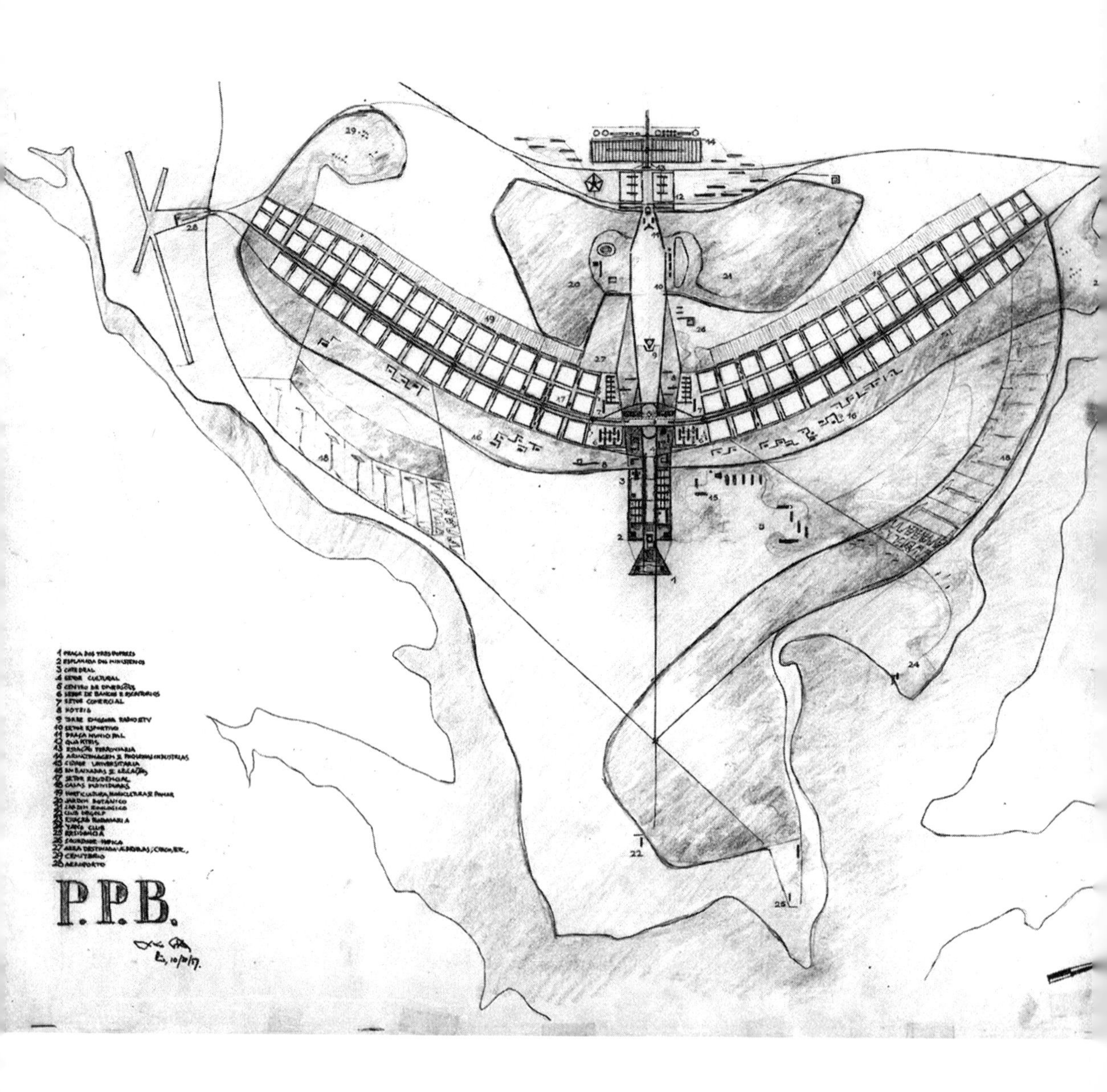

FIGURE 6.1.
Lúcio Costa, competition drawing for the *plano piloto* of the new capital of Brasília, 1957
Arquivo Público do Distrito Federal

CHAPTER 6

Military Gardens

Concurrently with Burle Marx's participation as an appointed member of the Conselho Federal de Cultura during the late 1960s and early 1970s, he obtained several commissions from the military regime for new projects in the capital city of Brasília. His earlier commission for the Parque Zoobotânico of 1961 was not executed; the continued occupation of the pioneer settlement of Candangolândia prevented what would have been a sweeping demolition of the community's buildings and redevelopment of the vast site. In addition, Brazil's general economic difficulties in the early 1960s, with skyrocketing inflation and a lack of international monetary aid, resulted in the virtual end of construction in Brasília after the city's official inauguration on April 21, 1960.[1] But in the late 1960s and early 1970s, with the rise of the Brazilian economic miracle, Burle Marx ultimately executed three significant designs for the government's ministries in Brasília, including two ministry palace gardens at the head of the monumental axis and a grand triangular plaza at the army headquarters in the military sector, all in collaboration with the architect Oscar Niemeyer. Like his early project for Vargas's Ministério da Educação e Saúde, these garden commissions were part of significant governmental ministry complexes: the Ministério das Relações Exteriores (Ministry of Foreign Affairs), known as the Palácio do Itamaraty (1965); the Ministério da Justiça (Ministry of Justice) or Palácio

FIGURE 6.2.
Praça dos Três Poderes, Palácio do Itamaraty, Palácio da Justiça, and the Ministérios at the Eixo Monumental, Brasília, 1973
Arquivo Público do Distrito Federal/Fundação Oscar Niemeyer © 2017 Artists Rights Society (ARS), New York/AUTVIS, São Paulo

da Justiça (1970–1971); and the Praça dos Cristais (Crystal Plaza, 1970–1971). This extensive thirty-acre triangular plaza, envisioned as a vast military parade ground, faces Niemeyer's monumental complex of the Quartel-General do Exército (Brazilian Army General Headquarters) and was commissioned in 1967 by the very Ministério do Exército (Ministry of the Army) that controlled the regime. The complex was finally inaugurated in 1973.[2]

FIGURE 6.3.
Praça dos Cristais with the Quartel-General do Exército, Brasília, ca. 1973
Photo by Marcel Gautherot/Instituto Moreira Salles Collection/Fundação Oscar Niemeyer © 2017 Artists Rights Society (ARS), New York/AUTVIS, São Paulo

Any discussion of Brasília and Burle Marx must acknowledge two rarely addressed moments of his career trajectory: his absence from the initial planning and execution of the new capital under President Juscelino Kubitschek, who served from 1956 through the end of 1960, and his later affiliation with Brazil's military dictatorship as a cultural counselor after the coup of 1964. Despite the efforts of Lúcio Costa, the planner of the new capital, Burle Marx did not sign a contract to develop a landscape plan for Brasília, even after Costa appealed to Niemeyer to speak with Kubitschek and Israel Pinheiro, the director of the Companhia Urbanizadora da Nova Capital (NOVACAP), to convince him to participate. In his letter to Niemeyer, Costa wrote eloquently that "it is not understandable that, having in our own country an internationally celebrated landscape architect, the capital might be built without a responsible person addressing the natural environment, especially when the description of the master plan of the city is entitled *City Park*."[3] The concluding sentence of Costa's 1957 narrative report accompanying his competition entry for the new capital, the *Relatório do plano piloto de Brasília*, insists on this technical integration of city and park: "Brasília, capital of aviation and the highway; city park. The greatest secular dream of the patriarchy."[4] But Burle Marx did not participate in the initial construction of this modern city park—instead he relocated his office to Caracas, Venezuela, from 1956 through 1960, the period of Brasília's construction, and did not execute any projects in Brasília until after Kubitschek's presidential term had ended.

After the inauguration of the new capital on April 21, 1960, Israel Pinheiro was appointed the first mayor of Brasília, a position he held until January 31, 1961, the last date of the Kubitschek presidency. During Pinheiro's mayorship, Costa wrote to him to express his interest in establishing a new Departamento Municipal de Parques e Jardins (Municipal Department of Parks and Gardens), with Burle Marx to serve as its director.[5] Though such a department was never established, Burle Marx would eventually work on many projects in Brasília, both public and private, in the 1960s and 1970s. His first post-Kubitschek project for Brasília was the unexecuted proposal for the Parque Zoobotânico of 1961. Later Burle Marx received commissions for the three government ministry gardens (the Ministério das Relações Exteriores, Ministério da Justiça, and Ministério do Exército) along with many others. All were completed in the early 1970s, during his tenure as an advisor to the military regime as a member of the Conselho Federal de Cultura from 1967 through 1974.

Roberto Burle Marx: The Ministry Gardens, 1970s

Palácio do Itamaraty

The design of Burle Marx's first ministry gardens in Brasília began in 1965 for Niemeyer's new building of the Ministério das Relações Exteriores. This project was initiated by the minister of foreign affairs and diplomat Wladimir Murtinho, whose leadership and vision led to the transfer of the ministry's headquarters from Rio de Janeiro to Brasília. The process of transitioning the ministry was a long one; Murtinho served as the president of a commission to transfer the Ministério das Relações Exteriores and the diplomatic corps from 1963 to 1969. The building for Brasília would be colloquially known as the Palácio do Itamaraty, a name transferred to Brasília because of its association with the previous headquarters of international diplomacy, the nineteenth-century Palácio do Itamaraty in Rio de Janeiro. Built in

FIGURE 6.4.
Palácio do Itamaraty, Avenida Marechal Floriano, Rio de Janeiro, ca. 1966
Photo by Marcel Gautherot/Instituto Moreira Salles Collection

1851 by the architect José Rebelo, a student of Grandjean de Montigny, this two-story neoclassical palace has large arched windows and doors opening onto an interior garden with a grand reflecting pool lined with imperial palms. Designed as the residence for the Count of Itamaraty, Francisco Jose da Rocha Leão, the palace later served as the diplomatic headquarters and residence of Brazil's various foreign ministers from 1899 through 1970.

Niemeyer's new building for the Ministério das Relações Exteriores was marked with a cornerstone in 1960, acknowledging its location determined by Costa's *plano piloto* at the head of the Esplanada dos Ministérios along the monumental axis of Brasília. Niemeyer did not begin work on the design until 1962. The project

FIGURE 6.5.
Palácio do Itamaraty, with the sculpture *O meteoro* (The Meteor) by Bruno Giorgi, Brasília, ca. 1975
Photo by Marcel Gautherot/Instituto Moreira Salles Collection/Fundação Oscar Niemeyer © 2017 Artists Rights Society (ARS), New York/AUTVIS, São Paulo

subsequently was stalled for various reasons, including the political turmoil surrounding the abrupt transition to military rule in 1964. The last official act of the first president of the military regime, Humberto de Alencar Castelo Branco, was the signing of the decree on April 20, 1967, that gave the nearly completed building its official name: Palácio do Itamaraty. The following day, on the national holiday of April 21 and the seventh anniversary of the inauguration of Brasília, Murtinho opened the Palácio to public visitation. In August 1968 the Palácio do Itamaraty received Queen Elizabeth II of England with a state dinner hosted by the subsequent military president, Artur da Costa e Silva. The palace held its definitive inauguration on April 20, 1970, this time with the third military president, Emílio Garrastazu Médici. Though initiated as part of Costa's *plano piloto* during Kubitschek's presidency, the Palácio do Itamaraty became a signature project of the military regime, anchored squarely in the economic context of the Brazilian miracle alongside the other grand

FIGURE 6.6.
Palácio do Itamaraty, looking toward the Praça dos Três Poderes, Brasília, ca. 1968
Photo by Marcel Gautherot/Instituto Moreira Salles Collection/Fundação Oscar Niemeyer © 2017 Artists Rights Society (ARS), New York/AUTVIS, São Paulo

FIGURE 6.7.
Salão de Banquetes at the Palácio do Itamaraty with tapestry of Brazilian flora by Roberto Burle Marx, Brasília, 1968
Photo by Marcel Gautherot/Instituto Moreira Salles Collection/Fundação Oscar Niemeyer © 2017 Artists Rights Society (ARS), New York/AUTVIS, São Paulo

projects of the Usina Hidrelétrica de Itaipu, the Rodovia Transamazônica, and even the successful 1970 Brazilian World Cup victory—Pelé was Médici's guest of honor at the Palácio's inaugural dinner.[6]

Niemeyer wrapped the square building with an open arcade of extruded three-story concrete fin arches encasing a glass box, allowing for vast long-span and column-free interiors. The building thus presented a modernist reference to its predecessor's neoclassical façade of arched windows. With another nod to the palace's courtyard garden in Rio de Janeiro, the building was suspended within a surrounding reflecting pool, and visitors entered the building by traversing a narrow walkway across the pool. Burle Marx's garden islands, replete with aquatic species from Amazônia, were deployed across the reflecting pool, anchoring this international political symbol of Brazil to the wealth of its native flora. Unlike the imperial palms

FIGURE 6.8.
Oscar Niemeyer, helicoid staircase at the Palácio do Itamaraty, state visit of Queen Elizabeth II, Brasília, 1968
Photo by Marcel Gautherot/Instituto Moreira Salles Collection/Fundação Oscar Niemeyer © 2017 Artists Rights Society (ARS), New York/AUTVIS, São Paulo

framing the garden pool at the Palácio do Itamaraty in Rio de Janeiro, however, Burle Marx chose to frame the Brasília building's site with stands of the native Brazilian buriti palm.

The building was masterfully designed to accommodate diplomats, ambassadors, and delegations for receptions, festivals, and dinners: visitors arriving along the bridge were brought into a vast column-free two-level reception space with an interior garden along one wall and then drawn upward via Niemeyer's graceful freestanding helicoid staircase to a third level with reception rooms and the grand state dining room, the Salão de Banquetes. There a wall of pivoting glass doors opened directly to Burle Marx's large trellised garden veranda, featuring the native species of Brazil's *cerrado* (tropical savanna). This seamless continuity of interior and exterior spaces established a visual connection across the roof garden through the frames of the façade's arches to both the modernist buildings of the Praça dos Três Poderes (Plaza of the Three Powers) and the horizon of the *cerrado* landscape beyond.

An echo of its predecessor in Rio de Janeiro, the Palácio do Itamaraty in Brasília was also a programmatic iteration of Vargas's Brazilian pavilion for the 1939 World's Fair Exhibition in New York. A showcase for foreign dignitaries, the ministry building presented the classical rationalist architecture of Niemeyer, important works of Brazilian painting, sculpture, and furniture both antique and modern as well as Burle Marx's landscapes of native flora transplanted to the central plateau of Brasília.[7] In addition to his interior and exterior gardens, the Salão de Banquetes featured a monumental wall tapestry by Burle Marx, representing abstracted Brazilian flora of the five ecological biomes of Brazil: the *caatinga*, *cerrado*, *mata atlântica*, Amazônia, and *pantanal* (floodplain grasslands).

FIGURE 6.9.
Roberto Burle Marx, trellised garden veranda at the Palácio do Itamaraty, Brasília, ca. 1968
Photo by Marcel Gautherot/Instituto Moreira Salles Collection/Fundação Oscar Niemeyer © 2017 Artists Rights Society (ARS), New York/AUTVIS, São Paulo

FIGURE 6.10.
Palácio da Justiça, Brasília, ca. 1972
Photo by Marcel Gautherot/Instituto Moreira Salles Collection/Fundação Oscar Niemeyer © 2017 Artists Rights Society (ARS), New York/AUTVIS, São Paulo

Palácio da Justiça

The Palácio do Itamaraty's twin ministry, the Ministério da Justiça or Palácio da Justiça, is located directly across the grassy esplanade of the Eixo Monumental. Designed by Niemeyer in 1962, it too is composed of a glass box wrapped with a structural concrete colonnade landing in a large reflecting pool—but here Niemeyer sets up dynamic counterpoints between the two buildings as they face each other across the esplanade. The columnar thin rectangular concrete fins along the east and west façades of the Palácio da Justiça pivot gradually from narrow to wide, visually

FIGURE 6.11.
Roberto Burle Marx, interior courtyard gardens of the Palácio da Justiça, Brasília, ca. 1972
Photo by Marcel Gautherot/Instituto Moreira Salles Collection/Fundação Oscar Niemeyer © 2017 Artists Rights Society (ARS), New York/AUTVIS, São Paulo

activating the colonnade and creating various lighting conditions for Burle Marx's narrow lateral gardens and walkways slipped between the fins and the glass box. A three-story open courtyard garden at the building's center, spanned with narrow vertical fins as at the Palácio do Itamaraty veranda's open roof, brings modulated light into all levels of the building. Planting beds with aquatic plants in the grand reflecting pool foreground the building's south façade when viewed from the Palácio do Itamaraty. The wide openwork of the half-arch concrete south arcade is punctuated by horizontally projecting water troughs, with cascades of water falling into the reflecting pool, animating the façade at various levels. The serene and balanced façade of the elegant palace of diplomacy thus faces its counterpoint, the dynamic and sonorous façade of the palace of law.

Praça dos Cristais

In 1970 Burle Marx designed a thirty-acre triangular formal garden plaza, the Praça dos Cristais, adjacent to Niemeyer's monumental Ministério do Exército military headquarters complex in Brasília, the Quartel-General do Exército. Niemeyer began work on the complex in 1967. Six years later construction was completed and the building was inaugurated in 1973. The headquarters complex, located to the northwest of the monumental axis at the Setor Militar Urbano (Urban Military Sector),

FIGURE 6.12.
Roberto Burle Marx, Praça dos Cristais with Oscar Niemeyer's Quartel-General do Exército beyond, Brasília, 1972
Arquivo Público do Distrito Federal/Fundação Oscar Niemeyer © 2017 Artists Rights Society (ARS), New York/AUTVIS, São Paulo

FIGURE 6.13.
Roberto Burle Marx, detail of the crystalline sculptures at the reflecting pool of the Praça dos Cristais, Brasília, ca. 1973
Photo by Marcel Gautherot/Instituto Moreira Salles Collection

consisted of a long linear administrative building, a series of parallel residential barracks and offices, the Pedro Calmon theater, and a proposed private residence intended for the minister of the army. Fronting the complex and facing the Praça dos Cristais was a large curvilinear concrete canopy and pylon—the Monumento à Caixas (Monument to the Duke of Caixas), a platform intended to accommodate the generals and their guests as they watched the military parades marching around the triangular plaza.[8]

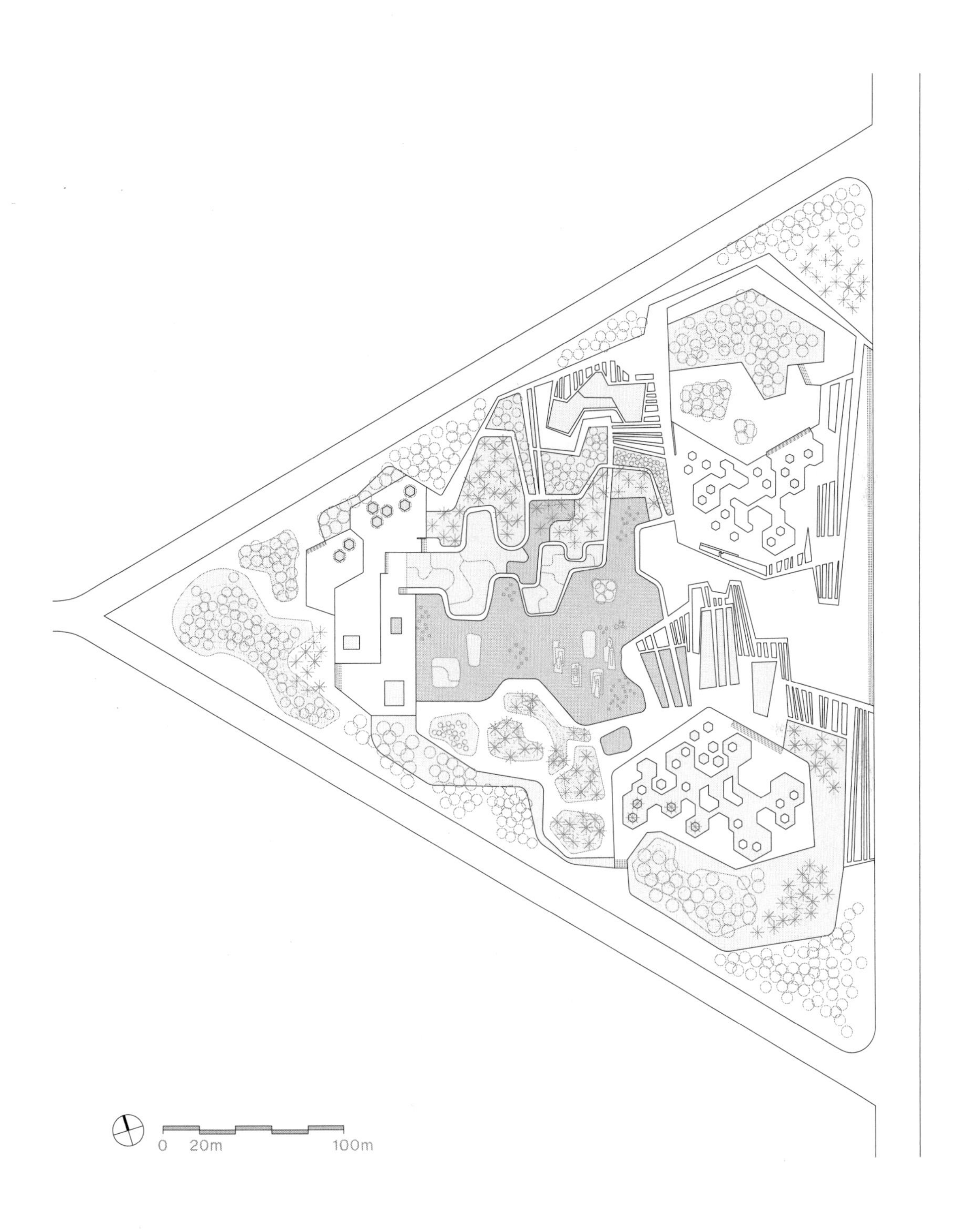

FIGURE 6.14.
Roberto Burle Marx, plan of the Praça dos Cristais, Brasília, ca. 1970
Drawing by Catherine Seavitt Nordenson

FIGURE 6.15.
Oscar Niemeyer, Quartel-General do Exército, Brasília, ca. 2004
Photo © Marcos Issa, Argosfoto/Fundação Oscar Niemeyer © 2017 Artists Rights Society (ARS), New York/AUTVIS, São Paulo

In addition to the Praça dos Cristais, Burle Marx also designed intertwined gardens and plazas for the Quartel-General do Exército complex, along with gardens for the generals' residential quarters to the north—though these two landscape plans were not executed. The guest curator William Howard Adams featured the Praça dos Cristais in his 1991 Museum of Modern Art exhibition "Roberto Burle Marx: The Unnatural Art of the Garden" but noted its isolation and neglect in the accompanying exhibition catalogue.[9] Reinaugurated in 2009 after almost two years of restoration, the Praça dos Cristais was registered as a historical and cultural heritage site by the municipal government of the Distrito Federal in 2011.[10] The garden plaza highlights the native species of Brazil's *cerrado* as well as symbolically referencing the mineral wealth of the state of Goías through the placement of large crystalline blocks of concrete within its vast central reflecting pools. The plaza's graphic geometric pavement patterns, executed in the *calçada portuguesa* technique using small black, white, and red stones, were echoed at his massive infrastructural project for the widening of the Avenida Atlântica sidewalk promenade in Copacabana, Rio de Janeiro, also completed in 1970.

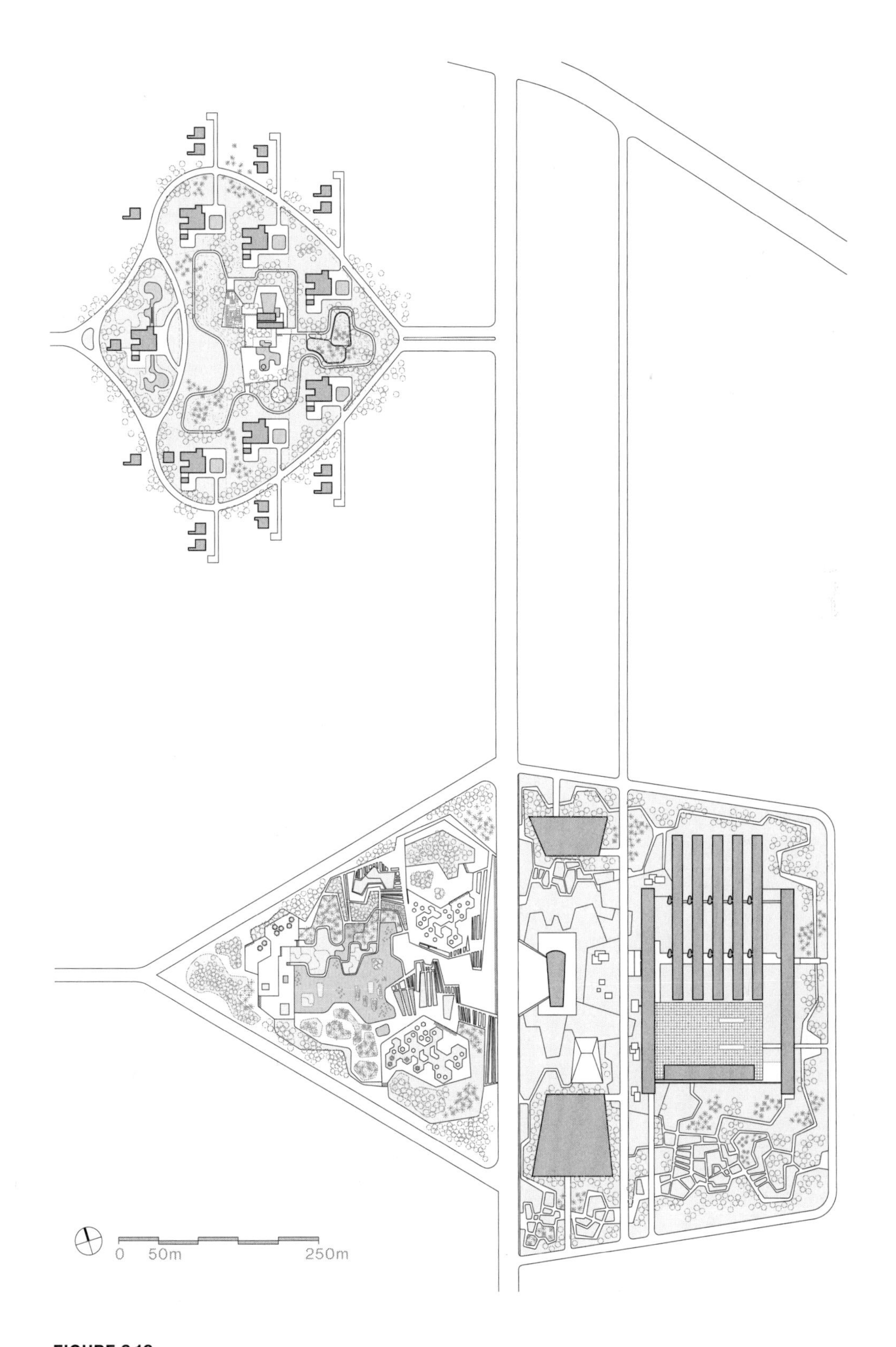

FIGURE 6.16.

Roberto Burle Marx, plan of proposed gardens for the Praça dos Cristais, Quartel-General do Exército, and Quadra Residencial de Generais, Brasília, ca. 1970
Drawing by Catherine Seavitt Nordenson

Deposition: The Brazilian Miracle

The modernization of Brazil—from Vargas's Estado Novo to the presidency of Kubitschek to the military regime after the 1964 coup—was often framed through an economic lens, particularly during the 1950s and 1960s with the rise of theories of economic developmentalism. Burle Marx, however, established a novel connection between modernism and ecology that countered the primacy of this economic narrative and presaged an environmental movement in Brazil that would continue to grow well into the 1970s and 1980s. His appointed position as a counselor on the Conselho Federal de Cultura provided him with an excellent platform for the presentation of this position. Though his association with the military regime is ethically questionable, his consular depositions were often quite critical of the regime's values, particularly its developmentalist interests in the expansion of road building, deforestation, and resource extraction. Burle Marx insisted on the protection of the country's unique natural and cultural landscapes, particularly its diverse native flora, as valuable components of a specifically Brazilian patrimony. His approach to cultural identity reflected the plurality of biodiversity present in a healthy ecology—he valued the richness of the Brazilian environment and sought to protect its differences not through the regime-sponsored infrastructural projects of unification but rather through an approach based on conservation, research, and education.

Burle Marx identified the established legal process of landmark and artwork declaration through the Serviço do Patrimônio Histórico e Artístico Nacional (SPHAN) as a strategy for protecting natural areas, thus defining the environment as part of a shared Brazilian cultural asset. For him, true modernity required the support of a robust ecology. This was particularly important for forested areas, yet Burle Marx went further to call for the protection of constructed and historic landscapes, such as urban plazas and parks. He saw these urban areas as benefiting the task of education and stewardship, creating associative connections between the metropolitan centers and the diverse ecologies of the far-flung phytogeographic regions of Brazil.

Brazil's military dictatorship, like Vargas's dictatorial regime of the Estado Novo that preceded it, sought to establish infrastructural connections throughout the vast terrain of the country. National integration had been a political goal for decades, from the interior exploratory efforts of the *bandeirantes*, to the establishment of railroad lines, to the Comissão Rondon's recommendation of a telegraph line connecting the farthest reaches of the country, to the shift of the Brazilian capital from the Atlantic coast to the country's central plateau. The goal of integration was not only to create a shared national and cultural identity but to allow for economic growth through access to and exploitation of natural resources. But this growth and development often led to unchecked environmental abuse. In 1967 President Castelo Branco launched Operação Amazônia (Operation Amazon), an effort to strengthen the regional economy of the Amazon basin as well as support the migration of communities to this area. The colonization and occupation of the Amazon region was also seen as an important step toward national border security. Castelo Branco's successor, President Médici, initiated the Programa de Integração Nacional (National Integration Program), initiating the Rodovia Transamazônica project in 1970, with significant international funding from the World Bank and the Inter-American Development Bank. The regime sought to penetrate the interior of the Amazon forest with roads and highways and incentivized deforestation in order to support development through new agricultural and grazing projects.[11] The Rodovia Transamazônica was seen as a pathway to the inexpensive land and fertile soils of the Amazon region. Farming was viewed as an extension of the regime's interest in resource extraction—but one that would have a disastrous environmental impact.

With his platform as cultural counselor, Burle Marx objected to the regime's developmentalist position of continental unification in the interest of resource extraction, particularly given the threat to species diversity and the increased risk of species extinctions. In addition to the acts of deforestation, state-owned companies extracted mineral resources, created hydroelectric power plants, and constructed nuclear reactors; these energy industries radically impacted the environment. The second president of the Conselho Federal de Cultura, Artur César Ferreira Reis, described Brazil as a *continente-arquipélago* (archipelago continent), thus poetically expressing the diverse and extensive geography of Brazil as well as the challenges of regional integration, which the military regime sought to overcome through development.[12] As a fellow counselor, Burle Marx defended this notion of the archipelago—not as an economic description but as a condition that had produced a rich and biodiverse ecological model. In his deposition "Jardim e ecologia" (Garden and Ecology), written in 1969 for the first issue of the Conselho Federal de Cultura's journal *Revista Brasileira de Cultura*, Burle Marx emphasized the importance of the plant as an ecological object of study. Reflecting on his thirty-five years of professional experience, he addressed the social mission of the landscape architect—to bring an understanding of the diversity of the vast Brazilian "archipelago" to urban gardens and parks, thereby sharing this knowledge and culture with Brazilian citizens. With this approach to the public landscape, Burle Marx sought to enhance support of both the natural and constructed landscapes of Brazil through a position of ecological modernity—the identification of the protection of biodiversity and its connection to human health and well-being as an integral aspect of Brazilian culture and modernity.

Roberto Burle Marx Deposition:

Garden and Ecology

July–September 1969

Garden and Ecology
July–September 1969

Published as Roberto Burle Marx, "Jardim e ecologia" (Garden and Ecology), *Revista Brasileira de Cultura* (Ministério da Educação e Cultura) 1, no. 1 (July–September 1969): 29–35.

Creationists and noncreationists, whatever their philosophical differences, fully agree that creation, or the emergence of life, did not originate as a singular action but rather through successive steps. The Book of Genesis relates the details of the acts of creation: first the earth; then the separation of the waters and the creation of plants, animals, and humans. By contrast, science has demonstrated that the plant, through photosynthesis, creates the conditions for an ongoing process of evolution. The plant modifies the composition of the earth's atmosphere. It has realized the dream of Prometheus, capturing solar energy and enabling the emergence of insects, birds, mammals, and humans as well as complex plants with their rich variety of forms, colors, and structures. It is through plants that life is disseminated. The phenomenon of plant reproduction is a beautiful spectacle, from pollination through the flowering stage. And it cannot be overemphasized that the composition of the earth's atmosphere, 21 percent of which is oxygen, is a phenomenon maintained and balanced by the photosynthetic activity of plants, foremost by the marine algae.

The plant is our object of study. And how should we consider the plant? On the one hand, it is a living being that is obedient to a fate conditioned by laws of growth, physiology, biophysics, and biochemistry. On the other hand, every plant is the result of a long evolutionary process that is incorporated into its very state of being. The plant embodies all of the experiences of a long line of ancestors, extending back to the very first living beings. This improvement and refinement of form, color, rhythm, and structure elevates the plant to another category—the level of an aesthetic being whose very existence is an enigma to humankind. The plant enjoys, to the highest degree, the property of instability. It is alive only if it is changing. It experiences a constant mutation, a continuous imbalance whose purpose is the pursuit of equilibrium. The more we deepen our knowledge of plants, the more we expand the realm of the unknown, almost in a logarithmic ratio. More knowledge merely elucidates even greater mysteries. The more questions we answer, the more "why" and "what for" questions accrue. For example, I recall a phenomenon that I witnessed deep in the *caatinga* of northeastern Brazil. Over a vast area at a particular hour of the night, all of the *Cereus jamacaru* rhythmically open their large white flowers in metronomic sequence.[13] Under the light of the moon, their multipetaled corollas open, exposing

FIGURE 6.17.

Grouping of notable Brazilian palms, including the *buriti*, *açaí*, and *bacaba*, upper Amazon River, ca. 1865

Photo by Albert Frisch/Instituto Moreira Salles Collection

their throats in order to attract multitudes of insects. Upon seeing this, I was reminded of the movements of sea anemones and could not stop thinking about the mysterious reasons for these strange convergences. Consider how each plant, possessing its own particular color, is enriched with meaning when juxtaposed with another color or another plant. In nature these relationships are not happenstance; rather, they occur because of the plants' compatibility with the complex factors of climate and soil as well as the interactions between plants and animals and between different plants. Ecologists call these defined groupings "associations."

The phenomenon of association is intimately linked to one of the most fascinating of all biological phenomena—adaptation. It seems almost impossible to address a topic as vast and profound as adaptation. However, we might briefly address the theory of mutual adaptation, so popular with today's modern biologists and students of evolution, demonstrating the simultaneous adaptation and association of flowering plants and pollinating insects. In the beginning, during the Mesozoic Era, the first flowering plants were pollinated by slow, clumsy insects of the order Coleoptera. The evolution of the flower from a cyclical form to a bilateral form (such as the Orchidaceae) or an asymmetrical form (such as the Cannaceae) is accompanied by the appearance of more adept and agile insects—the butterflies and the Hymenoptera order or the "membrane-winged" bees, wasps, and ants. It goes without saying that the next entrance onto the stage is that of the most refined pollinator—the hummingbird.

On the earth's surface, no region has a greater variety of plant associations than the tropical belt. This spectacle is stronger and more impressive, even astounding, to the inhabitants of temperate countries upon their first contact with the tropics. The wonder evoked by this world, one tumultuous and wild with activity, heat, and life, transformed the perspective of various European naturalists during the period of great discoveries, such as Martius, [Joseph] Banks, [Auguste de] Saint-Hilaire, Prince Maximilian of Wied-Neuwied, [George] Gardner, and others. Even today the flora of the tropical zone is so diverse that I can attest from my own experience on plant excursions that I have always found and collected plants that were completely unknown to me; indeed, some of these were unknown to science. Consequently, it is clear that the garden should be anchored within an ecological base, above all in a country with such extraordinarily varied environments as Brazil. From this emerges the simple problem of the introduction, cultivation, and domestication of wild plants. This is a topic that has been explored very little or not at all.

The landscape architect in Brazil enjoys the liberty of creating gardens in this environment of overflowing abundance. While acknowledging the requirements of ecological and aesthetic compatibility, one can create artificial associations or relationships with great expressiveness. To create an artificial landscape is not to negate or imitate nature in a servile manner. It is to know how to transpose and associate plants by using one's selective and personal criteria, developed over time from intense and prolonged observation. From my own experience, I am grateful for all I learned through my friendships with knowledgeable botanists. I acknowledge their collaboration as indispensable to this personal project of the profound act of making landscapes that incorporate the vast patrimony of our exuberant Brazilian flora. These plants are poorly understood by landscape architects and by those who love gardens. Despite having at our disposal a massive selection of approximately 5,000 species of trees within a forest complex that has an estimated total of 50,000 different species, our gardens primarily display cosmopolitan domesticated flora and our street tree planting is often done with exotics, such as plane trees, privet shrubs, and so forth. I reject this conception of landscape and have fought against strategies of urbanization that completely destroy the natural landscape in order to create a vegetal composition with exotic plants. This ruins the masterpiece that represents the climax state of the landscape, a state of equilibrium achieved after thousands of years of activity, expressing the dynamic forces of nature. Ideas are derived from our experiences, through a long process of interpretation and an understanding of natural associations. Of these, I might cite my personal observations of the flora of the *canga* region, a geological formation composed of iron-rich matter that produces the soils of extensive areas of central Brazil. Ascending a mountain after traversing a grassy meadow, I came across a grayish stain of rocks. As I came closer, I suddenly encountered a world completely new to me. This extraordinary association of plants appeared to have been created in order to work together compositionally—the strong yellow cadmium tones of the lichens and the *Laelia flava* contrasting with the deep violets of the quaresmeiras while harmonizing with the Venetian reds of the underside of the leaves of the *Mimosa calodendron*, a plant that is notable because of the defensive movements of its leaves when touched. All this polychromy is set against a background where form, rhythm, and color are united, and each season is enhanced by a predetermined cycle of blossoming. One of the great secrets of nature is this instability, of which we never tire. Nature is constantly rejuvenated by the effects of light, wind, rain, and shadows that shape new forms and mutations. And one might consider the flora of the *calcáreo*, the limestone outcrops whose rocks are marked with distinctive stratification. The roots of these plants plunge greedily for the nutrients of the rich biogenous sediment that accumulates in the fissures of the rocks. This spectacle is distinguished by groups or communities of the palm *Acrocomia* and by *Ficus calcicola*.[14] Their flexible roots have a special ability to envelope and dominate various supports, such as rocks, trees, and palms. I have visited regions of strange beauty such as the valley formed by the Rio Pancas, which just thirty years ago still sheltered indigenous tribes. This valley region is enclosed by mountains with tapering conical forms, beautifully arrayed like a stage set. On these slopes there grows a flora entirely sui generis, including species of *Vellozias*, *Bombax*, orchids, *Merianias*, *Mandevillas*, *Allamandas*, and so forth. From the mountain heights one glimpses the sinuous course of rivers nourished by rivulets along the slopes. It is a

FIGURE 6.18.
Efflorescence of the *Corypha taliera* palm specimen, Jardim Botânico, Rio de Janeiro, March 1933
Acervo Museu do Meio Ambiente/Instituto de Pesquisas Jardim Botânico do Rio de Janeiro

shame that these geological formations do not enjoy the advantages of protection that would be offered to a sacred tabernacle. This region is gradually being destroyed at the hands of the local people who do not understand the value of this landscape. Nor is it valorized by European immigrants to Brazil, whose standards of beauty have not yet been adapted to this country.

Finally, I would like to include in this statement a discussion of one of the most impressive vegetal formations of the tropical Americas—the *buritizal* ecosystem.[15] The buriti—*Mauritia vinifera*—is the largest of the native Brazilian palms, and its trunk can reach a height of fifty meters. Communities of hundreds or even thousands of individual trees gather in moist lowlands or swamps. The effect produced by this landscape of dense clusters of stately palms, supporting thousands of berries armored with copper-colored scales, is intense and even savage. Here and there a pair of showy macaws, blossoming with color, traverse the landscape in search of a resting place in their fronds. The buriti palm is propagated by its seeds being carried along by rivers, resulting in its clustering in terraced rectilinear lines parallel to the riverbank. Enhancing the beauty of the *buritizal*, an exquisite grouping of understory plants appears in the midst of this palm forest. This includes the buritirana—*Mauritiella armata*—a delicate miniature of the buriti palm; and the flowering *Urospatha*, a member of the Araceae family whose arrow-shaped leaves and helicoidal inflorescence resemble a baroque ornament.

The plant lives in harmony with its environment and is correlated with the conditions of the seasons and the requirements for its germination, growth, and reproduction.

The life of the plant is cyclical, with intervals marked by germination and death. This fact of crystalline clarity is revealed in both annual and monocarpic plants, most dramatically by the beautiful *Corypha taliera* that waits forty or fifty years before its singular and spectacular flowering.[16]

In addition to its general conditions within a region, the climate subdivides and diversifies into a series of microclimates due to various factors (topographic, edaphic, altitudinal, and so forth). From the point of view of the garden, this perspective is very important.

In fact, to make gardens is often to create and harmonize microclimates, while always maintaining the concept of associations—that the plants must be placed side by side in particular relationships.

The value of a plant in a composition, like the value of a color in a painting, is always relative. A plant is valued for its contrast or harmony with other plants.

Regarding microclimates, I am reminded of a region where I was able to learn from valuable personal observation. I am referring to the region of the Serra do Cipó, about one hundred kilometers from Belo Horizonte in the state of Minas Gerais. The flora of this place is essentially determined by the soils produced by its quartzitic and sandstone geologic formations.

To take this journey is to travel from microclimate to microclimate, from surprise to surprise. In some areas, certain plants are transformed by various environmental forces, resulting in shared exterior resemblances among representatives of very distant families of the evolutionary tree. Such is the case with the similar appearance of *Sipolisia* (family Compositae) and *Vellozia*, and *Eryngium bromelifolium* and *Lychnophora*. Here, as in other regions of Brazil (for example, the region of Cabo Frio, known for an intense wind that blows from a constant direction), one can appreciate the modeling effect of wind on various plants. Certain trees thrive in the humid microclimate of protected depressions where biogenous matter is accumulated, sheltering an unexpected world of orchids, lichens, and other epiphytes. These plants have not developed roots but derive moisture and nutrients from the air. At the highest elevations, an unusual community of plants appears, a misty flora characterized by stunted trees with small wrinkled leaves. The bark of these trees supports an unprecedented wealth of epiphytes, particularly corticolous lichen with intense colors harmonizing with ruby-red flowers such as *Sophronitis*. The *Tillandsia usneoides* form oscillating strands. It is a phantasmagoric landscape. At one moment the plants dissolve and disappear into the mist; then they reappear in all their fullness, as the sunlight illuminates different planes with various inflorescences.

Illustrious figures such as Auguste de Saint-Hilaire passed through these very places, documenting their erudite observations despite the great difficulties of travel at that time. I followed these same voyages with a beloved friend, the now-departed botanist Henrique Lahmeyer de Mello Barreto.

From an anthropocentric point of view, one might state that the plant was created for humankind. And this notion is consistent with the Bible. In Europe, with its highly domesticated flora, humans maintained a relative equilibrium with the tree and the forest. By contrast, the tropical forest of the conquered New World was filled with fear. The forest was the refuge of the Indian and of aggressive beings: the puma, the serpent, the spider, the caiman, and the mosquito. Thus the conqueror believed it necessary to create strategic clearings in the forest and developed an obsession with cutting down trees, with destroying the woods. The creation of pastures and farmland required extensive clearcutting. Civilization distinguished itself through the practice of *coivara*, a technique developed by the Indian for establishing fields for nomadic agriculture.[17] And the *coivara* expanded, gaining strength. Today this is done with an intensity never before achieved, because the tools used for this forest destruction, the machines and bulldozers, are much more powerful. One of these monstrous machines can destroy the work of thousands of years of evolution in just one hour. This is the melancholy situation that enlightened people are witnessing, helpless in the face of this violence that surpasses any moral, economic, social, or psychological logic of our contemporary world. Yet there still exists a world of plant life to conserve, a world that until now remained mysterious because there have been so few experts and specialists in this field. The implications of our mercantile way of life provide little compensation for the noble task of cultivating, preserving, and disseminating the treasure represented by the plants of our tropical flora. Massive population growth has intensified serious problems, including a "deficit" of culture. This in turn has led to the degradation and disinterest of the collective attitude of the public regarding issues surrounding the conservation of nature, the respect for trees, and the role of the garden. Consider the relationship of the binomial human-plant. This interdependence is so intimate that, despite the misunderstanding of each by the other, there remains a sentiment, a desire for intimacy. Often we find that reality is exchanged for mere appearances or for a routine that is followed mindlessly. Consider the example of plants and flowers made of plastic that have invaded and infested today's markets. In Miami, Florida, the winter garden of a grand international hotel does not have a single live plant—all of them are formed and modeled from plastic. A great horticulturalist of this country was obliged to close his exemplary nursery because he was unable to compete with the fabricators of these pseudo-plants. There are thousands of human beings who are unable to perceive and understand that the plant is something dynamic and cyclical. The life of a plant consists of a sequence of modifications that produce its charm—this is nonexistent in a static and lifeless plastic model.

Focusing on the theme of deforestation—an issue more serious in tropical countries than in temperate ones—we must emphasize that one of its principal consequences is the impact on the climate and microclimates as well as the destruction of the social capital inherent in fertile soil. Subsequently we will see the extinction of fauna and the desertification of extensive areas that are difficult to restore. This destruction represents an attack on humanity, an affront to the sources of life, and an assured means of destroying future generations.

The social mission of the landscape architect includes the didactic aspect of communicating with the public, imparting a sense of appreciation and an understanding of the value of nature through interactions with parks and gardens. In Brazil, where there seems to be a dislike for all that is planted, experience has taught me that it is necessary to continuously insist on the importance of the plant. A collision between two opinions provides an opportunity to communicate an understanding of the importance of our actions, thereby provoking a change of behavior. In relation to the future, our conduct has a projective purpose—to demonstrate that we are concerned with preserving the important legacy of both aesthetics and usefulness for our descendants.

The dominant conditions at the moment in Brazil, and possibly in other tropical countries, permit the delineation of a policy of preservation for enhancing that which already exists through the creation of a series of reserves with private, public, and international funding. The principal goal should be to maintain for the present and conserve for the future these regions of nature in its pristine state or even in its altered condition.

Considering the diversity of our flora, these reserves—veritable natural gardens—should be distributed across different botanical regions, preserving both the typical communities of plants and the rarest endemic species. Landscape architects deploy, by means of creative expression, plants that are the vocabulary with which they write their compositions. Arranging this material expressively allows for the possibility of applying the laws of contrast, harmony, and proportion to the designed landscape, reflecting the creative human mind. An idea can translate plant material into form; however, to accomplish this, it is necessary that the plant material capable of embodying that idea indeed exists.

In conclusion, I declare that landscape architecture is an art—however, it is a highly elaborated art that is the result of a network of concepts and knowledge, and this interlacing is done throughout the evolution of the artist's individual life, with all of his experiences, doubts, anxieties, mistakes, and successes.

FIGURE 6.19.
Field of buriti palms, Pouso Alto, Goiânia, date unknown
Acervo Museu do Meio Ambiente/Instituto de Pesquisas Jardim Botânico do Rio de Janeiro

Epilogue

The Counselor

FIGURE 7.1.
Roberto Burle Marx at the Sítio Santo Antônio da Bica, Barra de Guaratiba, ca. 1970
Photo by Alair Gomes/Acervo da Fundação Biblioteca Nacional do Brasil

An examination of the work of Roberto Burle Marx as both landscape architect and environmental activist situates him as an integral character in the long narrative of the history of the Brazilian state and the construction of Brazilian culture. This trajectory begins with the arrival of the Portuguese court in 1808, continuing through the empire and the República Velha, the era of Getúlio Vargas, into the democratic period dominated by Juscelino Kubitschek, and even to the military regime from 1964 through 1985. The state's support of culture may be traced through a reading of successive Brazilian Constitutions. The first Constitution of the Republic, dating from 1891 and amended in 1926, established a cultural foothold, yet without the use of the word "culture." Under chapter 4: Of the Attributions of Congress, article 35, item 2: "It is further the duty of Congress, but not its exclusive prerogative, to stimulate in the country the development of letters, arts, and sciences, as well as immigration, agriculture, industry and commerce."[1] In this nascent legislation, cultural support is conflated with economic development, both critical to the success of the newly independent Republic of Brazil. The cultural mission of the state is not explicitly formalized until Vargas's Brazilian Constitution of 1934, under article 148: "It appertains to the Union, to the States and to the Municipal districts, to favor and animate the development of sciences, of the arts, of letters and of culture in general."[2] This direct demand for the state support of culture is a principal contribution of Vargas's presidency. Cultural construction continued, under varying levels of control, during the military regime that held power from 1964 through 1985, with the regime's 1967 Constitution vigorously asserting: "Support of culture is a duty of the state."[3]

The formation of the Conselho Federal de Cultura in 1967 by President Humberto de Alencar Castelo Branco was a manifestation of this constitutionally mandated duty. The council was tasked with the mission of producing a Plano Nacional da Cultura (National Cultural Plan) for Brazil. As one of twenty-four appointed counselors, Burle Marx was selected not only due to his position as a member of the cultural elite but also as an expert witness. He would oblige, presenting firsthand testimony to the recently renamed Ministério da Educação e Cultura and, by extension, to the president of the Republic. His record of eighteen depositions, published as proceedings of the plenary meetings in the council's three journals, *Cultura*, *Boletim*, and *Revista Brasileira de Cultura*, presents a privileged view of both his skill at rhetorical argument and a wealth of experience drawn from over thirty years of practice as a landscape architect. His position on the necessity of the conservation and preservation of both cultural and natural landscapes as critical aspects of national heritage was clear and unwavering.

In many ways, the construction of culture in Brazil was a completely state-led, top-down initiative—particularly the development of modern architecture and Burle Marx's corollary tropical modernist landscapes. Vargas's dictatorial Estado Novo and the appointment of Gustavo Capanema as his minister of education were especially significant factors in the development of modern architecture in Brazil. Kubitschek's progressive vision brought a modern capital to an empty plateau in just five years. Yet each character in this story took a particular approach to the state support of culture. The military regime of 1964–1985 proved itself a complex cultural patron, and the responses of individuals to the regime's actions varied. As in many oppressive regimes, human rights were often suppressed, but the firm support of a state-defined view of culture was elevated as a nationalist mission of the regime. Did the elite form-givers of buildings and landscapes see themselves as continuing a longer trajectory of the construction of a national culture, spanning beyond a temporary dictatorial visage?

Oscar Niemeyer was a particularly ambiguous figure in this respect—an avowed Communist, he both attacked and was attacked by the military regime, yet he continued to work for the dictatorship in Brasília.[4] Lúcio Costa, as both a historian and an architect, developed a particular affinity for the relationship between the landscape and built form and saw Brazil's modern architecture in this respect as an extension of the neoclassical relationship between the formal palace and the informal garden, the legacy of Grandjean de Montigny. Costa worked as a government civil servant at the Serviço do Patrimônio Histórico e Artístico Nacional from 1937 through his retirement in 1972, spanning multiple presidential administrations and his tenure from

FIGURE 7.2.
Getúlio Vargas, fourteenth president of Brazil, Rio Grande do Sul, ca. 1932
Arquivo Gustavo Capanema/Fundação Getúlio Vargas, Centro de Pesquisa e Documentação

1957 to 1960 as the urban planner of the new capital city of Brasília. Roberto Burle Marx did not appear to flaunt his activities as counselor to the regime as a member of the Conselho Federal de Cultura, but neither did he seem to disguise them. For Burle Marx, enhancing his view of cultural patrimony in the realm of the country's natural and constructed landscapes was achieved through the careful construction of an ecological modernity that identified the protection of rich associations of biodiverse species alongside the connection of landscapes to human health and well-being as integral aspects of a modern national culture.

Yet it must be noted that, by accepting this appointment to the Conselho Federal de Cultura, Burle Marx placed himself (or perhaps found himself) as an advisor to

FIGURE 7.3.
Juscelino Kubitschek, twenty-first president of Brazil, visiting the future site of Brasília, 1956
Photo by Dmitri Kessel/The LIFE Picture Collection/Getty Images

FIGURE 7.4.
Humberto de Alencar Castelo Branco, twenty-sixth president of Brazil and first president of the military regime, with Gen. Artur da Costa e Silva and Gen. Ernesto Geisel (both future military presidents) at his right, Brasília, ca. 1965
Arquivo Ernesto Geisel/Fundação Getúlio Vargas, Centro de Pesquisa e Documentação

an oppressive regime that repressed human rights and censored free speech. The depositions themselves bear witness that Burle Marx, as an activist, spoke carefully yet boldly, working within the strictures of power and law. He judiciously selected and invoked legal precedents—the published proceedings of international convenings, the Brazilian Forestry Code, the autocratically imposed decree-law regarding the protection of Brazil's historic and artistic heritage, and the Brazilian Constitution itself—to develop arguments for positions often at odds with the theory of economic developmentalism supported by the regime. Burle Marx's ability to leverage his position of authority as both a cultural counselor to the state and an experienced designer of public spaces was unique, providing valuable advocacy for a nascent environmentalist movement in Brazil.

Well before his appointment to the Conselho, Burle Marx, the son of European immigrants to Brazil, had developed close affiliations with those holding political power in Brazil, beginning with his early projects for the plazas of Recife commissioned by the governor of the state of Pernambuco, Carlos de Lima Cavalcanti, and the gardens of the Ministério da Educação e Saúde in Rio de Janeiro developed for President Getúlio Vargas and its minister, Gustavo Capanema. Burle Marx was contracted by the governor of Minas Gerais, Benedito Valadares, for the project of the Parque do Barreiro at Araxá and by the mayor of Belo Horizonte, Juscelino Kubitschek, for the gardens of Oscar Niemeyer's architectural suite of buildings at Pampulha. He collaborated with the mayor of São Paulo and future president Jânio Quadros on the Parque do Ibirapuera. Returning to Brazil after a brief period in Caracas, Venezuela, Burle Marx worked with the governor of the Estado da Guanabara, Carlos Lacerda, on the development and construction of the Parque do Flamengo in Rio de Janeiro. And during the military dictatorship, concurrent with his tenure as cultural counselor, he developed ministry gardens in Brasília for the first three presidents of the regime: Humberto de Alencar Castelo Branco, Artur da Costa e Silva, and Emílio Garrastazu Médici.

"The Modern Le Nôtre"

The most significant projects of Burle Marx's career were commissioned by the most powerful figures in political power, with whom he established careful alliances. It is therefore not particularly surprising, if somewhat troubling, that he would accept the invitation of the military regime in 1967 to join the Conselho Federal de Cultura as a cultural counselor. Many other artists, writers, and intellectuals were represented on the council, and their personal agendas and motivations for participating were likely equally complex. What is fascinating is Burle Marx's use of this position as a platform for the delivery of a particularly modern message from which to develop his cultural program. But what makes this alliance unique is Burle Marx's role as counselor and the subsequent publication of his written political position pieces. He speaks quite frankly and honestly in his role as counselor, despite the surrounding political context in which many public speech acts were censored or repressed.[5] Burle Marx exhibits a certain boldness in several of his testimonies that are surprisingly critical of governmental policies. He took on the acts that drove the economic miracle—hydroelectric power production, commercial forestry exploitation, Amazonian highway construction—and identified their environmental consequences. Burle Marx indeed influenced culture through his public works prior to the onset of the military dictatorship in 1964, but it is arguably these assertive rhetorical depositions that shaped culture even more, through the resonance and persuasiveness of speech and text.

One of the most insightful assessments of Burle Marx is from the pen of American poet Elizabeth Bishop, who lived in Brazil from 1952 through 1967 with her partner Maria Carlota de Macedo Soares, head of the Grupo de Trabalho for the Parque do Flamengo project. Bishop met Burle Marx on several occasions and visited his

FIGURE 7.5.

The Comissão Rondon, construction of the telegraph line at the Rio Jamarí, Amazonas (now Rondônia), ca. 1910

Photo by Joaquim de Moura Quineau/Acervo do Museu do Índio/Fundação Nacional do Índio, Brasil

FIGURE 7.6.
Earthworks at the future Praça do Cruzeiro and the monumental axis of the *plano piloto*, Brasília, 1958
Photo by Mario Fontenelle/Arquivo Público do Distrito Federal

FIGURE 7.7.
Construction of the BR-230 Rodovia Transamazônica, Amazonas, ca. 1972
Folhapress, São Paulo

FIGURE 7.8.
Roberto Burle Marx, untitled drawing (*Fora Ludwig*), ca. late 1960s

Sítio in Barra de Guaratiba as well. In a June 1961 letter to her friend the poet Robert Lowell, Bishop astutely noted that Burle Marx was known as "the modern Le Nôtre," and identified him as "one of the real Brazilian geniuses."[6] André Le Nôtre (1613–1700) was the master of the *jardin à la française*, while Burle Marx's style, formally quite different, descended from a French colonial line of the *jardin à l'anglaise* in Brazil. But both men mastered the nuanced methods of working within an authoritarian regime. Le Nôtre was the royal gardener to King Louis XIV at Versailles, while Burle Marx's patrons were the political elite, a long line of Brazil's presidents and politicians—including, as Bishop quips, "our pal the Governor," Carlos

Lacerda, whose patronage and journalistic advocacy both brought the masterful Parque do Flamengo to completion and supported the military coup of 1964. In some respects, this patronage continued with Burle Marx's appointment by President Castelo Branco to the Conselho Federal de Cultura and the later commissions from the military government of presidents Castelo Branco, Costa e Silva, and Médici. But, unlike Le Nôtre, Burle Marx was given the authority of counsel to the regime as its advisor. This is where taking Burle Marx at his word becomes most insightful. The depositions, faithfully transcribed and published in *Cultura*, *Boletim*, and the *Revista Brasileira de Cultura*, are on the record. The public gardens, as silent witnesses, willingly present themselves for cross-examination.

Yet another artifact that speaks for Burle Marx is an unusual drawing that is part of the collection of drawings and paintings held at the Sítio, his home and experimental garden on the outskirts of Rio de Janeiro in Barra de Guaratiba. It might be described as a protest drawing, inscribed with the words *Fora Ludwig*, a message opposing the American Daniel Ludwig's 1967 purchase and subsequent deforestation of a massive 1.6 million acres of the Amazon forest, the Jari Project, for paper pulp production. The drawing is a striking and sobering reminder of the role that the United States played in the deforestation of the Amazon as well as its collusion with Brazil's military regime.

As both a designer and a counselor, Burle Marx articulated a position for the landscape as an important and integral component of Brazilian cultural heritage. He leveraged the design of the public realm as a means of supporting the protection of the natural landscape, a particularly modern approach to aesthetics, ecology, and the conservation of culture. Throughout his professional career, Roberto Burle Marx explored the role of ecology, and specifically a celebration of the rich biodiversity of Brazil, as a key element of the expression of Brazilian modernity. The development of an ecological and cultural narrative through the design of the public landscape is one of his greatest contributions—not only to Brazil's modern architecture and public spaces but to the very conception of landscape architecture as a civic act.

Acknowledgments

I am happy to have the opportunity to thank the many individuals and institutions who supported the successful completion of this book. The Graham Foundation for Advanced Studies in the Fine Arts deserves special mention, as it provided both a research grant in 2001, enabling me to study the work of Roberto Burle Marx in Brazil, and most recently a publication grant in 2017, generously supporting the production of this book. I am indebted to the United States Fulbright Program for making my first extended research trip to Brazil possible, and I am honored to have been a fellow of this significant international educational exchange program. I am also grateful to the Foundation for Landscape Studies for selecting this project for a 2017 David R. Coffin Publication Grant.

I would like to acknowledge the continuing support of my home institution, the City College of New York, the flagship college of the City University of New York. Thanks are due to the interim dean of the Bernard and Anne Spitzer School of Architecture, Gordon Gebert, who supported this project with a faculty enhancement award from the Spitzer Endowment in 2016, as well as to the chair of the school, Julio Salcedo-Fernandez, and the director of the graduate landscape architecture program, Denise Hoffman Brandt, for their encouragement of the project. The Professional Staff Congress, in partnership with the City University of New York, provided jointly funded support for this publication with a 2016 PSC-CUNY Faculty Research Award, and the CUNY Office of Research provided additional support with a 2017 Book Completion Award. I am particularly grateful to the City College libraries for enabling my research, and thanks are due to Charles Steward, chief librarian at the Cohen Library, Nilda Sanchez-Rodriguez, division chief of the Architecture Library, and their dedicated and helpful staff. I am also grateful to the Spitzer School of Architecture administrative staff who have supported my work on this project, with particular thanks to Camille Hall and Michael Miller. I would also like to acknowledge my City College faculty colleagues who have provided a rich and stimulating academic environment, especially Michael Sorkin, Marta Gutman, Denise Hoffman Brandt, Elisabetta Terragni, Michael King, and Sean Weiss. Beyond my own campus, I am grateful to Barry Bergdoll at Columbia University, Bruno Carvalho at Princeton University, and Anita Berrizbeitia and Edward Eigen, both at the Harvard University Graduate School of Design, for their continued support and enthusiasm for this project as well as the inspiration of their own scholarly pursuits. Finally, I would like to recognize my thesis advisor at Princeton University, Georges Teyssot, who first introduced me to the work of Roberto Burle Marx, and my thesis advisor at the Cooper Union for the Advancement of Science and Art, the late John Hejduk, who insisted on the social and political activism of the architect.

Three individuals deserve a very special mention for their help in the realization of this book. Kjirsten Alexander aided in the preparation of the scaled plans of Burle Marx's public gardens, and her care and precision are evident throughout these drawings. Jacob R. Moore's structural and stylistic edits of the evolving manuscript were both insightful and invaluable, as were his enthusiastic comments on the importance of translation. Lígia Mathias provided essential support in obtaining image rights and permissions from numerous archives throughout Brazil, as well as training a careful eye on my translations of irregular Portuguese verbs. I am indebted to the generosity of many archives in Brazil, the United States, Berlin, and Paris, with particular thanks due to the archivists and directors at the Instituto Moreira Salles, Burle Marx Landscape Design Studio, Sítio Roberto Burle Marx, and Biblioteca Nacional do Brasil.

I am very grateful to the University of Texas Press and its editor-in-chief, Robert Devens, who supported this project from its beginnings as a simple prospectus and whose insights and advice regarding its advancement were consistently on the mark. Robert's shaping of an exemplary peer review process was critical to the vast improvement of the manuscript, and I am deeply grateful to the two anonymous readers whose helpful comments, suggestions, and provocations led to my significant restructuring of the manuscript and reshaping of its arguments. My thanks to the University of Texas Press extend to editorial assistant Sarah Rosen McGavick, the copyediting team under the direction of managing editor Robert Kimzey, and production designer Derek George for their exceptional work throughout the book's editing and design process.

Finally, my greatest acknowledgment is to my family, especially my husband, Guy Nordenson, and my two boys, Sébastien and Pierre, for their enduring support, patience, and love throughout this and many other projects.

Notes

Introduction

1. Burle Marx had a significant roster of patrons holding political power. Commissions were received from President Getúlio Vargas's minister of education and public health, Gustavo Capanema; the mayor of Belo Horizonte and future president, Juscelino Kubitschek; Benedito Valadares, governor of the state of Minas Gerais; and Carlos Lacerda, governor of Rio de Janeiro's Estado da Guanabara and a key promoter of the right-wing coup of 1964 that led to the military dictatorship.
2. An excellent reference for the political context of Brazil during the military regime is Thomas E. Skidmore, *The Politics of Military Rule in Brazil: 1964–1985* (New York: Oxford University Press, 1990).
3. Niemeyer, an avowed Communist, was harassed by the military even before the 1964 coup. Yet, despite his establishment of an architectural practice in Paris in the late 1960s, he traveled freely back and forth to Brazil and never ceased working on projects for the new capital of Brasília during the dictatorship—although some projects, such as his proposed airport and a bridge for the Lago Paranoá, were canceled by the military.

Chapter 1: Constructing Culture in Brazil

1. See João Barbosa Rodrigues, *Lembrança do primeiro centenário do Jardim Botânico do Rio de Janeiro, 1808–1908* (Rio de Janeiro: Oficinas da Renascença, E. Bevilacqua e Companhia, 1908).
2. The group known as the Missão Artística Francesa was led by the professor Joaquim Lebreton and composed of the following artists: the painters Jean-Baptiste Debret and Nicolas-Antoine Taunay;

the sculptors Auguste Marie Taunay, Marc Ferrez, and Zéphirin Ferrez; and the architect Auguste-Henri-Victor Grandjean de Montigny. Note that recent scholarship questions the notion that the Missão Artística Francesa was a cohesive mission contracted by the Portuguese state; see Lilia Moritz Schwarcz, *O sol do Brasil: Nicolas-Antoine Taunay e as desventuras dos artistas franceses na corte do d. João* (Rio de Janeiro: Companhia das Letras, 2008). I am grateful to Bruno Carvalho for bringing this work to my attention.

3. Alexandre Rodrigues Ferreira's expedition journal, the *Diário da Viagem Filosófica*, was not fully compiled and published until almost one hundred years later, in 1887. Ferreira's biography first appeared in the Brasiliana collection, a prestigious Brazilian publishing house inaugurated in 1931 that reflected the rising nationalist interest in Brazilian history and heritage after the Revolução de 1930. See V. Correia Filho, *Alexandre Rodrigues Ferreira: Vida e obra do grande naturalista brasileiro* (São Paulo: Companhia Editora Nacional, 1939). From 1971 to 1974, the Ministério da Cultura and the Conselho Federal de Cultura sponsored a comprehensive multivolume republication of the *Viagem Filosófica*, proudly positioning Ferreira as the first Brazilian naturalist. See Alexandre Rodrigues Ferreira, *Viagem Filosófica pelas capitanias do Grão Pará, Rio Negro, Mato Grosso e Cuiabá: 1783–1792* (Rio de Janeiro: Conselho Federal de Cultura, 1971).
4. The naturalist Alexander von Humboldt (1769–1859), who traveled extensively in Venezuela, Colombia, Ecuador, Peru, and Chile from 1799 to 1804, was never permitted to cross the border into Brazil—the Portuguese authorities feared that he was a Spanish spy.
5. Carl Friedrich Philipp von Martius and August Wilhelm Eichler, *Flora brasiliensis: Enumeratio plantarum in Brasilia* (Munich and Leipzig: R. Oldenbourg, 1840–1906). Martius's works also include *Nova genera et species plantarum brasiliensium* (1823–1832) and *Historia naturalis palmarum* (1823–1850).
6. The Herbarium Martii was acquired by the Belgian government in 1870 and is now part of the Jardin Botanique Meise of Belgium.
7. The entrance façade of the Academia Imperial de Belas Artes now stands as a fragment at the entrance to the Jardim Botânico of Rio de Janeiro, appropriately framing the allée of imperial (no longer royal) palms. The academy's original location was on the Travessa das Belas Artes between Avenida Passos and Rua Gonçalves Ledo in the center of Rio de Janeiro. When it was demolished in 1938, Lúcio Costa organized the salvage and relocation of the building's façade to the garden in 1940.
8. For an excellent biography of the life of Pedro II, see Roderick J. Barman's *Citizen Emperor: Pedro II and the Making of Brazil, 1825–91* (Stanford, CA: Stanford University Press, 1999).
9. Anna Maria Fausto Monteiro de Carvalho, *Mestre Valentim* (São Paulo: Cosac & Naify, 1999).
10. José Marianno Filho, *O Passeio Público do Rio de Janeiro* (Rio de Janeiro: C. Mendes Jr., 1943).
11. Francisco José Fialho, "Passeio-Publico: Glaziou, no châlet do Passeio," in *Almanak administrativo mercantil e industrial da corte e provincia do Rio de Janeiro* (Rio de Janeiro: Eduardo e Henrique Laemmert, 1862), p. 313.
12. Formerly named the Campo de Santana, the field was the site of an unexecuted neoclassical urbanistic proposal for the imperial capital by Grandjean de Montigny in 1827, giving the park its new name of Campo da Aclamação. The park would be renamed again in 1890 as the Praça da República, as it was the site of Manuel Deodoro da Fonseca's proclamation of the Brazilian Republic in 1889. Today it is again known as the Campo de Santana.
13. Guilherme Mazza Dourado, *Belle epoque dos jardins* (São Paulo: Editora Senac, 2011).
14. Anna Paula Martins, *Glaziou e os jardins sinuosos* (Rio de Janeiro: Dantes Editora, 2011).
15. Itatiaia was the site of an expedition by the botanist Auguste de Saint-Hilaire over sixty years earlier. During the República Velha, the area was purchased by the government and used as a research annex of Rio de Janeiro's Jardim Botânico. In 1937 it was transformed by Getúlio Vargas into Brazil's first national park. For more on the princess's expedition with Glaziou, see Carlos Fioravanti,

"A princesa e as plantas da serra," in *Revista Pesquisa: Fundação de Amparo à Pesquisa do Estado de São Paulo (FAPESP)* 231 (May 2015): 88–89.

16. The Floresta da Tijuca became a national park, Parque Nacional Floresta da Tijuca, in 1961 and remains the world's largest urban forest.
17. José Drummond, "The Garden in the Machine: An Environmental History of Brazil's Tijuca Forest," *Environmental History* 1, no. 1 (January 1996): 83–104.
18. Raymundo Ottoni de Castro Maia, *A Floresta da Tijuca* (Rio de Janeiro: Centro de Conservação da Natureza, 1966).
19. In one of his final accomplishments before abdication, Pedro II supported the abolition of slavery in Brazil. It was in fact his daughter Princesa Isabel, serving as regent in 1888 while her father was traveling in Europe, who actively promoted and signed the Lei Áurea (Golden Law), emancipating all slaves in Brazil.
20. The name became Estados Unidos do Brasil (United States of Brazil) in 1937 with Vargas's new Constitution. In the 1967 Constitution the name was changed to República Federativa do Brasil (Federative Republic of Brazil) by the military dictatorship that assumed power in 1964.
21. Cited in Ernesto Silva, *História de Brasília: Um sonho, uma esperança, uma realidade* (Brasília: Coordenada-Editora de Brasília Ltda., 1971), p. 31.
22. Through Joaquim Nabuco, Luíz Cruls was introduced to Dom Pedro II in 1874 and was soon hired at the Observatório Imperial, located at Morro do Castelo in Rio de Janeiro, becoming its director in 1881. The observatory was renamed the Observatório do Rio de Janeiro at the dawn of the República Velha and the Observatório Nacional do Brasil in 1909.
23. Glaziou's letter is included in Luíz Cruls's *Relatório da comissão exploradora do planalto central do Brasil (Relatório Cruls)* (1894). The report was republished in 1947 as volume 258 of the prestigious Brasiliana collection (São Paulo: Companhia Editora Nacional, 1947).
24. In his 1951 essay "Muita construção, alguma arquitetura e um milagre: Depoimento de um arquiteto carioca," Costa reflects on the role and history of the ENBA, arguing that the neocolonial style was merely another manifestation of eclectic historicism. First written for the Rio de Janeiro newspaper *Correio da Manhã*, the essay is reprinted in Costa's *Lúcio Costa: Registro de uma vivência* (São Paulo: Mirante das Artes, 1995).
25. In 1913–1914 Hoehne joined the Roosevelt-Rondon Scientific Expedition to the Rio da Dúvida in the current-day state of Rondônia, which takes its name from Rondon. The River of Doubt, now renamed the Roosevelt River, was at that time one of the least explored tributaries of the Amazon River. Hoehne went on to direct the Instituto de Botânica (Botanical Institute) at the Jardim Botânico de São Paulo, which he led for over forty years.
26. The extension of the commission's production of scientific research through imagery—photographs and silent films—is captured in Thomaz Reis's *Ao redor do Brasil* (Around Brazil), a silent film released in 1932, with footage of the native peoples of Brazil making contact with the "civilizing progress" delivered by the Comissão Rondon.
27. Dominichi Miranda de Sá, "Inventário da natureza do Brasil: As atividades científicas da Comissão Rondon," *História, Ciências, Saúde-Manguinhos* 15, no. 3 (July–September 2008): 779–810.
28. As an alternative "religion of humanity," positivism also presented clear ethical and moral positions: an influential group of Brazilian positivists was instrumental in ending slavery, overthrowing the country's monarch, and founding a new Republic.
29. Comte's original positivist mantra is "L'amour pour principe et l'ordre pour base; le progrès pour but" (Love as the beginning and order as the foundation; progress as the end; in Portuguese: O amor por princípio, e a órdem por baze; o progrésso por fim).
30. It should be noted that Epitácio Pessoa, the president of the Republic from 1919 through 1922, expressed discomfort that Brazil was the only country possessing great forests that did not have a forestry code.

31. Cited in Warren Dean, *With Broadax and Firebrand: The Destruction of the Brazilian Atlantic Forest* (Berkeley: University of California Press, 1997). Torres also addresses the specific problem of conservation in Brazil: "Os brasileiros são, todos, estrangeiros em sua terra, a qual não aprendem a explorer sem destruir" (All Brazilians are strangers in their own land, which they have not yet learned to explore without destroying), as quoted by Carlos Haag, "Entre o homem e a natureza," *Revista Pesquisa: Fundação de Amparo à Pesquisa do Estado de São Paulo (FAPESP)* 176 (October 2010): 86.
32. Jeffrey Lesser, *Immigration, Ethnicity, and National Identity in Brazil, 1808 to the Present* (New York: Cambridge University Press, 2013), p. 62.
33. This expression was used to describe the regime of the powerful oligarchs of São Paulo and Minas Gerais, named after the two main agricultural products of those states.
34. This argument is articulated by Carlos Eduardo Comas in his 1989 essay "Identidade nacional, caracterização arquitetônica," reprinted with commentary in José Pessoa et al., eds., *Moderno e nacional* (Niterói: Editora da Universidade Federal Fluminense, 2006). In the application of *brasilidade* to an architectural style intended to represent national identity, Comas identifies the neocolonial style advocated by José Marianno Filho as an "essentialist" position and the Brazilian inflection of modern International Style architecture as a "constructionist" position. As an example of the latter position, Comas identifies Lúcio Costa's report on the University of Brazil project, which indicates (among other aspects) "the use of appropriate vegetation" as supporting an unmistakable local character. See "Cidade Universitária" (1936–1937), reprinted in Costa's *Lúcio Costa: Registro de uma vivência* (São Paulo: Mirante das Artes, 1995).
35. Though the 1922 Semana de Arte Moderna focused on the art and literature of the avant-garde, it was soon followed by a claim for vanguard architecture with Gregori Warchavchik's 1930 inauguration of his Casa Modernista da Rua Itápolis, a six-week open house held at his newly constructed modernist house in São Paulo.
36. The full title of Andrade's novel in Portuguese is *Macunaíma, o herói sem nenhum caráter* (Macunaíma: A Hero with No Character). The novel follows Macunaíma, born in the Amazon forest, through his adventurous journey to São Paulo to recover his stolen magical amulet. Descriptions of the native flora of Brazil feature prominently.
37. Gilberto Freyre, *Casa-grande e senzala* (Rio de Janeiro: Maia e Schmidt, 1933). Translated into English as *The Masters and the Slaves* in 1946, the book's title literally means "the big house and the slave quarters," establishing an architectonic condition for the argument of miscegenation.
38. For an excellent analysis of the relationship of modernist Brazilian architecture and the cultural anthropophagy theories of the literary and artistic vanguard, see Carlos Eduardo Comas, "Niemeyer's Casino and the Misdeeds of Brazilian Architecture," in *Transculturation: Cities, Spaces, and Architectures in Latin America*, ed. Felipe Hernández, Mark Millington, and Iain Borden (Amsterdam: Editions Rodopi, 2005), pp. 169–188.
39. Blaise Cendrars, the Swiss poet, first visited Brazil in 1924. He influenced the work of Oswald de Andrade, including the *Manifesto antropofágico*, a text that reaffirmed the unique specificity of Brazilian cultural values. Le Corbusier was fascinated by Rio de Janeiro during his first South American tour in 1929 and famously crossed out classical architecture during a lecture in Buenos Aires, insisting on the necessity of the application of modernist principles. He returned to Rio de Janeiro in 1937, by then highly influential and admired by the young architects of Brazil, to consult on Costa's new projects for the Ministério da Educação e Saúde Pública (Ministry of Education and Public Health): the ministry building itself and the University of Brazil. Claude Lévi-Strauss, in his anthropological memoir *Tristes tropiques* (Paris: Plon, 1955), identified the multitude of intellectual elites whom he had met in the 1930s in São Paulo, admiring this set of experts on specific subjects who joined him at dinner parties and in drawing rooms.

40. "Tupi, or not Tupi, that is the question" is a pun on Prince Hamlet's famous soliloquy that opens with "To be, or not to be" in William Shakespeare's play.
41. The oppositional Movimento Tenentismo (Lieutenant Rebellion) consisted of a group of junior military officers resistant to the ruling coffee oligarchy of the República Velha. They organized a revolt in 1922 amid demands for various forms of social modernization, including agrarian reform, the formation of cooperatives, and nationalization of mines. The revolt failed, but it led to the rise of the Brazilian Communist Party later that same year.
42. The ministry was renamed the Ministério da Educação e Saúde (Ministry of Education and Health) by the ministerial reforms of January 13, 1937. It would be renamed the Ministério da Educação e Cultura (Ministry of Education and Culture) in 1953, when the health department became autonomous as the Ministério da Saúde.
43. Fernando de Azevedo's seminal book *A cultura brasileira* (São Paulo: Serviço Gráfico do Instituto Brasileiro de Geografia e Estatística, 1943) brought this notion of the relationship of culture and education in Brazil to an international audience. William Rex Crawford, a University of Pennsylvania sociologist and former cultural relations attaché at the American Embassy in Brazil, translated the book into English in 1950.
44. Vargas's first presidency, from 1930 to 1945, like the military dictatorship that began in 1964, was very much dedicated to the construction of a public policy in support of Brazilian modernist cultural identity and the controlled construction of *brasilidade*. Even as governor of the state of Rio Grande do Sul, Vargas funded the preservation of the ruins of the Jesuit missions in the late 1920s. As president, Vargas began by emphasizing the importance of a national policy of education.
45. For his presentation of the complexities of cultural construction and Brazilian modern architecture, I am indebted to Carlos Eduardo Comas's doctoral dissertation, "Précisions brésiliennes sur un état passé de l'architecture et de l'urbanisme modernes d'après les projets et les oeuvres de Lúcio Costa, Oscar Niemeyer, MMM Roberto, Affonso Reidy, Jorge Moreira et cie" (Paris: Université de Paris VIII, 2002).
46. The Código Florestal Brasileiro was established with Decreto No. 23.793, January 23, 1934; the Serviço do Patrimônio Histórico e Artístico Nacional (SPHAN) was established with Decreto-Lei No. 25, November 30, 1937.
47. For a complete chronology, see Caio Nogueira Hosannah Cordeiro, "A reforma Lúcio Costa e o ensino da arquitetura e do urbanismo: Da Escola Nacional de Belas Artes à Faculdade Nacional de Arquitetura (1931–1945)" (Ph.D. dissertation, Universidade Federal de Mato Grosso do Sul, 2015), accessed at repositorio.cbc.ufms.br:8080/jspui/handle/123456789/2464.
48. By 1937 the Escola Nacional de Belas Artes had been separated into two schools: fine arts and architecture. These would be absorbed as part of the University of Brazil, not at the Quinta da Boa Vista as first planned, but north of the center of Rio de Janeiro at the Ilha do Fundão in Guanabara Bay. In 1946 the fine arts school was renamed the Escola de Belas Artes and the new school of architecture became the Faculdade Nacional de Arquitetura. Both have been absorbed into the current Universidade Federal do Rio de Janeiro.
49. The public agency of SPHAN was founded by Mello Franco de Andrade in 1937 just before the initiation of the Estado Novo. It was transformed into the Departamento Patrimônio Histórico e Artístico Nacional (DPHAN) from 1946 to 1970 and subsequently became the Instituto do Patrimônio Histórico e Artístico Nacional (IPHAN) in 1970. In 1979 IPHAN was subdivided into two sections: SPHAN (the secretariat) and the Fundação Nacional Pró-Memória (National Pro-Memory Foundation), the executive arm of the organization. Both branches were reunited as the Instituto Brasileiro do Patrimônio Cultural (IBPC: Brazilian Institute of Cultural Heritage) in 1990, and the agency was again renamed the Instituto do Patrimônio Histórico e Artístico Nacional (IPHAN: Institute of National Historical and Artistic Heritage) in 1994.
50. Decreto-Lei No. 25, *Diário Oficial da União* (Brasília: Imprensa Nacional), December 6, 1937,

section 1, p. 24056. A note on Brazilian legislation is useful here. Since 1862 all of the government's legal acts have been published in the *Diário Oficial da União* (Official Gazette of the Union) by the Imprensa Nacional (National Press). The legislative branch of the government is composed of the National Congress, consisting of a Chamber of Deputies and the Federal Senate. Congress has the power to legislate, producing both *leis ordinárias* (ordinary laws) and *leis delegadas* (delegated laws). The president, as head of the executive branch of the government, has the power to create decrees. *Decretos* (decrees) are executive statements emanating from the president, often addressing or clarifying existing laws. *Decretos-leis* (decree-laws) were historically issued by the president of the Republic with the force of law and no oversight by the Congress. The term *decreto-lei* was used only during Brazil's two dictatorial periods: Vargas's Estado Novo (1937–1946) and the military regime through redemocratization (1965–1988). The use of the presidential *decreto-lei* was eliminated by the Constitution of 1988.

51. Both the Ministério do Trabalho, Indústria e Comércio and the Ministério da Educação e Saúde Pública were new ministries established by Vargas in November 1930.
52. For a comprehensive reading of the pavilion and its political, cultural, and architectural importance, see Carlos Eduardo Comas, "A feira mundial de Nova York de 1939: O Pavilhão Brasileiro," in *Revista ArqTexto* 16 (Porto Alegre, Brazil: Universidade Federal do Rio Grande do Sul, 2010): 56–97.
53. "Termo do julgamento do concurso de ante-projetos para o Pavilhão Brasileiro na feira de New York," *Arquitetura e Urbanismo* (March–April 1938): 99.
54. Philip L. Goodwin, *Brazil Builds* (New York: Museum of Modern Art, 1943), p. 194.
55. The snake pit was intended to evoke the Serpentário, the snake habitat at the toxicology research center Instituto Butantan in São Paulo, the world's foremost biomedical center for venom and antivenom research, founded in 1901 by the Brazilian scientist and immunologist Vital Brasil (1865–1950).
56. Armando Vidal, *O Brasil na feira mundial de Nova York de 1940: Relatório geral, primeira parte* (Rio de Janeiro: Imprensa Nacional, 1942).
57. Decreto No. 50.293, February 23, 1961, at www2.camara.leg.br/legin/fed/decret/1960-1969/decreto-50293-23-fevereiro-1961-390034-publicacaooriginal-1-pe.html.
58. The four individual councils were the Câmara de Artes (Council of Arts), Câmara de Letras (Council of Letters), Câmara de Ciências Humanas (Council of Social Sciences), and Câmara do Patrimônio Histórico e Artístico Nacional (Council of National Historical and Artistic Heritage).
59. Decreto-Lei No. 74, November 21, 1966, at www2.camara.leg.br/legin/fed/declei/1960-1969/decreto-lei-74-21-novembro-1966-375931-publicacaooriginal-1-pe.html.
60. Brazil had several military presidents during Burle Marx's tenure on the Conselho Federal de Cultura from 1967 to 1974: Humberto de Alencar Castelo Branco (1964–1967), who appointed the members of the first Conselho; Artur da Costa e Silva (1967–1969); the two-month military junta of Augusto Rademaker, Aurélio de Lira Tavares, and Márcio de Sousa e Melo (September–October 1969); and Emílio Garrastazu Médici (1969–1974).
61. The inaugural Conselho Federal de Cultura consisted of twenty-four counselors, one of whom served as its president. President of the Conselho: Josué Montello; Câmara de Artes: Clarival do Prado Valladares (president), Ariano Suassuna, Armando Sócrates Schnoor, José Cândido de Andrade Muricy, Octávio de Faria, and Roberto Burle Marx; Câmara de Letras: Adonias Aguiar Filho (president), Cassiano Ricardo, João Guimarães Rosa, Moysés Vellinho, and Rachel de Queiroz; Câmara de Ciências Humanas: Arthur César Ferreira Reis (president), Augusto Meyer, Djacir Lima Menezes, Gilberto Freyre, Gustavo Corção, and Manuel Diégues Júnior; Câmara do Patrimônio Histórico e Artístico Nacional: Afonso Arinos de Mello Franco (president), Hélio Vianna, Marcos Barbosa, Pedro Calmon, Raymundo Castro Maya, and Rodrigo Mello Franco de Andrade.
62. *Revista Brasileira de Cultura* was a quarterly journal, published for five years, from July–September 1969 until April–June 1974. The editorial director was Mozart de Araújo, and Clarival do Prado

Valladares was on the editorial council. Valladares was also the editor of *Cadernos Brasileiros* and first met Burle Marx during his early career as director of parks and gardens in Recife.

63. For a comprehensive study of the Conselho Federal de Cultura, see Tatyana de Amaral Maia, *Os cardeias da cultura nacional: O Conselho Federal de Cultura na ditadura civil-militar (1967–1975)* (São Paulo: Itaú Cultural, Iluminuras, 2012).
64. Lia Calabre, "A cultura e o estado: As ações do Conselho Federal de Cultura," in *Direitos e didadania: Memória, política e cultura*, ed. Angela de Castro Gomes (Rio de Janeiro: Editora FGV, 2007), pp. 155–173.

Chapter 2: Forest Narratives

1. Código Florestal Brasileiro (Brazilian Forestry Code), instituted by Decreto No. 23.793, on January 23, 1934, during the Vargas administration; revoked and replaced by Lei No. 4.771, on September 15, 1965, under the military dictatorship. The most recent Código Florestal Lei No. 12.651 was signed into law on May 25, 2012, by President Dilma Rousseff.
2. The conference has been identified as an important turning point in the history of the environmental movement in Brazil. See José Luiz de Andrade Franco and José Augusto Drummond, "Wilderness and the Brazilian Mind (II)," *Environmental History* 14, no. 1 (January 2009): 82–102; "Wilderness and the Brazilian Mind (I)," *Environmental History* 13, no. 4 (October 2008): 724–750; and *Proteção à natureza e identidade nacional no Brasil, anos 1920–1940* (Rio de Janeiro: Editora FIOCRUZ, 2009).
3. The conference did not specifically address species extinction as an argument for conservation, as extinctions had not yet been effectively documented. Hoehne, however, would go on to research orchid extinction as part of his future work at the Instituto de Botânica in São Paulo.
4. "Incessant life, development, and movement are in her, but she advances not. She changes for ever and ever, and rests not a moment. Quietude is inconceivable to her, and she has laid her curse upon rest. She is firm. Her steps are measured, her exceptions rare, her laws unchangeable" (Goethe, *Aphorisms on Nature*, ca. 1780). Read at the opening of the First Brazilian Conference on Nature Protection.
5. The conference included proposals for the creation of *berçários de árvores* (tree nurseries), envisioned as large-scale areas for the production of lumber.
6. Legislative details of the three codes: Código Florestal (Decreto No. 23.793, January 23, 1934), Código de Minas (Decreto No. 24.642, 1934), Código de Aguas (Decreto No. 24.643, 1934).
7. On the politics of environmental policy in Brazil, see Robert P. Guimarães, *The Ecopolitics of Development in the Third World: Politics and Environment in Brazil* (Boulder, CO: Lynne Rienner Publishers, 1991).
8. André Rebouças, "O parque nacional: Notas e considerações gerais," in *Provincia do Paraná: Caminhos de ferro para Mato Grosso e Bolívia, Salto do Guayra* (Rio de Janeiro: Typographia Nacional, 1876), p. 73.
9. Note that slavery was not abolished in Brazil until 1888, twenty-three years after emancipation in the United States. Brazil was the last country in the Western Hemisphere to end slavery, when Princess Isabel, the daughter of Emperor Pedro II, declared the Lei Áurea (Golden Law) for emancipation on May 13, 1888, while acting as regent during her father's absence abroad.
10. This book is now in the collection of the Muséum d'Histoire Naturelle in Paris, France, along with Glaziou's plant herbarium created while in Brazil.
11. Dean, *With Broadax and Firebrand*. Loefgren was also responsible for bringing the North American tradition of Arbor Day to Brazil in 1902.
12. Wanderbilt Duarte de Barros, *Parques nacionais do Brasil* (Rio de Janeiro: Imprensa Nacional,

1952). Duarte de Barros was the director and administrator of the Parque Nacional de Itatiaia from 1941 through 1957.

13. In 1973 the military dictatorship demonstrated that economic development trumped these natural wonders by beginning construction on a binational project with Paraguay for a massive hydroelectric project, the Usina Hidrelétrica de Itaipu. The dam, 7 kilometers wide and 185 meters high, was designed to generate 12.6 megawatts of hydroelectric energy. The project's artificial lake flooded over 1,500 square kilometers on the Brazilian side and 2,200 square kilometers on the Paraguayan side, submerging Sete Quedas within fourteen days in 1982.
14. Dean, *With Broadax and Firebrand.*
15. Note that Humboldt's research in South America focused on the Orinoco River basin of Venezuela and Amazônia north of the Rio Negro. He never traveled to Brazil due to the contested border between the Spanish and Portuguese territories.
16. Two of Luiz Nunes's early buildings in Pernambuco were the Usina Higienizadora de Leite (Milk Pasteurization Factory) in Recife (1934) and the Prédio da Caixa d'Água (Water Tank Building) in Olinda (1936). Both were influenced by the factory architecture of Peter Behrens and Walter Gropius; the Caixa d'Água was included in Philip Goodwin's 1943 exhibition "Brazil Builds" at the Museum of Modern Art, New York.
17. Unfortunately, Luiz Nunes died prematurely of tuberculosis the same year (1937), at the age of twenty-eight.
18. Roberto Burle Marx, "Jardins e parques do Recife," *Diário da Tarde* (Recife, Pernambuco: March 14, 1935): 1.
19. Many years later, in 1956, Joaquim Cardozo would write a widely disseminated essay for the architectural journal *Revista Módulo* 2, no. 4 (March 1956), entitled "Dois episódios da história da arquitetura moderna brasileira." Cardozo describes two significant moments in the history of Brazilian modern architecture. The first was the brief but fruitful period of 1934–1937 in Recife, during the directorship of Luiz Nunes at the Diretoria de Arquitetura e Construções (DAC: Office of Architecture and Construction). The second is the construction period of the complex of buildings at Pampulha, near Belo Horizonte, by Oscar Niemeyer, from 1941 to 1945. *Revista Módulo* was founded by Niemeyer in 1955 in Rio de Janeiro; Cardozo collaborated with Niemeyer as his engineer for decades.
20. The *caatinga* is one of Brazil's six major ecoregions (along with the Amazon basin, *pantanal, cerrado,* Atlantic forest, and pampas). Its vegetation consists of xeric shrubland and thorny forests. The Portuguese word *caatinga* is adapted from the Tupi language, translating as "white forest," a reference to the visual transparency through the leafless and stunted trees of this very dry region.
21. *Sertão* is also used as a generalized term to refer to the vast backlands or hinterland of Brazil, capturing everything but the densely populated coastal zones. The politician and physician Júlio Afrânio Peixoto stated: "In Brazil, the *sertão* begins where Rio de Janeiro's Avenida Central ends." Cited in Gilberto Hochman, *A era do saneamento* (São Paulo: Hucitec Editora, 1998), p. 65.
22. For an excellent chronology of the process of the ministry's design and construction, see Mauricio Lissovsky and Paulo Sergio Moraes de Sá, *Colunas da educação: A construcão do Ministério da Educação e Saúde* (Rio de Janeiro: Ministério da Cultura/IPHAN and Fundação Getúlio Vargas/CPDOC, 1996).
23. The design process of the Ministry of Education building and the contribution of Le Corbusier to the collective authorship of the Brazilian scheme has been studied extensively by Brazilian scholars since the late 1980s, but much of this research is not well known by American and European scholars. Seminal texts include the previously cited *Colunas da educação* by Lissovsky and Sá; Cecilia Rodrigues dos Santos, Margareth da Silva Pereira, Romão da Silva Pereira, and Vasco Caldeira, *Le Corbusier e o Brasil* (São Paulo: Tessela/Projeto Editora, 1987); Carlos Eduardo Comas, "Protótipo e monumento, um ministério, o ministério," *Revista Projeto* (São Paulo) 102 (August 1987): 136–149;

Carlos Eduardo Comas, "Projeto arquitetônico, obra coletiva: O caso do Ministério da Educação," in Cristiane Rose Duarte et al., *O lugar do projeto: No ensino e na pesquisa em arquitetura e urbanismo* (Rio de Janeiro: Contra Capa Livraria, 2007); and Roberto Segre, *Ministério da Educação e Saúde: Ícone urbano da modernidade brasileira, 1935–1945* (São Paulo: Romano Guerra, 2013). Brazilian scholars agree that Le Corbusier's sketch of the ministry building appearing in the *Oeuvre complète 1934–38* and repeated in the *Oeuvre complète 1938–1946* is apocryphal, based on the plans and model photo sent by Costa to Le Corbusier in Paris in 1938.

24. I am indebted to Carlos Eduardo Comas and our conversations regarding the configuration of the nineteenth-century amoeboid landscape plazas as forecourts to the neoclassical palace in Brazil, their precedent in the early work of Grandjean de Montigny of the Missão Artística Francesa, and this influence on Burle Marx at the Ministério da Educação e Saúde and elsewhere.
25. Bruno Giorgi's *Juventude* (Youth) replaced the controversial *Homem brasileiro* (Brazilian Man), the proposed but unexecuted monumental statue by Celso Antônio rejected by Capanema as misrepresenting the modern Brazilian man. Two additional statues were commissioned by Capanema and placed at the minister's roof terrace gardens: *Mulher* (Woman) by Adriana Janacópulos and *Moça reclinada* (Reclining Girl), also by Celso Antônio. *Moça reclinada* had been displayed at the Brazilian Pavilion at the 1939 New York World's Fair.
26. Goodwin, *Brazil Builds*, p. 92.
27. Segre, *Ministério da Educação e Saúde: Ícone urbano da modernidade brasileira, 1935–1945.*
28. This early adoption of landmark status for modernist buildings and landscapes is a prescient aspect of SPHAN's work, which also protected a significant number of Brazil's baroque colonial buildings. Costa's 1951 essay was translated by Elisabeth Sprague Smith and republished in the *Atlantic* in 1956: Lúcio Costa, "Testimony of a Carioca Architect: Concrete, Sun, and Vegetation," *Atlantic* (Boston) 197, no. 2 (February 1956): 137–139.
29. Costa, "Testimony of a Carioca Architect," p. 137.
30. Note that a new Forestry Code was signed by President Dilma Rousseff in 2012, superseding the previous Forestry Code of 1965. The new code has been criticized by scientists and environmentalists for its significant reduction of the areas designated for permanent preservation and the amnesty granted to landowners who illegally deforested their lands before 2008. This legislation will likely cause serious impacts on biodiversity and ecosystem services, given the new value standards for "preservation."
31. The Berlin-Dahlem Botanical Garden was constructed under the direction of the botanist Adolf Engler from 1897 to 1910 and today is part of the Free University of Berlin. Its initial mission was to house exotic and tropical plant specimens that were collected in the German colonies. The garden now includes more than 20,000 plant species from around the world. The Große Tropenhaus (Great Tropical Pavilion), where Burle Marx first viewed the collection of Brazilian flora, is the property's largest glasshouse, with a surface area of over 1,750 square meters.
32. Lúcio Costa was a close family friend of the Burle Marx household and admired young Roberto's planting beds in the garden of the family's house in the Leme neighborhood of Rio de Janeiro. Costa would commission Burle Marx's first landscape project in 1932, the roof garden of the Schwartz residence in Copacabana, designed by Costa and his partner Gregori Warchavchik.
33. By comparison, note that the number of North American tree species is estimated at approximately 1,000.
34. The Atlantic Coast *restinga* is a distinct tropical and subtropical ecoregion found in eastern Brazil along the coast from the state of Rio Grande do Norte in northeastern Brazil to the state of Rio Grande do Sul in southern Brazil. The *restinga* complex is formed on spits of sandy, acidic soils and is characterized by species of the tropical and subtropical moist broadleaf forest that are adapted to nutrient-poor conditions.
35. Burle Marx uses the term *saxícola* to describe this rock-dwelling plant, and he is likely referring

to *Aechmea saxicola*, a species endemic to eastern Brazil found in the Atlantic rainforests of Rio de Janeiro and the state of Espírito Santo. A member of the Bromeliaceae family, it is an epiphyte, a rootless plant that derives its moisture and nutrients from the air and rain or the debris that accumulates around it.

36. Adolpho Ducke (1876–1959) was a Brazilian botanist and entomologist of German heritage who specialized in the tree systems of the rainforests of Amazônia.
37. Burle Marx is referring to Prince Alexander Philipp Maximilian of Wied-Neuwied (1782–1867), a Prussian explorer, naturalist, and ethnologist who led an expedition to southeastern Brazil from 1815 to 1817. This expedition produced the album *Reise nach Brasilien* (Journey to Brazil), which included the first illustrations of native Brazilians seen by European readers. His later publication of his expedition, *Beiträge zur Naturgeschichte von Brasilien* (Contributions to the Natural History of Brazil), was published in Weimar, 1825–1833.
38. Quaresmeira is the common name of *Tibouchina granulosa*, a stunning purple-blossomed tree that flowers during the period of Lent (*quaresma*), the religious observance that begins on Ash Wednesday and continues for forty days until Easter Sunday in the liturgical calendar of many Christian denominations.
39. A note on the translation: Burle Marx consistently uses the term *essência* to refer to tree species that have a commercial value; I have translated this term simply as "tree species."
40. By the early 1940s mahogany was known to grow in forests as far east as the Tocantins River, but exploitation in the state of Pará was delayed by access and transport difficulties. Initiation of the construction of the Belém-Brasília and Transamazônica highways in the mid-1960s opened this region to a broad spectrum of socioeconomic interests, including the logging industry. An excellent history of mahogany exploitation is James Grognan, Paulo Barreto, and Adalberto Veríssimo, *Mahogany in the Brazilian Amazon: Ecology and Perspectives on Management* (Belém: Institute of People and the Environment in the Amazon, 2002). Burle Marx is likely responding to the beginnings of the discussions regarding the construction of the Rodovia Transamazônica by the military generals.
41. Burle Marx is referring to the devastating landslides, mudflows, and flooding provoked by torrential rains that occurred in January and March 1966 in the city of Rio de Janeiro, killing over 1,000 people, and in January 1967 in the nearby western mountains of Serra das Araras in the state of Rio de Janeiro, killing over 1,700 people.
42. The *Carta de Brasília* was the summary Plano Nacional da Agropecuária (National Plan of Farming and Ranching) developed in 1967 by President Artur da Costa e Silva's minister of agriculture, Ivo Arzua Pereira. The document was the result of the Primeiro Congresso Nacional de Agropecuária (First National Congress of Farming and Ranching), held from July 25 to 28, 1967, in Brasília. This agricultural reform plan sought to improve the quality of life of rural farmworkers as well as to increase their productivity, thereby integrating them into national development.
43. Article 16 of the Forestry Code: "As florestas de domínio privado, não sujeitas ao regime de utilização limitata e ressalvadas as de persevação permanente, previstas nos artigos 2o e 3o desta lei, são suscetíveis de exploração, obedecidas as seguintes restrições: c) na região Sul as áreas atualmente revestidas de formações florestais em que ocorre o pinheiro brasileiro, 'Araucaria angustifolia' (Bert.) O. Ktze, não poderão ser desflorestadas de forma a provocar a eliminação permanente das florestas, tolerando-se, somente a exploração racional destas, observadas as prescrições ditadas pela técnica, com a garantia de permanência dos maciços em boas condições de desenvolvimento e produção."
44. See Dammis Heinsdijk and A. de Miranda Bastos, *Boletim No. 6: Inventários florestais na Amazônia* (Rio de Janeiro: Ministério da Agricultura: Serviço Florestal, Setor de Inventários Florestais, 1963).
45. Article 15 of the Forestry Code: "Fica proibida a exploração sob forma empírica das florestas primitivas da bacia amazônica que só poderão ser utilizadas em observância a planos técnicos de condução e manejo a serem estabelecidos por ato do Poder Público, a ser baixado dentro do prazo de um ano."

46. D. Heinsdijk, R. O. Soares, and H. Haufe, "O pinheiro brasileiro em Santa Catarina: Dados e conclusões dum inventário florestal piloto," *Anuário brasileiro de economica florestal* (Rio de Janeiro) 12, no. 12 (1960): p. 91.
47. *Araucaria angustifolia* is currently listed as "critically endangered" by the Red List of Threatened Species of the International Union for Conservation of Nature (IUCN).
48. Article 10 of the Forestry Code: "Não é permitida a derrubada de florestas, situadas em áreas de inclinação entre 25 a 45 graus, só sendo nelas tolerada a extração de toros, quando em regime de utilização racional, que vise a rendimentos permanentes."
49. This is a reference to the massive landslide along the Serra das Araras escarpment in January 1967, which impacted the Ponte Coberta Reservoir.
50. Recognizing this risk, the Parque Nacional da Serra da Bocaina was created by federal decree in 1971, encompassing an area of 134,000 hectares and rich biodiversity. The park was created not only to protect the native flora of the slopes of the Serra do Mar but also to establish a protective buffer in the event of a possible nuclear accident at the Angra I and Angra II nuclear reactors, part of the military government's nuclear program.
51. The Gran Chaco is the name of the lowland region in the Río de la Plata basin of South America, including areas of Paraguay, Bolivia, northern Argentina, and southern Brazil.
52. The geological Archean eon dates from 4 billion to 2.5 billion years ago; it was preceded by the Hadean eon and followed by the Proterozoic eon.
53. Burle Marx is referring to the Secretaria do Patrimônio Histórico e Artístico Nacional (SPHAN), the name by which the national heritage office (first founded by Vargas in 1937) was known from 1970 through 1990.

Chapter 3: Landscapes of the Baroque Interior

1. SPHAN continues to be active today but was renamed Instituto do Patrimônio Histórico and Artístico Nacional (IPHAN) in 1970. A note on translation: the word *patrimônio* in Portuguese is similar to the English "heritage," used more commonly than "patrimony." In this context, patrimony is connected to a notion of cultural inheritance passed from one generation to the next.
2. *Tombamento* is derived from the verb *tombar*, meaning "to register lands." This is in turn derived from the Latin word *tumulum* (archive or repository). *Tombamento* was an archaic term associated with the official registration of property or wealth. In the context of Brazilian legislation, the term referred to an administrative process of formally inscribing important historical sites or works of art into official registries, known as the *livros do tombo* (registration books). For an illuminating analysis of this topic in the context of cultural definition during the Vargas era, see Daryl Williams, *Culture Wars in Brazil* (Durham, NC: Duke University Press, 2001).
3. From Decreto-Lei No. 25, article 1, section 2: "Equiparam-se aos bens a que se refere o presente artigo e são também sujeitos a tombamento os monumentos naturais, bem como os sítios e paisagens que importe conservar e proteger pela feição notável com que tenham sido dotados pelo natureza ou agenciados pelo indústria humana."
4. In Portuguese the categories are *artes, letras, ciências humanas*, and *patrimônio histórico e artístico nacional*. Note that article 216 of the Federal Constitution of 1988 amplifies the concept of patrimony established in Decreto-Lei No. 25, replacing "Patrimônio Histórico e Artístico" with "Patrimônio Cultural Brasileiro," in order to capture and recognize cultural assets of a more ephemeral quality.
5. Rodrigo Mello Franco de Andrade had been the chief-of-staff to Capanema's predecessor, Francisco Campos, the first minister of education appointed by Vargas.
6. Vargas's presidency was indebted to the interior state of Minas Gerais: the Revolução de 1930 that had put him into power was largely supported by the powerful coalition of Minas Gerais, Rio Grande

do Sul (Vargas's home state), and the northeastern states of Brazil against the established political and economic power of São Paulo.

7. Cited in Daryl Williams, *Culture Wars in Brazil: The First Vargas Regime, 1930–1945* (Durham, NC: Duke University Press, 2001), p. 105.
8. The first design for the Grande Hotel de Ouro Preto was a neocolonial scheme proposed by Carlos Leão, a member of Costa's design team for the Ministério da Educação e Saúde. The design and construction oversight of the hotel was to be provided by SPHAN, but construction costs were paid with municipal and state funds. In 1938 Costa successfully advised Mello Franco de Andrade to reject Leão's scheme in favor of a modernist design by Oscar Niemeyer. For more on these stylistic debates during the Vargas era, see Williams, *Culture Wars in Brazil.* For specifics of the debate regarding the Grande Hotel de Ouro Preto, see Lauro Cavalcanti, *As preocupações do belo: Arquitetura moderna brasileira dos anos 30/40* (Rio de Janeiro: Taurus Editora, 1995), pp. 151–170.
9. For a complete analysis of the complex of Niemeyer's buildings at Pampulha, see Carlos Eduardo Comas's doctoral dissertation, "Précisions brésiliennes sur un état passé de l'architecture et de l'urbanisme modernes," chapter 6.
10. Sigfried Giedion, in his preface to Henrique E. Mindlin's book *Modern Architecture in Brazil* (Rio de Janeiro: Colibris Editora Ltda., 1956), p. x, makes an unequivocal declaration: "Brazil has given us also Burle Marx, one of the few great landscape architects."
11. The transcript of Max Bill's June 1953 lecture in São Paulo was published as "O arquiteto, a arquitetura e a sociedade," *Habitat* (São Paulo) 14 (January–February 1954): 26–27. A second assessment by Bill appears in "Report on Brazil," *Architectural Review* (October 1954): 239. Despite the critique of Niemeyer's work, Bill praised Affonso Eduardo Reidy's Conjunto Residencial Pedregulho in Rio de Janeiro (1947). Burle Marx participated on this project, designing both the landscapes and *azulejo* tile murals. See Lúcio Costa's response, "Max Bill e a arquitetura brasileira vistos por Lúcio Costa: Oportunidade perdida," *Arquitetura e Engenharia* (Belo Horizonte, Brazil) 5, no. 26 (May–June 1953): 20–21.
12. Oscar Niemeyer also responded to Bill's critique; see his "Depoimento," *Módulo* (Rio de Janeiro) 9 (February 1958): 3–6.
13. Joaquim Cardozo, "Dois episódios da história da arquitetura moderna brasileira," *Módulo* (Rio de Janeiro) 4 (March 1956): 32–36.
14. For an analysis of the casino in the context of a modernizing Brazil, see Carlos Eduardo Comas, "Niemeyer's Casino and the Misdeeds of Brazilian Architecture," in *Transculturation: Cities, Spaces, and Architectures in Latin America*, ed. Felipe Hernández, Mark Millington, and Iain Borden (Amsterdam: Editions Rodopi, 2005), pp. 169–188. Comas interprets Pampulha as a modern interpretation of the eighteenth-century picturesque circuit park exemplified by the Stourhead gardens in Wiltshire, England; see "Rio, Pernambuco, Rio Grande e Minas: Contextualismo e hetermorfismo," in *Arquitetura moderna no norte e nordeste do Brasil: Universalidade e diversidade*, ed. Fernando Diniz Moreira (Recife: FASA, 2007), pp. 35–51.
15. In the early twentieth century it was believed that drinking the region's "radioactive" spring waters was a health benefit. The waters of many hot springs contain radon gas, produced by the decay of thorium and uranium deep in the earth, which permeates the spring waters. Bottled radon water was a popular health drink; luckily for consumers, the short half-life of radon meant that it had disappeared completely before consumption.
16. Signorelli was part of the lobby of neocolonialist architects who opposed the construction of Oscar Niemeyer's modernist Grande Hotel de Ouro Preto in 1940, a project defended by Lúcio Costa, who insisted that Brazilian modernism was compatible with the colonial baroque; Burle Marx also designed the gardens for that hotel.
17. This region, between the towns of Ouro Preto and Mariana, was designated a conservation area called the Parque Estadual do Itacolomi in 1967.

18. For a complete list of the plant selections for the Parque do Barreiro, see Daniele Resende Porto, "O Barreiro de Araxá: Projetos para uma estância hidromineral em Minas Gerais" (Ph.D. dissertation, Escola de Engenharia de São Carlos, Universidade de São Paulo, São Carlos, 2005).
19. Dona Beja, the popular name given to Ana Jacinta de São José, a nineteenth-century resident of Araxá of legendary beauty, gave the town of Araxá notoriety in the 1980s as the site for the filming of the popular television soap opera *Dona Beija*. It is said that she bathed daily in a secret "fountain of youth" that gave her this beauty. The *telenovela*, filmed in Araxá, selected the site of the Hotel Rádio for this secret source.
20. The Constitution of 1967 was written when the military presidents had dropped all pretense of democracy and it became clear that a return to civilian rule would not be forthcoming. President Humberto de Alencar Castelo Branco commissioned a team of lawyers to write the Constitution in 1967, which extended the powers of the military and radically restricted political and civil rights. It also granted the president the right to issue decrees (*decretos-lei*) that would be enforced upon publication. The amendment of 1969, developed by the triumvirate military junta in power between the presidential terms of Castelo Branco and Emílio Garrastazu Médici, made the 1967 Constitution even more repressive, giving the president the right to suspend constitutional freedoms, declare a state of emergency, and banish individual citizens from the country. The amendment of 1969 also suspended habeas corpus.
21. Roberto Burle Marx, "Defêsa das reservas naturais" (Defense of Nature Reserves), *Cultura: Conselho Federal de Cultura* (Ministério da Educação e Cultura) 3, no. 25 (July 1969): 44.
22. See Robert Caro's biography of Robert Moses: *The Power Broker* (New York: Alfred A. Knopf, 1974). In 1956 Moses ordered bulldozers to tear up a Central Park playground, but Stanley Isaacs, the Manhattan Borough president at the time, stood up to Moses and rallied the neighborhood mothers to protest with their children in strollers. The event became known colloquially as "The Battle of Central Park."
23. The Fábrica Carioca de Tecidos (Textile Factory of Rio de Janeiro) was established in 1890 in the area of the Jardim Botânico. Over one hundred units of workers' housing were constructed near the factory.
24. The Jockey Club Brasileiro was founded in 1932 when two horse racing clubs merged—the Derby Club and the Jockey Club. The Jockey Club's 400,000 square meter racecourse, a formerly marshy area along the edge of the Lagoa Rodrigo de Freitas near the Jardim Botânico, was obtained from the city of Rio de Janeiro in 1922 through a land transfer of the club's previous racecourse site at Prado Fluminense in Rio's northern zone. In 1926 the elaborate Hipódromo da Gávea (Gávea Hippodrome) was completed by the French architect André Raimbert at the Lagoa site.
25. These are all exotic tree species, many used for reforestation.
26. Burle Marx is likely referring to his garden at the Igreja de São Francisco de Assis, Pampulha.
27. The garden of the Capela da Jaqueira, Recife, was designed by Burle Marx in 1951 and then renovated in the early 1970s. The baroque chapel was built in 1766 but fell into disrepair by the early nineteenth century. The Serviço do Patrimônio Histórico e Artístico Nacional initiated a restoration project in 1944.
28. The Sala Cecília Meireles, located in the Lapa neighborhood of Rio de Janeiro, was opened in 1965 by the Ministério da Cultura as a theater to promote chamber music and concerts. The building was constructed as the Grande Hotel da Lapa in the late nineteenth century and in 1948 was renovated as a film theater, the Cine Colonial. Its conversion to a space for classical music in 1965 was developed as part of the celebration of the fourth centenary of the city of Rio de Janeiro.
29. This section is extracted from the Constitution of the Federal Republic of Brazil of 1967, which was amended on October 17, 1969. Burle Marx is providing commentary on the draft of this constitutional amendment, appearing under article 15 of Title I: National Organization, chapter 3. The States and Municipalities section of the Constitution addresses the assurance of municipal autonomy and conditions under which state governors may appoint municipal mayors. The following draft text

from this article was not included in the final amended version of the Constitution: "as well as the mayors of municipalities with assets registered as part of the national historic and artistic heritage, or those that have notable urban ensembles with artistic and historic assets declared by the appropriate section of the federal administration." The English translation of the final version is found in this OAS document: *Constitution of Brazil 1967 (As Amended by Constitutional Amendment No. 1 of October 17, 1969)* (Washington, D.C.: General Secretariat, Organization of American States).

30. Note that Burle Marx applauds the proposed amendment to grant governors the power (with the previous consent of the president of the Republic) to nominate the mayors of significant artistic and historic cities, in the same way that they would have the power to nominate the mayors of border towns considered to be of interest for national security. Those cities would thus not have the power to choose their own mayors by direct election.
31. The "sole paragraph" appears in the Constitution of the Federal Republic of Brazil of 1967, amended on October 17, 1969, under Title IV: The Family, Education, and Culture, article 180: Support of culture is a duty of the state. The English translation provided here is found in the OAS document *Constitution of Brazil 1967 (As Amended by Constitutional Amendment No. 1 of October 17, 1969).*
32. This referenced article does not appear in the Constitution of the Federal Republic of Brazil of 1967, amended on October 17, 1969, under Title III: The Economic and Social Order. It was likely struck from the final version.
33. Burle Marx is referring to the pilgrimage church in the town of Congonhas do Campo, the Santuário de Bom Jesus de Matosinhos.
34. Burle Marx is probably referring to the growing occupation of these particular granite hills in Rio de Janeiro by informal settlements *(favelas)*. This process is often referred to in Portuguese as an *invasão* (invasion).
35. Burle Marx is likely describing the Pico dos Quatro and Irmão Menor rock formations at the Pedra da Gávea.
36. Corcovado is the highest granite dome in Rio de Janeiro, upon which the famed statue of Cristo Redentor stands with arms outstretched.
37. The Festa de São João or Festa Junina, occurring annually on June 23, is a lively rural street festival dating back to the Portuguese colonial midsummer celebrations. The festival pays tribute to Saint John the Baptist and celebrates the beginning of the Brazilian winter. Illuminated flame-propelled paper lanterns are traditionally launched skyward. In 1998 the Brazilian government passed a law making the release of these lanterns an environmental crime (Lei de Crimes Ambientais, Lei No. 9.605, art. 42).

Chapter 4: Large Parks, Statues, and Disfigurement

1. The failed assassination attempt against Carlos Lacerda, an anti-Vargas newspaper editor and congressional hopeful, on August 5, 1954, became known as the "atentado da rua Tonelero" (attack of Rua Tonelero). It is believed by historians to have been masterminded, without Vargas's knowledge, by Gregório Fortunato, Vargas's long-serving chief personal bodyguard. Fortunato later confessed to the crime.
2. Costa's competition entry consisted of several typewritten sheets of paper presenting a first-person narrative annotated with small sketches, elaborating his proposed step-by-step idea for building the new city. Evocatively capturing the 1883 dreamlike vision of the Italian priest Dom Bosco of a promised land of milk, honey, and great wealth in the interior of Brazil, Costa wrote in his preamble: "I did not intend to compete, and in truth, I did not compete—a possible solution that was not even sought just came to me—it emerged, so to speak, fully formed." Lúcio Costa, *Relatório do plano piloto de Brasília* (Brasília: Governo do Distrito Federal, 1991), p. 18.
3. Costa sought to include Burle Marx as a member of the planning team along with Niemeyer, but

Burle Marx refused to sign a contract. The historical evidence is unclear, but according to Grady Clay, the longtime magazine editor of *Landscape Architecture*, there was an unresolved dispute between Kubitschek and Burle Marx regarding payment for the landscape architect's earlier work at Pampulha. Two letters in the Casa de Lúcio Costa archive are of interest. Document VI.A.01-02172 is a letter from Costa to Niemeyer, telling him to remind Kubitschek and Israel Pinheiro, president of NOVACAP, of his interest in hiring Burle Marx to work on the landscape plan for Brasília. Another letter (Document VI.1A.01-01811) from Costa to Pinheiro suggested that Burle Marx be appointed to a position of responsibility regarding Brasília's parks and gardens.

4. The Ibirapuera site was formerly a wetland; the name means "rotten wood." Following the recommendation of the scientist Edmundo Navarro de Andrade, an expert in reforestation strategies employed in the early twentieth century by the Companhia Paulista de Estradas de Ferro (São Paulo Railroad Company), the Ibirapuera site was planted with native Australian eucalyptus trees in the 1920s to drain the land as well as to allow it to serve as a municipal tree nursery for both fuel and reforestation projects.
5. Octávio Augusto Teixeira Mendes was an agronomist and landscape architect and in the 1950s became the director of the Serviço Florestal do Estado de São Paulo (Forestry Service of the State of São Paulo). He designed the landscape of the Parque do Ibirapuera as well as the gardens of the Fundação Maria Luisa e Oscar Americano in São Paulo.
6. Roberto Burle Marx, "A Garden Style in Brazil to Meet Contemporary Needs," *Landscape Architecture* (Boston) 44, no. 4 (July 1954): 201.
7. The traditional Portuguese hardscape paving technique of *pedra portuguesa* consists of a mosaic of small black basalt and white limestone stones of irregular sizes pounded into a substrate of sand. This labor-intensive but durable paving was developed in the 1840s in Lisbon, Portugal, by Eusébio Pinheiro Furtado, the governor of Castelo de São Jorge, to improve the streets of his district; it is now used extensively on the sidewalks of Lisbon as well as throughout Brazil.
8. See Claude Vincent, "Jardins do Parque Ibirapuera: Roberto Burle Marx," in *Brasil Arquitetura Contemporânea* (Rio de Janeiro) 2–3 (November 1953–January 1954): 55–59, for her descriptive text on the fourteen ornamental gardens.
9. There may have been a disagreement between Niemeyer and Burle Marx over the cancellation of the ornamental gardens at Parque do Ibirapuera. Years later, in the *Estado do São Paulo* (January 15, 1992), Burle Marx was quoted as saying that he would not under any circumstances ("de jeito nenhum") work together with Niemeyer on the landscape restoration work at Parque do Ibirapuera. The basis of this alleged dispute remains unproven in the archival material, but it is notable that Niemeyer makes no reference at all to Burle Marx in his 1998 memoir, *As curvas do tempo: Memórias* (Rio de Janeiro: Editora Revan, 1998).
10. The associates at Burle Marx's Caracas office included Maurício Monte, Júlio César Pessolani, John Godfrey Stoddart, and Fernando Tábora. He did continue to execute several private gardens in Brazil during this period, but most of the landscape work was international.
11. For more on the initial project for the Exposición Internacional, see Anthony Walmsley's article "South America: Appraisal of a Master Artist," *Landscape Architecture* (Boston) 53, no. 4 (July 1963): 263–270.
12. From my interviews with Roberto Burle Marx's former associate, John Godfrey Stoddart, in Caracas, June 2002.
13. The Estado da Guanabara was short-lived (1960–1975), consisting only of the city of Rio de Janeiro after the national capital, the Distrito Federal, moved to the new city of Brasília in 1960. The new Federal District was carved out of the state of Goiás, while the old Federal District was renamed the Estado da Guanabara. In 1975 the states of Guanabara and Rio de Janeiro were merged into a new state of Rio de Janeiro, and the city of Rio de Janeiro became its new capital. Lacerda, the governor of the Estado da Guanabara, began his career as a journalist and was a staunch opponent of Gétulio

Vargas. Lacerda also opposed the subsequent presidency of Juscelino Kubitschek and was elected governor of the Estado da Guanabara in 1960. Larceda initially supported the military coup of 1964, hoping to be elected president, but he began to oppose the regime upon the cancellation of elections in 1965 and sought to restore democracy. He was arrested in 1968.

14. In both the Praça Senador Salgado Filho and the Parque do Flamengo, Burle Marx worked closely with the director of the city's department of parks and gardens, the botanist Luiz Emygdio de Mello Filho (1914–2002), as well as with Mello Barreto, who had relocated to Rio de Janeiro from Minas Gerais to assume the directorship of the municipal Jardim Zoológico. The airport terminal building was designed by the brothers Marcelo, Milton, and Maurício Roberto.
15. Burle Marx describes both of these botanical gardens in his essay "Projetos de paisagismo de grandes áreas" (1962), reprinted in *Arte e paisagem: Conferências escolhidas*, ed. José Tabacow (São Paulo: Livraria Nobel S.A., 1987), pp. 21–25.
16. This pattern is derived from traditional *calçada portuguesa* paving techniques developed in Lisbon, Portugal, and transferred to colonial Brazil. The double-wave pattern is found at the Copacabana *calçada* and also at the Praça São Sebastião in front of the Teatro Amazonas opera house in Manaus. The two native species of grass used at the museum gardens are *Stenotaphrum americanum* Schrank and *Stenotaphrum americanum* var. *variegata* Hort. The allée of imperial palms consists of *Roystonea oleracera.*
17. The planned theater at the northeastern sector of the MAM complex was not initially executed due to a lack of funding, although the foundation piles were built in the 1950s. The theater was finally built in 2006, based on Reidy's original plans.
18. Maria Carlota de Macedo Soares was a well-connected and ambitious self-taught architect and urban planner. As head of the Work Group, she would coordinate the city's administrative units of the Departamento de Parques da Secretaria Geral de Viação e Obras (Department of Parks of the General Secretariat of Transportation and Public Works) and the Superintendência de Urbanização e Saneamento (SURSAN: Superintendency of Urbanization and Sanitation).
19. The Work Group included Affonso Eduardo Reidy, Jorge Machado Moreira, Sérgio Bernardes, Hélio Mamede, Maria Hanna Siedlikowski, Juan Derlis Scarpellini Ortega, and Carlos Werneck de Carvalho (architects); Berta Leitchic (engineer); Luiz Emygdio de Mello Filho (botanist) and Maria Agusta Leão da Costa Ribeiro and Flávio de Britto Pereira (assistant botanists); Ethel Bauzer Medeiros (recreation specialist); Alexandre Wollner (graphic designer); Roberto Burle Marx e Arquitetos Associados, with Fernando Tábora, John Godfrey Stoddart, Júlio César Pessolani, and Maurício Monte (landscape architects); Sérgio Rodrigues e Silva and Mário Ferreira Sophia (designers); and Fernanda Abrantes Pinheiro (secretary). The team also included the Laboratório de Hidráulica de Lisboa (hydraulic studies) and Richard Kelly (lighting designer). For another perspective on the politics and conflicts within the Work Group, see Carmen L. Oliveira's *Flores rares e banalíssimas* (Rio de Janeiro: Editora Rocco Ltda., 1995).
20. Clarival do Prado Valladares, "A unidade plástica na obra de Burle Marx," *Cadernos Brasileiros* (Rio de Janeiro) 19 (September–October 1963): 74. Like Burle Marx, Valladares would soon be appointed a member of the Conselho Federal de Cultura, serving as the president of the Câmara de Artes.
21. See Luiz Emygdio de Mello Filho (the Work Group's botanist), "A arborização do aterrado Glória-Flamengo," *Revista de Engenharia do Estado da Guanabara* (Rio de Janeiro) 1–4 (January–December 1962): 9–13.
22. Roberto Burle Marx, "O jardim de hoje para o homem de amanhã," *Cadernos Brasileiros* (Rio de Janeiro) 59 (May–June 1970): 34.
23. Known since 1989 as the Fundação Parques e Jardins (FPJ: Parks and Gardens Foundation) of Rio de Janeiro, this governmental department of the city was created in 1893. Its first director was Auguste François Marie Glaziou. The department's responsibilities include the creation and

conservation of parks and plazas, monuments, fountains, and playgrounds, reforestation, arborization, and the nursery production of plants for use in municipal public spaces.

24. French architect and urbanist Donat-Alfred Agache created a Beaux Arts master plan for Rio de Janeiro in 1930, a 300-page document that drew upon sociological ideas to provide the Brazilians with a plan for urban and national development along with socioeconomic and moral reform. The Praça Paris, a formal garden, was constructed near the center of downtown Rio de Janeiro along the Bay of Guanabara in the open space that was produced by the flattening of the Morro do Castelo, an "insalubrious" hill in the center of town. The hill had been the site of informal housing erected by the poor.

25. Burle Marx is referring to the monument to Marechal Floriano Peixoto (1839–1895), the second president of Brazil, in the center of Praça Floriano. Cast in Paris and erected in 1910, it was the work of the sculptor Eduardo Sá. This plaza was created as part of a 1920s development of the area of downtown Rio called Cinelândia, named after the many movie theaters that were developed on the ground floors of the new office buildings framing the western edge of the plaza.

26. These are the traditional itinerant photographers who took outdoor portrait photographs in the parks and plazas of Brazil, using the park as a backdrop. Occasionally they would provide their own painted canvas backdrops, often a picturesque natural scene. *Lambe-lambe* translates literally as "wheat-paste," an adhesive glue used to paste up outdoor posters.

27. Rodolfo Bernadelli (1852–1931) is one of Brazil's most significant sculptors. He trained at the Academia Imperial de Belas Artes (Imperial Academy of Fine Arts) and later became its director during the República Velha, when it was renamed the Escola Nacional de Belas Artes (National Academy of Fine Arts). The sculpture referenced by Burle Marx is Bernadelli's 1899 equestrian sculpture of the imperial marshal Duque de Caxias (Luís Alves de Lima e Silva, 1803–1880), who is considered the patron of the Brazilian army because of the critical role that he played in Brazil's struggle for independence. The statue was installed at the Largo do Machado, an urban plaza renovated by Glaziou in 1872 at the Catete neighborhood of Rio de Janeiro, for which Burle Marx proposed a renovation in 1948. In 1949 the statue was transferred to the Praça da República to a massive plinth housing a pantheon with the remains of the duke in front of the former Ministério da Guerra (Ministry of War) building on Avenida Presidente Vargas.

28. The Passeio Público is the oldest public park in Brazil. It was designed by the sculptor Mestre Valentim da Fonseca e Silva in the 1780s and renovated by the French landscape architect Auguste François Marie Glaziou in the 1860s. In the early twentieth century the Passeio was ornamented with many busts of famed Brazilians; by 1912 the park was referred to as the *parque de hermas* (statuary park). The bust cited by Burle Marx is of the writer Júlia Lopes de Almeida (1862–1934). It was executed by her daughter, Margarida Lopes de Almeida, in 1935 (who was also the model for the hands of the statue of Cristo Redentor on the peak of the Morro do Corcovado).

29. Saint Sebastian is the patron saint of the city of Rio de Janeiro; in fact, the official name of the city is São Sebastião do Rio de Janeiro. In the polytheistic religions of Macumba and Condomblé, widely practiced in Brazil, Catholic saints were syncretized with specific African deities, called *orixás*. Saint Sebastian is associated with Oxossi, the god of the forest and hunting, and offerings to him are often left at the statue.

30. This monument commemorates thirty soldiers of the Third Infantry Regiment Military School of Praia Vermelha, killed during the Intentona Comunista (Communist Conspiracy) of November 1935, an attempted coup by the Brazilian Communist Party against the government of Getúlio Vargas.

31. Burle Marx, at the age of twenty-five, was appointed as the director of parks and gardens in the northeastern city of Recife, where he worked from 1934 to 1936. The renovation of the Praça de Casa Forte in 1935 was one of his first public park designs. The plaza is the historic site of the Casa Forte uprising, a 1645 conflict between the residents of the state of Pernambuco and the Dutch army known as the Insurreição Pernambucana (Pernambuco Insurrection).

32. Burle Marx is referring to the stabilization and reinforcement of the city's granite hills, subject to erosion and rockslides. Much of this "patching and stitching" work was begun in 1966 by the engineer Raymundo de Paula Soares (1926–1992), the chief public works engineer of the Estado da Guanabara. Paula Soares also insisted on a vast reforestation project in order to prevent further erosion of the hills.
33. This statue is an homage to Professor Oswaldo Diniz Magalhães (1904–1998), the "radio gymnast," who broadcast a morning radio gymnastics program ("Hora da Ginástica") for fifty-one years.
34. King Albert I of Belgium (1875–1934) indeed visited Brazil once.
35. Burle Marx is referring to the bust of Clarisse Índio do Brasil (1869–1919) by the sculptor Honório Cunha Melo, erected in 1923 at the Largo dos Leões.
36. The Theatro Municipal do Rio de Janeiro is located in the center of the city's downtown at Praça Floriano, also known as Cinelândia. The mayor (and engineer) Francisco Pereira Passos included the building as part of his "hygienic" reconstruction of the city's downtown in the early twentieth century. The theater was inaugurated in 1909. Inspired by Charles Garnier's Paris Opera, it is one of the most important theaters in South America.
37. The baroque colonial town of Ouro Preto was one of the very first sites in Brazil to be landmarked by SPHAN. The entire city was designated a historic and artistic site of Brazilian heritage (a national monument) in 1933.
38. Burle Marx indicated the following footnote in his text: "As there is a federal law that prohibits the alteration of historic monuments, it is troubling that modifications are deemed necessary; in the case of paintings, the law should be applied to prevent such modifications."
39. Burle Marx is referring to the sculptor Flori Gama's proposed 35-meter high monumental sculptural composition for the city of Rio de Janeiro's fourth centennial, including a 7-meter high statue of Estácio de Sá and a 25-meter high tower with an observation deck, to be installed at the plaza in front of the Morro da Viúva in Burle Marx's Parque do Flamengo.
40. The Parque do Flamengo was registered as a protected national historic and artistic landmark in July 1965, just months after its inauguration.
41. Jorge Machado Moreira was one of the team of architects participating with Lúcio Costa on the Ministério da Educação e Saúde and later was appointed the chief architect of the new campus of the Universidade do Brasil on the Ilha do Fundão. Burle Marx, who often collaborated with Moreira, is referring to Moreira's May 1970 letter addressed to Francisco Negrão de Lima, the governor of the Estado da Guanabara, in which he insists on the importance of protecting the landscape of the Morro do Pasmado. This issue is emblematic of the conflict between landscape preservation and the pressure of *invasões* (invasions) of informal settlements on the granite hills of Rio de Janeiro. The Morro do Pasmado was one of the first sites of forced relocation of those living in informal housing to state-built housing complexes far from the center of Rio de Janeiro. The forced evictions at the Morro do Pasmado were finalized with a massive controlled burn, operated by the city's fire department, just months before the beginning of the military dictatorship in March 1964. The *favela* removal program was soon implemented as policy by the regime.
42. The Agulha do Inhangá (Needle of Inhangá) is a dramatic rock formation rising between the neighborhoods of Copacabana and Humaitá in Rio de Janeiro. Geotechnical slope stabilization in Rio de Janeiro was initiated by Francisco Negrão de Lima, governor of the Estado da Guanabara from 1965 to 1971. He created the Instituto de Geotécnica (Geotechnical Institute), a division of the Serviço de Pedreiras do Departamento de Obras (Quarry Service of the Department of Public Works), now the Secretaria Municipal de Obras (Municipal Secretariat of Public Works) led by the engineer Raymundo de Paula Soares. This slope stabilization program was a response to a series of catastrophic mudslides in 1966 and 1967.
43. Samba schools, usually associated with a particular *favela* neighborhood, are the community centers where the dances being prepared for the annual carnival parades in Rio de Janeiro are rehearsed.

44. Note that Burle Marx uses *mesológico* here, a term used only in French and Portuguese and essentially equivalent in meaning to "ecological." The term "mesology" was introduced by Louis-Aldolphe Bertillon in 1860, while the German biologist Ernst Haeckel is credited with establishing the first definition of "ecology" in 1866 as the study of the relationship of beings with their environment.
45. The Companhia Caminho Aéreo Pão de Açúcar (Sugar Loaf Mountain Airway Company) is the corporation that developed the first aerial tramway line to access the Pão de Açúcar in 1912; the company still owns and operates the cable car system and the complex. The last trip of the old *bondinho* (cable car) was on January 19, 1973, shortly before the company's sixtieth year in operation (and just months before this opinion piece by Burle Marx). The company modernized its cable car system with a duplication of cable lines, inaugurating the new *bondinho* cars in 1973. The modernization of the Caminho Aéreo in the early 1970s also included the reconstruction of the cable car stations in a brutalist concrete architectural style, likely unappealing to Burle Marx.
46. The Conselho Superior de Planejamento Urbano da Guanabara was established by the governor Antônio de Pádua Chagas Freitas in 1971, as a regulatory agency with jurisdiction over the planning of public works within the Estado da Guanabara. Architects Lúcio Costa and Jorge Machado Moreira were members of this council. As a privately owned company, the development initiatives of the Companhia Caminho Aéreo Pão de Açúcar on public land represent an interesting case.
47. In 1970 the reforestation plan called Plano de Reconstituição Vegetal dos Morros da Urca e Pão de Açúcar (Plan for the Restoration of the Vegetation of Urca and Sugar Loaf Hills) was begun by the Companhia Caminho Aéreo. The plan was developed by the Instituto de Conservação de Natureza (Institute of Nature Conservation), part of the Secretaria de Ciência e Tecnologia do Estado da Guanabara (Secretariat of Science and Technology of the State of Guanabara). This initiative to reestablish the forests of these granite hillsides was likely part of a strategy to also prevent the growth of informal housing settlements, which were then appearing at the base of the Pão de Açúcar. At the same time, *favelas* were cleared from the top of the nearby Morro da Babilônia, which was also reforested.
48. Burle Marx's appeal was successful. In August 1973 the Instituto do Patrimônio Histórico e Artístico Nacional (IPHAN) granted landmark status to the Complexo do Pão de Açúcar (Rio de Janeiro), inclusive of the hills of Pão de Açúcar, Urca, and Babilônia, for their importance as part of the cultural landscape of Rio de Janeiro. The *bondinho* was also landmarked by IPHAN the same year. In 2000 the hill of Pão de Açúcar was designated an archaeological reserve.
49. Riotur, the Empresa de Turismo do Município do Rio de Janeiro S.A. (Tourism Company of the City of Rio de Janeiro), is a subsidiary of the Secretaria Especial de Turismo (Special Secretariat of Tourism) of Rio de Janeiro, charged with executing tourist policies developed by the municipal administration. It was created in July 1972 as Riotur S.A., Empresa de Turismo do Estado da Guanabara.
50. In 1969 Lúcio Costa developed a pilot plan for the urbanization of the coastal lowlands west of the center of Rio de Janeiro—Barra da Tijuca, Pontal de Sernambetiba, and Jacarepaguá. Burle Marx provided advice regarding the arborization of the project, and Niemeyer proposed a number of the commercial buildings. The project was rejected in 1972 by the governor of the Estado da Guanabara, Antônio de Pádua Chagas Freitas.

Chapter 5: The Scientific Park

1. Conrad Hamerman, "Roberto Burle Marx: The Last Interview," *Journal of Decorative and Propaganda Arts* 21 (1995): 178.
2. The Universidade do Brasil is now known as the Universidade Federal do Rio de Janeiro (UFRJ). It was first established as the Universidade do Rio de Janeiro in 1920 by President Epitácio Pessoa then restructured as the Universidade do Brasil in 1937 by President Gétulio Vargas's minister of

education, Gustavo Capanema. The Quinta da Boa Vista was the site of Le Corbusier's unexecuted 1937 proposal for the new campus of the Universidade do Brasil.

3. Roberto Burle Marx, "Projetos de paisagismo de grandes áreas," in *Arte e paisagem: Conferências escolhidas* (São Paulo: Livraria Nobel S.A., [1962] 1987), p. 23.
4. Ibid.
5. P. M. Bardi, *The Tropical Gardens of Burle Marx* (Rio de Janeiro: Colibris Editora Ltda., 1964), p. 154.
6. Burle Marx, "Projetos de paisagismo de grandes áreas," p. 23. "The characteristics of the Jardim Botânico de São Paulo are, at the same time, a scientific garden, a reserve for the conservation of flora and fauna, and a place of recreation for the people of this immense and hardworking metropolis."
7. Hitoshi Nomura, "João Moojen de Oliveira (1904–1985)," *Revista Brasileira de Zoologia* 10, no. 3 (1993): 553–558.
8. Bardi, *The Tropical Gardens of Burle Marx*, p. 152.
9. Considered *invasões* (invasions) by the Distrito Federal, these pioneer settlements were not incorporated as legal entities in Brasília until after the redemocratization in the 1980s. They are now incorporated into the city, alternative urban settlements within the *plano piloto*. For an excellent history of the development of the satellite cities of Brasília, see James Holston, *The Modernist City: An Anthropological Critique of Brasília* (Chicago: University of Chicago Press, 1989).
10. The plan was completely abandoned in 1969. A much smaller Jardim Zoológico was eventually built at the northern margin of Candangolândia, but without the participation of Burle Marx.
11. Burle Marx, "Projetos de paisagismo de grandes áreas," p. 23.
12. Vera Beatriz Siqueira, "Um jardim sem igual," *Revista de História da Biblioteca Nacional* (Rio de Janeiro: Sociedade de Amigos da Biblioteca Nacional/Ministério da Cultura) 40 (January 2009): 52–57.
13. Giulio G. Rizzo, *Il giardino privato di Roberto Burle Marx: Il Sítio* (Rome: Gangemi Editore, 2009), p. 45.
14. Roberto Burle Marx, "Paisagismo e flora brasileira," in *Arte e paisagem: Conferências escolhidas* (São Paulo: Nobel, [1975] 1987), p. 49.
15. The Banco Nacional de Habitação (BNH) was established by the military regime with Lei No. 4.380, August 21, 1964, as a self-governing federal agency linked to the Ministério da Fazenda (Ministry of Finance). It was then transferred to the Ministério do Interior (Ministry of the Interior) by decree in June 1967. In December 1971 the BNH was transformed into a public company. The bank provided housing loans to other banks and housing companies. Banco Nacional de Habitação was responsible for the funding and construction of social housing complexes, usually at the periphery of cities, for people displaced by the forced removal of *favelas*. Dissolved in 1986, BNH was replaced by the Caixa Econômica Federal (Federal Savings Bank).
16. Several years later, the 1973 IPHAN record for the landmark registration of the Horto Florestal notes that the site has been "muito prejudicada por várias ocupações" (seriously damaged by the encroachment of various *favelas*). Strong debate about the ongoing "occupation" of the Horto Florestal and its environmental preservation continues today.
17. Burle Marx is referring to his own 1961 proposal for the Parque Zoobotânico de Brasília.
18. Note that the scientific nomenclature of the giant water lily has been changed from *Victoria regia* to *Victoria amazonica*, a postcolonial revision.
19. The director of the Jardim Botânico when this deposition was delivered (February 1968) was Gil Sobral Pinto, an appointee of the military regime who served from February 1965 through May 1968. An agronomist engineer, Sobral Pinto had previously been the director of the Parque Nacional da Serra dos Órgãos from 1943 to 1951. He responded to Burle Marx's accusations with an interview with the *Correio da Manhã* on February 10, 1968, admitting that the garden's collections had

suffered during the previous directorship and acknowledging the presence of a *favela* within the garden's grounds.

20. In the minutes of the 102nd plenary session of the Conselho Federal de Cultura of September 26, 1968, Djacir Menezes asks for Burle Marx's opinion on a report in the *Correio da Manhã* on the same day that a significant area of the Horto Florestal was being divided into plots for future development. The report included an interview with the new director of the Jardim Botânico, Luiz Edmundo Paes, who would serve from 1968 through 1971. President Artur da Costa e Silva's Decreto No. 62.698 of May 14, 1968, conceded through eminent domain an area of 35 acres of the Horto Florestal to the Banco Nacional da Habitação. The decree was later retracted on November 6, 1970.
21. Burle Marx is referring to Artur da Costa e Silva, the second president of Brazil's military regime.
22. Decreto No. 9.015, *Diário Oficial da União* (Brasília: Imprensa Nacional), March 18, 1942, section 1, article 2, paragraph 1, p. 4293 (cited in "General que dá gleba ao BNH planta árvore no Jardim Botânico," *Correio da Manhã*, September 29, 1968, p. 14). Decreto No. 9.015 confirmed the entities over which the Serviço Florestal had oversight, including the Seção de Botânica that was responsible for the maintenance of both the Jardim Botânico and the Horto Florestal da Gávea.
23. Burle Marx is referring to Carlos Lacerda, governor of the former Estado da Guanabara (Rio de Janeiro) from 1960 to 1965.
24. The Ministério de Minas e Energia was created by executive decree in 1960. Decreto No. 58.469 of May 17, 1966, claimed territory at the Horto Florestal for a substation and a power transmission line right-of-way for Central Elétrica de Furnas.
25. Novo Código Florestal de 1965, Lei No. 4.771, *Diário Oficial da União* (Brasília: Imprensa Nacional), September 15, 1965, section 1, article 1, p. 9529.
26. This law, signed by President Humberto de Alencar Castelo Branco in 1967, established the Instituto Brasileiro de Desenvolvimento Florestal (IBDF: Brazilian Institute for Forest Development). Decreto-Lei No. 289, *Diário Oficial da União* (Brasília: Imprensa Nacional), February 28, 1967, section 1, p. 2465. The item cited by Burle Marx addresses afforestation and reforestation for ecological, touristic, and scenic purposes.
27. See article 1 of the Novo Código Florestal de 1965.
28. Decreto No. 52.442 of September 3, 1963, was signed into law by President João Goulart with his minister of agriculture, Oswaldo Lima Filha, establishing the rules of procedure of the Departamento de Recursos Naturais Renováveis (DRNR). With this law, the Jardim Botânico was placed under the jurisdiction of the DRNR.
29. Furnas is an electric company and subsidiary of Centrais Elétricas Brasileiras S.A.–Electrobras and is associated with the Ministry of Mines and Energy. The original company, Central Eléctrica de Furnas, was created by federal decree in 1957 in order to construct and operate the first large-scale hydroelectric power plant in Brazil, the Usina Hidrelétrica de Furnas (Furnas Hydroelectric Plant), located on the Rio Grande near Passos, Minas Gerais. The plant began operation in 1963.
30. The Morro da Margarida, named for the daisies that once lined its pathways, is one of the highest points in the Horto Florestal and the site of a colonial structure thought to be the slave quarters of a plantation.
31. Formerly a plantation site, the territory of the Instituto Agronômico (Agronomic Institute) was claimed by the state in 1912 with the goal of establishing an experimental agriculture station. In 1953 it was established as the Instituto Agronômico of Belo Horizonte's Universidade Federal de Minas Gerais. It is now known as the Horto Florestal.
32. Burle Marx uses the geological term *canga*, translated here as iron ore. *Canga* is an auriferous iron conglomerate formation about four feet thick, unique to the state of Minas Gerais in the so-called Quadrilátero Ferrífero (Iron Quadrangle), a rectangular territory within south-central Minas Gerais characterized by its rich mineral deposits. *Canga* produces an iron-rich soil supporting rare flora, and numerous endemic adapted species of metal-tolerant plants are found in the unique

environment of these *canga* outcrops. As it is the most important mining region of southeastern Brazil, these ecosystems are particularly vulnerable. See Charles Frederick Hartt and Louis Agassiz, *Geology and Physical Geography of Brazil* (Boston: Fields, Osgood, and Co., 1870), produced as the summary report of the Thayer Expedition of 1865 and 1866. See also Jay Backus Woodworth, *Geological Expedition to Brazil and Chile, 1908–1909* (Cambridge, MA: Museum of Comparative Zoology at Harvard College, 1912).

33. Fundação Nacional do Bem Estar do Menor (FUNABEM) was established by the military dictatorship in 1964 as a restructured nationalized version of the Fundação Estadual do Bem Estar do Menor (FEBEMS: State Foundation for Child Welfare). The mission of this new unified agency was the creation of a national policy providing direct help for the well-being of minors. SENAI was created by Getúlio Vargas in 1942 as an entity providing quality professional education for those working in the developing nationalized industries of Brazil.
34. The Caixa Econômica Federal is a government-owned Brazilian bank, founded in 1861 by Emperor Pedro II as the Caixa Económica e o Monte de Socorro (Savings and Loan Bank) in Rio de Janeiro as a financial institution established to collect national savings, mainly from the poor, and provide loans. Several similar institutions developed over time and merged to form the Caixa Econômica Federal in 1967. Today it is the second-largest government-owned financial institution, after the Banco do Brasil.
35. *Mineiro* is the Brazilian Portuguese term for the inhabitants of the state of Minas Gerais.
36. The eucalyptuses (*Eucalyptus robusta*) of the Praça Getúlio Vargas (formerly known as the Praça dos Eucaliptos and prior to that as the Praça Quinze de Novembro) in Novo Friburgo were planted between 1877 and 1883 by the physician Carlos Éboli and landscape architect Auguste François Marie Glaziou, the designer of the Campo da Aclamação and the Quinta da Boa Vista in Rio de Janeiro. The eucalyptus planting was intended to help with the drainage of the marshy terrain. The plaza was landmarked by IPHAN in 1972, two years after the delivery of this deposition.
37. Burle Marx uses the term *patrimônio florestal*, translated here as "forestry heritage."

Chapter 6: Military Gardens

1. For an excellent analysis of the political and economic conditions leading to the military coup of 1964, see Thomas E. Skidmore, *Politics in Brazil 1930–1964: An Experiment in Democracy* (Oxford: Oxford University Press, 1967). For the period of the military regime, see his book *The Politics of Military Rule in Brazil: 1964–1985* (Oxford: Oxford University Press, 1988).
2. The Ministério do Exército was established by the military regime in 1967, under the presidency of Costa e Silva; this name replaced its previous title from 1808 until 1967, the Ministério da Guerra (Ministry of War). The Ministro do Exército (Minister of the Army) from March 1967 through October 1969 was Aurélio de Lira Tavares, who also served as one of the three members of the interim Junta Governativa Provisória de 1969 (Provisional Governing Junta of 1969) between the presidencies of Costa e Silva and Médici. Tavares was succeed by Orlando Geisel from October 1969 through 1974, during the presidency of Médici. In 1999 the ministry was renamed again, this time as the Ministério da Defesa (Ministry of Defense).
3. Lúcio Costa, undated letter to Oscar Niemeyer, Acervo Casa Lúcio Costa. See Document VI.A.01-02172, Brasília, "Oscar, Acho que seria bom você falar com o president."
4. Costa's original text is as follows: "Brasília: Capital aérea e rodoviária; cidade parque. Sonho arqui-secular do partriarca." Lúcio Costa, *Relatório do plano piloto de Brasília* (Brasília: Governo do Distrito Federal, 1991), p. 34.
5. Lúcio Costa, undated letter to Israel Pinheiro, Acervo Casa Lúcio Costa. See Document VI.A.01-01811, Brasília, sobre Roberto Burle Marx, "Prezado Dr. Israel, Confirme instruções do Oscar."

6. See Eduardo Pierrotti Rossetti, "Palácio do Itamaraty: Questões de história, projeto, e documentação de arquitetura (1959–1970)," *Fórum Patrimônio* 4, no. 2 (2011): 55–67.
7. Two paintings by Cândido Portinari exhibited at the Palácio do Itamaraty were in fact shown at the Brazilian pavilion of the 1939 World's Fair. The Palácio also includes works by the sculptors and painters Jean-Baptiste Debret, Pedro Américo, Bruno Giorgi, Althos Bulcão, Sergio Camargo, and many others.
8. A residence for the minister of the army was designed as well but was not constructed.
9. William Howard Adams, *Roberto Burle Marx: The Unnatural Art of the Garden* (New York: Museum of Modern Art, 1991), p. 35.
10. The Praça dos Cristais was landmarked on July 14, 2011, along with several other gardens in Brasília designed by Burle Marx. These include the Palácio do Itamaraty (1970), Ministério da Justiça (1970), Tribunal de Contas da União (1972), Superquadra 308 Sul (1972), Palácio do Jaburu (Residência da Vice-Presidência da República, 1975), Teatro Nacional Cláudio Santoro (1976), Banco do Brasil (1962), and Parque Pithon Farias (Parque da Cidade Dona Sarah Kubitschek, 1976).
11. For an excellent analysis of the economics of developmentalism and its impact on Latin American architecture and urbanism, see Jorge Francisco Liernur, "Architectures for Progress: Latin America, 1955–1980," in *Latin America in Construction: Architecture 1955–1980*, ed. Barry Bergdoll, Carlos Eduardo Comas, Jorge Francisco Liernur, and Patricio del Real (New York: Museum of Modern Art, 2015), pp. 69–89.
12. Tatyana de Amaral Maia, *Os cardeais da cultura nacional: O Conselho Federal de Cultura na ditadura civil-militar, 1967–1975* (São Paulo: Itaú Cultural Iluminuras, 2012). Artur Ferreira Reis was the former governor of the state of Amazonas and came from its capital city, Manaus.
13. Also known as the "queen of the night," *Cereus jamacaru* is a drought-resistant cactus common to the Brazilian northeast and often reaches a height of twenty feet. Its flowers last for only one night, blooming at nightfall and withering by dawn.
14. Burle Marx is likely referring to *Acrocomia aculeata*, a species of palm identified by Martius in his *Historia naturalis palmarum* (1824). It is native to the tropical regions of the Americas. *Ficus calcicola* is a fig tree well adapted to the calcium-rich environments of the *calcáreo*.
15. Burle Marx's fellow counselor on the Conselho Federal de Cultura, João Guimarães Rosa, wrote extensively and poetically about the oasis landscapes of buriti palms found in the dry savanna-like hinterlands of the Brazilian interior in his great novel *Grande sertão: Veredas*.
16. Monocarpic plants flower, seed, and then die. *Corypha taliera* is a species of palm, originally native to Myanmar and the Bengal region of India and Bangladesh but now very close to extinction and considered extinct in the wild. A specimen of *Corypha taliera* was planted at the Jardim Botânico in Rio de Janeiro; it bloomed in 1933; a second tree bloomed in 1980. A close relative is *Corypha umbraculifera*, planted by Burle Marx at both the Sítio and the Parque do Flamengo.
17. *Coivara* is the practice of creating a clearing in a forest through the process of clear-cutting and controlled burning.

Epilogue

1. The English translation of the text of the Brazilian Constitution of 1891, as amended in 1926, is included in Ernest Hambloch's *Complete Text of the Brazilian Constitution of 1934 Done into English* (São Paulo: Graphica Paulista, 1935).
2. This article is extracted from the Constitution of the Republic of the United States of Brazil of 1934, Heading V: Of the Family, of Education, and of Culture, chapter 2: Of Education and of Culture, article 148. The English translation is quoted from Hambloch, *Complete Text of the Brazilian Constitution of 1934*, p. 55.

3. Constitution of the Federal Republic of Brazil of 1967, amended on October 17, 1969, under Title IV: The Family, Education, and Culture, article 180: "Support of culture is a duty of the state."
4. Although he was harassed, Niemeyer was not "exiled" by the military regime. He did leave Brazil to live and work in Europe, but he traveled freely back to Brazil and continued to work in Brasília in the late 1960s and 1970s. He designed and completed annexes to the Congress, the Planalto, the Supreme Court, the ministries, and the vice-presidential palace, Palácio do Jaburu. He did not return from Europe to live permanently in Brazil until a general amnesty was declared by the military government in 1979. See Josep Maria Botey, *Oscar Niemeyer* (Barcelona: Editorial Gustavo Gili, 1996) for a complete chronology of Niemeyer's projects in both Brazil and elsewhere, indicating his significant ongoing work in Brasília.
5. The issuance of Institutional Act Number Five (Ato Institucional Número Cinco, AI-5) in December 1968 suspended habeas corpus, closed the Congress, and instituted features of a totalitarian state, including the use of torture to silence opponents.
6. See the epigraph to this book and Elizabeth Bishop and Robert Lowell, *Words in Air: The Complete Correspondence between Elizabeth Bishop and Robert Lowell*, ed. Thomas Travisano and Saskia Hamilton (New York: Farrar, Straus and Giroux, 2008), p. 361.

Index

Note: Page numbers in *italics* indicate photographs and illustrations.